Epicurus and Democritean Ethics

The Epicurean philosophical system has enjoyed much recent scrutiny, but the question of its philosophical ancestry remains largely neglected. It has often been thought that Epicurus owed only his physical theory of atomism to the fifth-century BC philosopher Democritus, but this study finds that there is much in his ethical thought which can be traced to Democritus. It also finds important influences on Epicurus in Democritus' fourth-century followers such as Anaxarchus and Pyrrho, and in Epicurus' disagreements with his own Democritean teacher Nausiphanes. The result is not only a fascinating reconstruction of a lost tradition, but also an important contribution to the philosophical interpretation of Epicureanism, bearing especially on its ideal of tranquillity and on the relation of ethics to physics.

JAMES WARREN is Assistant Lecturer in Classics at the University of Cambridge and Fellow of Corpus Christi College. He was previously Henry Lumley Research Fellow in Ancient Philosophy at Magdalene College, Cambridge. He has published a number of articles in respected journals in classics and philosophy.

CAMBRIDGE CLASSICAL STUDIES

EPICURUS AND DEMOCRITEAN ETHICS

An Archaeology of *Ataraxia*

JAMES WARREN
University of Cambridge

CAMBRIDGE
UNIVERSITY PRESS

PUBLISHED BY THE PRESS SYNDICATE OF THE UNIVERSITY OF CAMBRIDGE
The Pitt Building, Trumpington Street, Cambridge, United Kingdom

CAMBRIDGE UNIVERSITY PRESS
The Edinburgh Building, Cambridge CB2 2RU, UK
40 West 20th Street, New York, NY 10011-4211, USA
477 Williamstown Road, Port Melbourne, VIC 3207, Australia
Ruiz de Alarcón 13, 28014 Madrid, Spain
Dock House, The Waterfront, Cape Town 8001, South Africa

http://www.cambridge.org

First published 2002

Printed in the United Kingdom at the University Press, Cambridge

Typeface Times 11/13 pt.   *System* LATEX 2ε   [TB]

A catalogue record for this book is available from the British Library

Library of Congress Cataloguing in Publication data

James, Warren.
Epicurus and Democritean ethics : an archaeology of ataraxia/Warren James.
p.   cm. – (Cambridge classical studies)
Includes bibliographical references and index
ISBN 0 521 81369 7
1. Epicurus–Ethics.   2. Democritus–Ethics.   3. Ethics, Ancient,   I. Title.   II. Series.

B573 .J36 2002
187–dc21

2001052631

ISBN 0 521 81369 7 hardback

For my family

CONTENTS

FIGURES

ACKNOWLEDGEMENTS

I have incurred a number of debts in writing this study. Above all I am indebted to David Sedley for his continuous assistance, advice, and criticism. David Blank, Jacques Brunschwig, Fernanda Decleva Caizzi, Dominic Scott, Gisela Striker, and Robert Wardy kindly read and commented on various sections of the work. David Blank also generously showed me preliminary versions of parts of his new edition of Philodemus *On Rhetoric*.

Portions of the work have been presented at the Annual Meeting of the American Philological Association in Chicago, 1997, the Annual Meetings of the Classical Association in Lampeter, 1998, and Liverpool, 1999, the Cambridge B Club, the Oxford Philological Society, and at various sessions of the Cambridge Graduate Interdisciplinary Seminar. I thank the audiences on all those occasions.

Much of this work first appeared in my 1999 Cambridge Ph.D. dissertation, 'An archaeology of *ataraxia*: Epicurus and Democriteanism'. During the writing of that thesis, financial assistance was received from the Humanities Research Board of the British Academy, and the Isaac Newton Trust. The Faculty of Classics, and Clare College, Cambridge, both provided funds to allow me to travel to and speak at various conferences. My examiners, Robert Wardy and Jacques Brunschwig, gave generous and thought-provoking reactions and criticisms. Portions of chapter six have appeared as parts of Warren (2000b); I thank the editors of the *Proceedings of the Cambridge Philological Society* for their cooperation. I also owe thanks to Michael Sharp and Pauline Hire for their editorial advice.

Three Cambridge institutions have been the venues for my philosophical formation. Clare College provided the environment in which I first took to ancient philosophy and where I pursued the bulk of the research which led to this work. Magdalene College then welcomed me and gave me the time and space to refine and continue those thoughts. Throughout my time in Cambridge the Faculty of Classics has been an excellent place in which to work, think, and learn.

More personally, I owe an enormous amount to my family (my parents would, I think, appreciate Democritus B275) and especially to Sara Owen, without whom the ταραχαί of writing would have been much greater. This book is for them.

ABBREVIATIONS

Arr.	G. Arrighetti (1973) *Epicuro opere*[2] (Turin)
Diels *Dox.*	H. Diels (1879) *Doxographi Graeci* (Berlin)
DK	H. Diels and W. Kranz (1952) *Fragmente der Vorsokratiker*[6] (Berlin)
EK	L. Edelstein, I. G. Kidd (1972) *Posidonius vol. 1, the fragments* (Cambridge)
FGrH	F. Jacoby (1923–) *Fragmente der Griechischen Historiker* (Berlin)
FHS&G	W. W. Fortenbaugh, P.M. Huby, R.W. Sharples, and D. Gutas (1993–) *Theophrastus of Eresus: sources for his life, writings, thought, and influence* (Leiden)
L-JP	H. Lloyd-Jones, P. Parsons (1983) *Supplementum Hellenisticum* (Berlin)
LSJ	H. G. Liddell and R. Scott, rev. S. Jones (1925–40) *Greek–English Lexicon*[9] (Oxford)
Luria	S. Luria (1970) *Democritea* (Leningrad)
PBerol.	Berlin Papyri
PHerc.	Herculaneum Papyri; see *Catalogo dei papiri ercolanesi* (Naples, 1979)
POxy.	Oxyrhynchus Papyri
RE	A. Pauly, G. Wissowa and W. Kroll (1893–) *Real-Encyclopädie der klassischen Altertumswissenschaft* (Stuttgart)
SSR	G. Giannantoni (1990) *Socratis et Socraticorum reliquiae* (Naples)
SVF	H. von Arnim (1903–5) *Stoicorum veterum fragmenta* (Leipzig)
Us.	H. Usener (1887) *Epicurea* (Leipzig)

INTRODUCTION: EPICURUS, DEMOCRITUS, AND *ATARAXIA*

Von der εὐθυμία oder εὐεστώ des Demokrit zu der ἀκαταπληξία des Nausiphanes und der epikureischen ἀταραξία ist ein langer Weg.[1]

The subject of this book is the philosophical background to the ethical theory of eudaimonistic hedonism proposed by Epicurus, a Hellenistic philosopher who founded a school in Athens at the very end of the fourth century BC. In particular, it describes the relationship between the philosophy of Epicurus and the tradition of philosophy founded by the earlier Greek atomist, Democritus. Although Epicurus has attracted his fair share of attention in the past, and Democritus has also been the subject of numerous works, no attempt has previously been made to give a full account of the philosophical tradition which links these two men.[2] Along the way this tradition takes in Pyrrho of Elis, whose importance for ancient thought is mainly due to his being chosen as the figurehead of the late and extreme scepticism of Pyrrhonist philosophers such as Sextus Empiricus. Of course, Pyrrhonism like Epicureanism advocated tranquillity, *ataraxia*, as the goal of life, *telos*. Why those two schools of thought came to promote a *telos* by this same name will also, I hope, be illuminated by examining the early history of such ideas.

[1] Sudhaus (1893) 337.
[2] Alfieri (1979) 160: 'Dal famoso saggio del Reinhardt, *Hekataios von Abdera und Demokrit,* che è del 1912, si può dire che non sia più stata studiata, almeno con indagini particolari, la questione dei rapporti tra il pensiero di Democrito e quello di Epicuro...Insomma, o si studia Epicuro da solo, cercando di inserire la sua dottrina nell'ambiente di pensiero dell'età sua e di spiegarne l'origine nelle polemiche contro platonismo e aristotelismo...; o si studia Democrito da solo...come fanno in generale quei pochissimi che si occupano della scuola di Abdera'. The situation has improved a little since Alfieri was writing, but nevertheless no single study of the ethical tradition has been attempted.

So this is not intended as prolegomena to the study of Epicurean ethics in the sense of being prior and auxiliary to that study. Nor is it primarily an assessment of the truth of Epicurean-style hedonism. Rather, my contention is that Epicurean ethics itself can profitably be studied through the relationships between Epicurus and other philosophers.

To call a study of a concept or idea an 'archaeology' risks recalling the Foucauldian 'archaeologies'. That is not my intention.[3] I use the term as a metaphor for the practice of gradual disclosure, inquiry, and reconstruction applied to the layers deposited by successive periods of history. The direction of archaeological excavation, from the most recent upper levels to the more ancient lower levels, will be paralleled in much of what follows. Our knowledge of the ethical goal of *ataraxia* is much better in the case of those Hellenistic schools, the Epicureans and the Pyrrhonists, than it is for the earlier thinkers who proposed goals related to this end. Furthermore, no clear and direct evidence has survived for the ethical thought of Democritus or his followers. No complete texts have survived, only brief quotations, summaries or anthologies of sayings in later authors. For those thinkers who precede Epicurus in the chronology of Greek philosophical history very little evidence survives which was written before Epicurus' life. Often the evidence for those thinkers comes from hostile Epicurean sources. So more excavation is required, both to see the thesis being criticised in the text, and also to reveal the intervening reception of that thesis. Archaeology does not simply uncover ancient remains – it places and interprets them in a particular context. In this way we might fully understand the final layer of deposition by seeing it in its proper relationship with what came before.

It is clear that Epicurus' thought was informed by what had come before and that if we wish fully to understand his thought and his hostility to this tradition, we ought to attempt to outline those pre-Epicurean philosophies. This will contribute both to a better understanding of those earlier thinkers, and also to a clearer view of their successors.

[3] See Foucault (1972) Introduction and 135–40.

Before I begin by introducing the cast of characters who form the philosophical tradition on which I will focus, let me first outline the very basic aspects of Epicurean ethical thinking in which I am particularly interested. Although the interpretation of Epicurus' ethical philosophy is a matter for no little debate and disagreement, the following can be stated as relatively uncontroversial. When Epicurus describes what he takes to be the goal of life, the *telos*, that goal has two aspects. First, it is identified as the absence of pain – where pain is understood to be not only physical pain but also the mental pains of anxiety, distress, or worry. Second, it is identified as pleasure, or at least as a certain kind of pleasure. Here is Epicurus' description of the good life from his summary of ethical teachings, the *Letter to Menoeceus*:

τούτων γὰρ ἀπλανὴς θεωρία πᾶσαν αἵρεσιν καὶ φυγὴν ἐπανάγειν οἶδεν ἐπὶ τὴν τοῦ σώματος ὑγίειαν καὶ τὴν τῆς ψυχῆς ἀταραξίαν, ἐπεὶ τοῦτο τοῦ μακαρίως ζῆν ἐστι τέλος. τούτου γὰρ χάριν πάντα πράττομεν, ὅπως μήτε ἀλγῶμεν μήτε ταρβῶμεν. ὅταν δὲ ἅπαξ τοῦτο περὶ ἡμᾶς γένηται, λύεται πᾶς ὁ τῆς ψυχῆς χειμών, οὐκ ἔχοντος τοῦ ζῴου βαδίζειν ὡς πρὸς ἐνδέον τι καὶ ζητεῖν ἕτερον ὧν τὸ τῆς ψυχῆς καὶ τοῦ σώματος ἀγαθὸν συμπληρώσεται. τότε γὰρ ἡδονῆς χρείαν ἔχομεν, ὅταν ἐκ τοῦ μὴ παρεῖναι τὴν ἡδονὴν ἀλγῶμεν· <ὅταν δὲ μὴ ἀλγῶμεν,>⁴ οὐκέτι τῆς ἡδονῆς δεόμεθα. καὶ διὰ τοῦτο τὴν ἡδονὴν ἀρχὴν καὶ τέλος λέγομεν εἶναι τοῦ μακαρίως ζῆν. (*Ep. Men.* 128)

For an unerring understanding of these things [sc. of what desires are natural and necessary] knows how to direct every choice and avoidance towards the health of the body and the tranquillity (*ataraxia*) of the soul, since this is the goal of the blessed life. For it is for the sake of this that we do everything – so that we may feel neither pain nor anxiety. And as soon as we achieve this, the whole storm of the soul is calmed, since the animal cannot go off as if towards something it needs and in pursuit of something else with which the good of the body and soul will be fulfilled. For the time when we need pleasure is whenever we feel pain through pleasure's absence. But when we feel no pain, then we no longer need pleasure. And for that reason we say that pleasure is the starting point and the goal of the blessed life.

This passage begins by emphasising what we might call the negative aspect of the Epicurean *telos* – the absence of mental and

---

⁴ Suppl. Gassendi.

physical pain. The prime motivational force which it identifies is the need to rid oneself of such pain.[5] It goes on, however, to relate this closely to the drive for pleasure. It is pleasure which is required to take away the pain, and as soon as pain and anxiety are removed then pleasure is no longer sought after. A little later in the same text, Epicurus explicitly identifies the *telos* as a kind of pleasure – and further identifies this with the absence of pain.

ὅταν οὖν λέγωμεν ἡδονὴν τέλος ὑπάρχειν, οὐ τὰς τῶν ἀσώτων ἡδονὰς καὶ τὰς ἐν ἀπολαύσει κειμένας λέγομεν, ὥς τινες ἀγνοοῦντες καὶ οὐχ ὁμολογοῦντες ἢ κακῶς ἐκδεχόμενοι νομίζουσιν, ἀλλὰ τὸ μήτε ἀλγεῖν κατὰ σῶμα μήτε ταράττεσθαι κατὰ ψυχήν· (*Ep. Men.* 131)

When we say that pleasure is the goal of life, then, we do not mean the pleasures of the profligates, and those which are to be found in extravagance – as some think mistakenly and in disagreement or through not understanding us correctly – but we mean neither feeling pain in the body nor being disturbed in the soul.

So the goal of life – if you are an Epicurean – is the pursuit of pleasure, understood to be the absence of physical and mental pain. We might call the Epicureans' advocacy of pleasure as the goal of life the positive aspect of their message. The combination of these two aspects – the pursuit of pleasure and the absence of disturbance – has often been thought to be an unstable mixture. The critics of Epicureanism were also quick to seize on the fact that Epicurus distinguished two species of pleasure, kinetic and katastematic. The latter he identified as the pleasure of the state of feeling no pain, the former he described as the pleasures which involve some sort of motion or change – the process of the removal of a need or lack and the variation of a state of painlessness.[6] These critics take the admission of kinetic pleasures to be the Epicureans' concession to what hedonism ought to be seeking – episodes of pleasurable sensation – and the promotion of katastematic pleasure merely to be some sleight of hand on Epicurus' part. Surely, this state of painlessness which Epicurus promotes is not itself pleasant, but is merely an intermediary state – a state in which one is feeling neither

---

[5] Other philosophers before Epicurus are known to have promoted a *telos* which can be described as the 'absence of pain', for example Speusippus (see Clem. *Strom.* 2.133) and Hieronymus of Rhodes (Clem. *Strom.* 2.127.3; Cic. *Fin.* 5.14, 19). See Dillon (1996), Dalfino (1993). Also cf. Purinton (1993) 300 n. 32.

[6] See DL 10.136–7 and Cic. *Fin.* 2.9–10.

pleasure nor pain? Cicero, for example, in his *De finibus* follows the general argumentative strategy of claiming that Epicurus ought to have advocated either hedonism or the avoidance of disturbance. He finds it quite implausible to identify the absence of pain as a pleasure itself – let alone the highest pleasure. And Cicero's overall stance has been supported by a number of modern commentators.[7]

My concern in this study is not to reopen the question of the coherence of Epicurus' overall ethical position, nor to offer a discussion of Epicurus' view of pleasure. Rather, I intend to offer a story which might explain how he came to advocate the position he did. In particular, I intend to show why the negative aspect of his message – namely the advocacy of a life free from disturbance – may have appealed. To do this, I will look at Epicurus' predecessors. One consequence of this approach is that it can also shed light on why it is that *ataraxia*, the absence of disturbance, was approved not only by the Epicureans. The Pyrrhonist sceptics in particular also promoted a vision of the best life which they characterised by the absence of disturbance, and they even used the same term, *ataraxia*, to describe this ideal state.[8]

Here is Sextus Empiricus' introductory description:

φαμὲν δὲ ἄχρι νῦν τέλος εἶναι τοῦ σκεπτικοῦ τὴν ἐν τοῖς κατὰ δόξαν ἀταραξίαν καὶ ἐν τοῖς κατηναγκασμένοις μετριοπάθειαν. (*PH* 1.25)

We say – up until now – that the goal of life for the sceptic is tranquillity in matters of opinion and moderation of passion in matters which are unavoidable.

Of course, there is an enormous difference between the life which Sextus promotes and that advocated by the Epicureans. Sextus asks us not to pursue nor to avoid anything too eagerly – certainly not with some opinion in mind that this particular object is to be pursued or avoided, while Epicurus insists that we must have opinions – the correct Epicurean opinions – about such matters. My point here, however, is much more basic. Both the Epicureans

---

[7] See e.g. Striker (1993). On Cicero's tactics, see Inwood (1990) and Stokes (1995). A number of approaches have been suggested in order to make Epicurus' position more plausible. Mitsis (1988) 18 argues that Epicurean *ataraxia* is an objective dispositional state – not a state immediately recognisable by introspection as 'pleasant'. For other views, see Brochard (1954), Gosling and Taylor (1982), Annas (1987) and (1993a) 334–50, Giannantoni (1984), Purinton (1993), Erler and Schofield (1999), Cooper (1999).

[8] For a survey of *ataraxia* as an ethical ideal, see Striker (1990).

and the Sextan Pyrrhonists, despite their other differences, promote something which they call *ataraxia* as the goal of life. Even earlier than Sextus, there is evidence of a Pyrrhonist promotion of *ataraxia*. In Eusebius' *Praeparatio Evangelica*, there is a section of Aristocles of Messene's *On Philosophy* which includes this report by Timon, the pupil of Pyrrho himself. The text is notoriously difficult to interpret, and I shall offer my own interpretation in chapter 4. However, the salient point for the moment is the following. Timon offers a description of the three things to which 'he who wishes to find *eudaimonia*' should attend. Then, he concludes:

τοῖς μέντοι γε διακειμένοις οὕτω περιέσεσθαι Τίμων φησὶ πρῶτον μὲν ἀφασίαν, ἔπειτα δ' ἀταραξίαν. (Eus. *PE* 14.18.4)

But for those disposed in such a way, Timon says there will first arise an absence of assertion, and then tranquillity.

Why should it be the case that the Epicureans and the Pyrrhonists – even the Pyrrhonists of Timon's time – should both promote *ataraxia* as a goal of life? My answer will be that both the Epicureans and the Pyrrhonists can trace their philosophical ancestry to the same tradition of thinkers – the tradition of philosophers who began by engaging with aspects of the thought of Democritus. This tradition includes Pyrrho himself, whom the Pyrrhonists later hailed as their founding father. The transformation and reinterpretation of the philosophy of Pyrrho is one of the concerns of chapter 4.

In one respect, of course, it is neither novel nor controversial in the slightest to claim that Epicurus owed a philosophical debt to Democritus. These two are undeniably linked by their physical theories. Democritus, and the rather more shadowy figure Leucippus, originated an atomistic view of the physical nature of the world. They described how the fundamental constituents of the world were discrete particles of matter – atoms – which move constantly within an infinite void. By their combinations and rearrangements the macroscopic world of changing objects is formed.

This general view was accepted by Epicurus, and although he took exception to a number of Democritus' ideas (some of which will be discussed in what follows), and although Epicurus did – it seems – seek to deny Democritus' influence, it would be foolish to deny that Democritus was the most obvious source of much of Epicurus' philosophy. It is also clear that to some degree their shared physical outlook also contributed to some shared ethical views. Atomism as a physical system has a number of ethical consequences which may have lent themselves to Epicurus' drive for *ataraxia*. An atomist view of the nature of the world promotes a generally anti-teleological outlook, and perhaps more importantly a theological view which does not require interventionist gods, or a divine maker of the world. It can also contribute to a life freed from moral demands imposed by such divinities. Similarly, it is easy to see how an atomist can hold that the soul or mind is physical and mortal – decaying and dying as does the body. So no part of an individual survives death, and there is no need to be concerned with an afterlife or punishment or reward after death. Some of these issues will also resurface as I describe the Democritean tradition. I will also claim, however, that some of the specifically ethical ideas promoted in the fragments of Democritus find echoes in later Epicurean theory.

More important for the story which follows, however, is another aspect of Democritean atomism which I must introduce before we proceed. Famously, once he had identified atoms and void as the fundamental existents and constituents of the world, Democritus went on to contrast these with other classes of things. There are a number of fragments of Democritus which relate this contrast, but perhaps the best known comes from Sextus Empiricus, and is fragment B9 Diels–Kranz:

νόμῳ γλυκύ, νόμῳ πικρόν, νόμῳ θερμόν, νόμῳ ψυχρόν, νόμῳ χροιή, ἐτεῇ δὲ ἄτομα καὶ κενόν. (Democritus B9 (SE *M*. 7.135))

By convention sweet, by convention bitter, by convention hot, by convention cold, by convention colour, but in truth atoms and void.

From the number of times it is quoted – with similar if not identical wording – it is clear that this was one of the more famous Democritean sayings.[9] I will refer to it in the rest of this study as Democritus B9. Its exact implications, however, are not so clear.

---

[9] It appears also in Galen *De medic. empir.* 15.7 (DK B125), and DL 9.72 (DK B117). See Gemelli Marciano (1998).

To some degree I welcome this, since part of the story I will tell involves different philosophers offering their own particular interpretations of the statement.

B9 offers a contrast between two sets of things. On the one side Democritus lists atoms and void. On the other he places various phenomenal qualities. The contrast is to some extent clear. Atoms and void are fundamental. They are what exists 'in truth' or 'in reality', ἐτεῇ. Everything else exists 'by convention', νόμῳ. Exactly what this latter means is not so clear. Perhaps Democritus means they exist only by human *fiat*. Or perhaps he means that – strictly speaking – such things do not exist *at all*; we merely and mistakenly talk as if they do.[10] Whatever the interpretation favoured, the contrast was generated as a result of Democritus' atomist theory which had identified atoms and void as in some sense the basic constituents of the universe.

Although B9 is a consequence of Democritean atomism, the influence it exerted over the tradition of philosophy which followed was by no means limited to those who shared Democritus' general physical theory. It is not difficult to see how it might appeal to those who are sceptically-minded, since it seems to relegate phenomenal qualities to a lesser existence or to non-existence, and so it is no surprise that Democritus was rapidly enlisted as a fore-runner of later ancient sceptical movements. Part of my story will be the description of different philosophers' views of what Democritus meant. For example, the Epicureans themselves took the view that Democritus was denying that anything other than atoms and void exists at all. But another part of my story will be the demonstration of other philosophers' adaptations of this claim and advocacy of related claims. Some, for example, restricted the class of things which exist merely 'by convention', νόμῳ, to moral properties such as 'the fine', or 'the shameful' – meaning that there is no objective existence in nature of such things; they are human constructs, and perhaps can be discarded or refashioned as we please. So the application of this contrast between reality and convention will vary from philosopher to philosopher, as will the exact terms in which it is expressed. Sometimes the contrast is between what is 'in truth',

---

[10] For discussions of this principle see Furley (1993) and O'Keefe (1997).

κατ᾽ ἀλήθειαν, and what is 'by convention', νόμῳ. Sometimes the contrast is between what is 'in nature', φύσει, and what is 'by convention'. Each case will have to be considered individually.

In my conclusion, I will come back to examine more specifically the Epicureans' approach to Democritus' claim and will outline the particular metaphysical issues about which they felt Democritus had been in error. Their particular perspective on Democritus can only be fully understood once it is placed in the context of the entire intervening tradition.

I

INTRODUCING THE DEMOCRITEANS

πάλιν δ' ἐν 'Αβδήροις ἀσύνετοι πολλοί, τοιοῦτοι δ' 'Αθήνησι ὀλίγοι.

Galen *QAM* 822

Again, in Abdera there are many fools, but in Athens there are few.

Democritus was born, and – so far as we know – spent most of his life, in Abdera. There is a curious irony in this fact, since in antiquity the inhabitants of this city were not known for their intelligence. Quite the opposite, in fact. The curious late-antique jokebook, the *Philogelos*, contains a number of jokes aimed at the residents of this city, and similar jokes appear regularly in Roman sources after the first century BC.[1] Nevertheless, Abdera was the centre for the group of thinkers whose rôle in the history of Greek thought is the subject of this work.

In this first chapter I introduce two sources to which I will refer constantly – Diogenes Laërtius' *Lives of the eminent philosophers* and a passage from Clement of Alexandria's *Stromateis* – and I begin to outline why and how they are to be used. They will introduce the cast of characters, and are examples of the practice common in later antiquity of attempting to arrange the history of philosophy into neat master–pupil relationships.

Diogenes Laërtius' succession

Diogenes Laërtius' account of the *Lives of the eminent philosophers* (DL) often provides information on a thinker otherwise lost

[1] On the *Philogelos* see Thierfelder (1968), Baldwin (1983). The 'Abderite jokes' are §§110–27. Also see Cic. *Ad Att.* 7.7.4, cf. 4.17.3, *ND* 1.120; Mart. 10.25.4; Mayor *ad* Juv. 10.50; Galen *QAM* 822; Lucian *Hist. conscr.* 1.

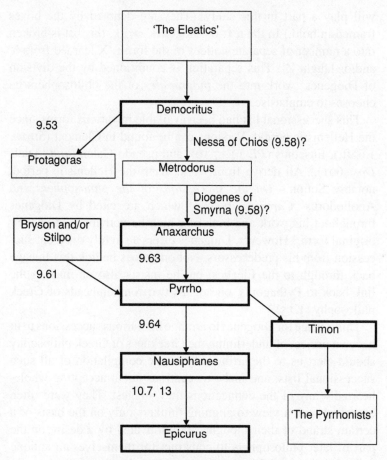

Fig. 1   Diogenes Laërtius' succession

in obscurity. Also, his work provides (sometimes colourful) illustrations in anecdotal form of the lives of the philosophers, which are in turn expected to offer some illustration of their respective philosophies.[2]

Figure 1 offers a reconstruction of a successional list of philosophical pupil–teacher relationships which can be extracted from the ninth and tenth books of Diogenes' *Lives*, starting with Democritus and passing to Epicurus. It includes the major figures who

[2] For a good introduction: Mejer (1992), Goulet-Cazé (1999b).

will play a part in this study. (They are denoted by the boxes framed in bold.) In the text of Diogenes' work, this list is broken into a number of separate notices of the form: 'X learned from Y and/or taught Z'. This separation is conditioned by the division of Diogenes' work into the *biographies* of the philosophers he chooses to emphasise.

This successional list had been available in various forms since the Hellenistic period. Versions can be found in Clement (*Strom.* 1.62ff.), Eusebius (*PE* 14.17.10), and pseudo-Galen (*apud* Diels *Dox.* 601).[3] All derive from works from the Hellenistic period, notably Sotion's *On the successions of the philosophers* and Apollodorus' *Chronica*, both of which are cited by Diogenes throughout his work and both of which he perhaps read in their original form.[4] However, Diogenes offers a slightly different succession from his predecessors. Not only does he link this lineage back through to the Eleatics, but he insists also on making the link back to Pythagoras, one of his two fountainheads of Greek philosophy (1.15).[5]

This licence for Diogenes to arrange his various successions to fit his own project of underlining the Greekness of Greek philosophy should alert us to the artificiality of the compilation of all such successional lists, and make us cautious about accepting wholeheartedly any of the connections they suggest. They were often compiled with a view to aligning thinkers only on the basis of a certain strand of their thought, and motivated by a desire on the part of later philosophers to construct for themselves an antique and noble lineage.[6] The tradition they describe, therefore, can only be a starting point for our philosophical history and none of the ties of influence they suggest can be accepted without thought. Nevertheless, we should also not descend into absolute scepticism ourselves; there is no need to discard the thought that some of

[3] See von Kienle (1961) 10ff. On successional lists in general: Giannantoni (1981a), Andria (1989).

[4] For the fragments of Sotion see Wehrli (1978). von Kienle (1961) 82 surveys the evidence for Diogenes' indirect knowledge of Sotion. Mejer (1978) 40–1, 70–1 argues that Diogenes followed the structure of Sotion's work and not Heracleides' epitome. Cf. Aronadio (1990).

[5] See Gigante (1986) 45ff.

[6] Cf. Giannantoni (1981a) 23–5; 30: even if these links are artificial, they are not arbitrary. Cf. Brunschwig (1999a) 1032–5.

the pupil–teacher relationships which appear in these successions should be accepted. That still, of course, offers no substantial help in analysing the *philosophies* of either of the thinkers thus linked.

Sceptical deformations

Although it is worth examining each of the proposed links in Diogenes' history of philosophy, a number of those which appear in my diagram will not be pursued in my history of the tradition from Democritus to Epicurus: the Eleatics, Protagoras, Diogenes of Apollonia and Bryson and Stilpo. They can be seen as later additions and elaborations to the story made by later philosophers trying to fashion for themselves a noble and antique heritage. This is itself an interesting phenomenon, and it is worth pausing briefly to consider it – especially since many of these links can be traced to a desire to find connections between 'sceptically minded' philosophers, and the relationship between Democriteanism and scepticism will become prominent in the story to come.

The Eleatic impulse

Xenophanes' position within this successional heritage as the first of the 'Eleatics' is a matter of some discussion among the ancient sources.[7] But Diogenes had strong reasons to include him in his story. Timon, Pyrrho's pupil, had made Xenophanes his guide in the second book of his *Silloi* (DL 9.111, SE *PH* 1.224). Sotion, the writer of a Hellenistic work on philosophical successions, is said to have written a commentary on Timon's poems (Athen. 336D), and apparently declared Xenophanes to be one of the first sceptics, since he had said that all things are 'inapprehensible' (ἀκατάληπτα, DL 9.20,[8] cf. SE *M.* 7.49[9]). Von Kienle explained Xenophanes' rôle in Sotion's successions as a reflection of the

---

[7] DL 8.91, 9.18. See von Kienle (1961) 88, Gigante (1983) 87–8.

[8] Diogenes rejects Sotion's evidence on this point and consequently leaves Xenophanes and Heraclitus as οἱ σποράδην. See DL 8.91, Brunschwig (1999a) 1032–3.

[9] Sextus compares Xenophanes with Xeniades of Corinth at *M.* 7.53. Democritus is here said to have mentioned Xeniades, but the nature of their relationship is obscure. For a speculative reconstruction: Brunschwig (1984). Morel (1996) 430 notes that Sextus himself opposes Xeniades and Protagoras (*M.* 7.388; cf. *PH* 2.76).

influence of Timon in shaping the doxographer's conceptions of past philosophers.[10] If this were true it would offer strong evidence of an early Hellenistic desire to tie Timonian scepticism to a supposed Eleatic origin. But this hypothesis is unlikely; the sources which Sotion used were probably more varied, and certainly included Academic writers.[11] It is more likely that the position of Xenophanes here, and the link it creates between Eleaticism and Democriteanism, were constructed by Sotion for a number of reasons: Timon grudgingly approves of the Eleatics for their resistance to accepting appearances, offered Xenophanes the partial compliment of being only 'slightly conceited' (ὑπάτυφος), and followed him in writing satirical verses (Silloi).[12] Further, various parts of Xenophanes' own work (for example, B34) could be marshalled in support of such an image of a 'sceptical' thinker.[13] There is no reason to conclude, however, that Timon himself saw Xenophanes as a direct philosophical ancestor, and the hesitancy over Xenophanes' position to be found in Diogenes strongly suggests that his appearance in book nine and in this successional tradition was at least in part the result of a search for hints of scepticism made by writers later than Timon.[14] Timon's use of Xenophanes in the Silloi may itself have influenced later readers' views of Xenophanes' own role in the successional story.

The upshot of all this is that it is not necessary for the story of the Democritean tradition to go all the way back to Xenophanes and the Eleatics. Their position in Diogenes' lineage is almost certainly a construction of the Hellenistic period and later based primarily upon the feeling that they were sceptics and provided a sceptical impulse for later members of the tradition.

Protagoras

Protagoras of Abdera, the relativist famed for his assertion that 'man is the measure of all things', is regularly linked with the

[10] Von Kienle (1961) 87, followed by Mejer (1978) 84.

[11] See Turrini (1982), Decleva Caizzi (1990) 43 n. 5, Brittain and Palmer (2001).

[12] See Bett (2000) 143–9.

[13] For similar forces at work in Hippolytus' treatment of Xenophanes, especially in relation to Metrodorus: Mansfeld (1992) 32–9.

[14] E.g. Sextus M. 7.46ff., esp. 48 (where not only Xenophanes but also Metrodorus of Chios, Anaxarchus and Monimus appear; Xenophanes B34 appears at M. 7.49 and 110).

scepticism of one of the followers of Democritus, one Metrodorus of Chios.[15] It is also sometimes claimed in the sources that Protagoras was a pupil of Democritus. It has been suggested that this is the result of a particular interpretation of Timon's report of Protagoras' theological views (fr. 5 Diels *apud* SE *M.* 9.56–7, cf. Protagoras B4), which may make him rather like Democritus in his view of the gods. But this interpretation is doubtful. Timon's Protagoras might not in fact have doubted whether there are gods and merely expressed agnosticism about the gods' nature.[16] In that case he is rather less like Democritus. In any case, the scepticism expressed in Protagoras B4, independently of Timon's view of Protagoras, would itself have been sufficient to warrant a place in Sextus' catalogue of thinkers who manifested some sort of scepticism (*M.* 7.46ff.). We should conclude that Protagoras' place in any succession of Abderites and Pyrrhonians is not, therefore, due to Timon.

Instead, his place is warranted by a combination of this sceptical air and – more importantly – the fact that he was from Abdera and roughly contemporaneous with Democritus.[17] As early as Aristotle's *On Education*, it is often claimed, we find traces of biographical anecdotes linking the two. Democritus discovered Protagoras carrying bundles of wood in a cunning fashion and as a result took Protagoras as a pupil (DL 9.53, Aulus Gellius 5.3, Athenaeus 354C, *Suda* s.v. κοτύλη, φορμοφόρος).[18] However, we

---

[15] E.g. Eus. *PE* 14.17.10, 19.8–10, Aristocles *apud* Eus. *PE* 14.20.1–2.

[16] Decleva Caizzi (1990) 50, cf. Bett (2000) 149–52. If the MSS reading of Timon fr. 5.5 is retained (οἵ rather than Bekker's εἰ), then Timon's Protagoras does not doubt whether there are gods, but what *kind of* gods they are. Decleva Caizzi points out that Diels–Kranz's B4 is a construction from DL 9.51 and Eus *PE* 14.3.7 (also cf. Cic. *ND* 1.63) and does not exactly correspond to the position expressed by Timon's Protagoras. Another version of B4 occurs immediately prior to Sextus' citation of the Timonian fragment at *M.* 9.56. Cf. Obbink (1989) 190. For an example of the inference of Protagorean atheism from his agnosticism: Diog. Oin. 16.II.8–12 Smith.

[17] The relative chronology of the two thinkers is unclear. Democritus' own chronology is debatable (Guthrie (1965) 386 n. 2, Salem (1996) 25–6; cf. D. O'Brien s.v. 'Démocrite d'Abdère' in R. Goulet ed. (1994) *Dictionnaire de philosophes antiques*, Paris). See also Steckel (1970) 193, Sassi (1978) 230 n. 53. Davison (1953) 39 notes that even on the earliest estimate Protagoras' career in Athens had already begun when Democritus was born, and suggests that Epicurean fabrications of the relationship between Protagoras and Democritus might have been responsible for some of the chronological confusion, and for Democritus' renowned longevity (Lucian *Macrob.* 18), by redating Democritus' birth in order to allow for such a relationship.

[18] See Schuhl (1968) 143–6.

should disentangle two sources for this particular anecdote. Aristotle perhaps reported only that Protagoras had invented a cunning way of carrying wood; this is all the *Suda* suggests. The further detail that this was approved by Democritus and that Protagoras became his secretary (γραφεύς), derives from Epicurus' work *On Ways of Life* (περὶ ἐπιτηδευμάτων). This latter work is cited by Athenaeus as his source for the whole tale, and Diogenes retains the identification of Protagoras as Democritus' assistant in his list of Epicurus' slanderous remarks about other philosophers (10.8), immediately following the story of Aristotle's profligate youth, also retained in Athenaeus.[19] Athenaeus is not an independent source; he is using information he found in Epicurus. Second, the link between Protagoras and Democritus cannot be shown to predate its appearance in Epicurus' work, a work in which he might also have humorously commented on Aristotle's *On Education* (his source for the story about Protagoras the hod-carrier) by including stories about Aristotle's own youth. The biographical connection between Democritus and Protagoras can be tied more closely to Epicurus than to Aristotle, and appears to be part of a humorous or slanderous commentary on earlier philosophers rather than an accurate report.[20] We are left, therefore, with the facts that Democritus and Protagoras are Abderites, and that both said some sceptical things, as the major grounds for Protagoras' inclusion in this succession.

In fact, there is another strong tradition in the ancient sources which sharply contrasts Democritus and Protagoras, viewing Democritus as a rationalist along somewhat Platonic lines. After all, Democritus was known to have argued against Protagoras (Plut. *Adv. Col.* 1109A). Sextus, the clearest example of this tendency, himself offers a discussion of how Democritus and Protagoras differ: *M.* 7.389ff. (cf. *PH* 1.213–14, 216–19).[21] There is little

---

[19] Sedley (1976a) 126.

[20] Cf. Alfieri (1957) 161–4, (1979) 32; Brunschwig (1999a) 1036.

[21] Barnes' (1979) vol. II, 231ff. discussion of Democritean epistemology derives mainly from the fragments contained in Sextus *M.* 7.135ff. In that case, his conclusion that Democritus held a remarkably 'Pyrrhonian' (251, 261) scepticism is not unexpected. Sedley (1992) 23 speculates that Sextus' knowledge of Democritus might derive from Epicurus. Cf. Decleva Caizzi (1980b), Spinelli (1997). For Sextus' view of Protagoras: Barnes (1994) 56–60.

notice of a sceptical Democritus in the writings of Timon (fr. 46 Diels).[22]

Nevertheless the linking of Democritus' epistemology and its metaphysical basis to the Protagorean position occurs quite early. Aristotle is happy to include Democritus alongside Protagoras in his discussion of those who use a 'no more' or 'indifference' (οὐ μᾶλλον) argument in cases of perceptual conflict to generate sceptical conclusions (*Met.* 1009b11ff.). In brief, this argument goes as follows. If there are two conflicting opinions or perceptions and there is 'no more' reason for one rather than another to be true, or 'no more' reason to prefer one to the other, then any acceptance of one rather than the other cannot be justified. We must suspend judgement on the question or reject both.[23] Epicurean criticism of Democritean metaphysics and epistemology as described in Plutarch's *Against Colotes* made use of similar claims, and it is significant that Plutarch begins his defence of Democritus by insisting on a distinction between him and Protagoras (1109A) and also in their use of such οὐ μᾶλλον arguments. Whereas Democritus advocates rejecting both perceptions of which there is 'no more' reason to accept one rather than another, Protagoras advocates a relativist position – each perception is true for that particular perceiver. In one sense, he accepts that *both* are true.[24] Perhaps the Epicureans had indeed elided these two Abderites in order to bolster their claims against Epicurus' philosophical ancestor; they

---

[22] He is called ἀμφίνοον λεσχῆνα in 46.2, but the meaning of this is unclear. Di Marco (1989) 218–19 suggests that it denotes that Democritus' νόμῳ/ἐτεῆ distinction was 'half right' (i.e. the *first* half) if compared with Pyrrho's view as reported in DL 9.61. On Pyrrho's liking for Democritus, see Sassi (1978) 227–36, Decleva Caizzi (1984b), and Bett (2000) 152–60, 187–8.

[23] Graeser (1970) 309–11, Burkert (1997); cf. Kullmann (1969). The Academics probably followed this lead and pointed to Democritus as an early sceptic: see Decleva Caizzi (1980b) 404ff., Brittain and Palmer (2001). For Academic lists of sceptical predecessors see Cic. *Acad.* 1.44ff., 2.14, 32, 73–4; Plut. *Adv. Col.* 1121F: Sedley (1983a) 24 n. 27 suggests that the list of philosophers attacked by Colotes might itself derive from an Academic list of 'predecessors'; cf. Gemelli Marciano (1998) 117–18. For Sextus' interpretation of Democritean epistemology: Graeser (1970) 309, Morel (1996) 393ff., (1998) 156.

[24] On these arguments: Sassi (1978) 227–36, Woodruff (1988) 146–7, Makin (1993) 66. On Colotes against Democritus: De Lacy (1964) 74 argues that Colotes cannot have simply assimilated Democritus to Protagoras because Democritus was known to have criticised Protagoras. He also has suggested (1958a) 59 that Plutarch therefore has misinterpreted Colotes. Cf. Vander Waerdt (1989) 247–53.

certainly seem to have read and manipulated Aristotle's *On Education*, so perhaps they were also using Aristotelian and Peripatetic doxography about Protagoras and Democritus.[25]

Once both Democritus and Protagoras had been taken into the sceptical ancestry, the fact of their both coming from Abdera, and being roughly contemporary, would have combined with Epicurus' tale to give a biographical explanation for their perceived philosophical similarity. Diogenes inherits this tradition, perhaps via Favorinus.[26]

Diogenes of Apollonia, Bryson, and Stilpo

Three more figures can be excluded from the story. The appearance in Diogenes Laërtius' work of a *Life* of Diogenes of Apollonia between Protagoras and Anaxarchus (9.57) has been viewed as a confusion for Diogenes of Smyrna, who appears as a teacher of Anaxarchus in 9.58, and in some sources is said to have had the same opinions as Protagoras (DK 71 A2).[27] This is certainly a possible explanation, but it is also not coincidental that Diogenes of Apollonia is mentioned alongside Democritus and Protagoras at Cic. *ND* 1.29, and with Leucippus at Theoph. *Phys. Op.* 2 (Diels *Dox.* 477). His appearance here might be a trace of a tradition which linked his cosmology to that of the atomists.[28]

Similarly, the suggestion at 9.61[29] that Pyrrho was taught by 'Bryson the son of Stilpo' or 'Bryson or Stilpo' is unlikely on chronological grounds,[30] and has plausibly been interpreted as an attempt to link Pyrrho via these Megarians to the Socratic schools, a manoeuvre designed to manufacture a tradition of 'eristic' or

---

[25] For an attempt to reconcile Peripatetic and Sextan versions of Democritus' epistemology: Asmis (1984) 339–48.

[26] Decleva Caizzi (1992b) 4236–8, esp. 4237 n. 89.

[27] Cf. Hicks ad loc; von Kienle (1961) 10, 27; Mejer (1978) 28.

[28] This was suggested by Laks (1983) 260, cf. Gigante (1986) 91. He appears after the entry on Metrodorus of Chios in ps.-Plut. *Strom.* (Diels *Dox.* 582–3): Laks (1983) 262. Cf. Brunschwig (1999a) 1037.

[29] Copied by *Suda* s.v. Πύρρων.

[30] The MSS read καὶ ἤκουσε Βρύσωνος τοῦ Στίλπωνος. Since Bryson is not thought to be sufficiently younger than Stilpo for this to be plausible, τοῦ is often emended to ἤ, as in Marcovich's edition. Even then the chronology is difficult to reconcile with Pyrrho: Decleva Caizzi (1981a) 132–5. Dörer (1997) provides no argument for his assertion that Bryson was indeed Pyrrho's teacher.

'dialectical' thinkers, to whom Pyrrho was felt to have some affinity.[31] At DL 1.16, the group of philosophers who left no writings includes Socrates, Stilpo, Bryson, and Pyrrho. Some methodological link between these thinkers might be implied by their lack of writings – which might in turn have suggested a successional link.

Now we have trimmed down the cast of characters from Diogenes Laërtius, this surviving list can be compared with that from another important source: Clement of Alexandria's *Stromateis*.

Clement of Alexandria

In his *Stromateis* Clement of Alexandria preserves a list of 'ends of life' or *telē* proposed by Democritus and his followers (2.130). As the title of the work ('Miscellanies') suggests, this is a long and often rambling collection of material, and it is therefore difficult to evaluate the exact rôle played by this list within Clement's larger concerns.[32] As a result, it is also difficult to evaluate the source and reliability of this account.

In this section of the work, Clement has turned his attention to the goals of life proposed by various ancient philosophers. He begins with an irritated attack on Cyrenaicism and Epicurus' impious hedonism (*Strom.* 2.127.1: this forms a frame to the section, closing it at 130.8)[33] and passes via the Peripatetics (128.3), and the Stoics (129.1), on to Anaxagoras, Heraclitus, Pythagoras, Democritus and 'the Abderites' (130). He then discusses Plato and the *Theaetetus*' vision of 'becoming like god' (131–3). All this then forms a preface to his account of the Christian *telos*, which is marked off from the preceding section with a promise that Clement will return to review and refute the various pagan positions when the time is right (2.134.1).

---

[31] Giannantoni (1981a) 25–30.

[32] Clement gives an account of his view of the work at *Strom.* 6.2.1 (and 1.11.1ff.). This places it in the tradition of *florilegia* and *gnomologia*: Méhat (1966) 99ff. Cf. de Fay (1906) 51ff. and Chadwick (1966) 31: the *Strom.* are 'unsystematic and surprisingly inconsequential notes on a large variety of themes'. Compare Ridings (1995) 132ff., Méhat (1966) ch. 1.

[33] On Clement's presentation of Cyrenaicism: Laks (1993) 41ff.

After his presentation of the Christian *telos* and before moving on to the next 'subject' of the book, marriage, Clement comments that the various pagan opinions he had canvassed can all be seen to have sprung from the one source, the Bible, but filtered and distorted through their transmission to pagan thinkers. This strategy of attempting to show the dependence of pagan philosophy on the Bible can be traced throughout the *Stromateis*.[34]

This general view offers some indications for our handling of the Abderite *telē*. With the possible exception of Plato, the other thinkers in this section are simply listed as a catalogue, with no comment of approval or disapproval on Clement's part. The presentation of a long and varied list of ethical *telē* from a wide diversity of schools is well suited to his overall aim of impressing upon his audience the rôle played in the development of pagan philosophy by its Biblical sources. There is no need for Clement to comment on the individual *telē*; he merely requires a long and impressive list which will demonstrate not only how fertile a source the Bible must have been (since it generated such a vigorous outpouring of thought) but also how mistaken this great variety of *telē* had become by Clement's own time.

If this is close to a simple catalogue, it is unlikely that Clement himself has manipulated the information to any large extent. His concern is simply to offer a list of opinions, and he might well have copied the information from a compilation of earlier philosophers' views on the goal of life (a *florilegium* περὶ τέλους). For once we might have a transparent source which preserves earlier information with little contamination (but perhaps some truncation). Our attention, therefore, should now turn to Clement's sources, and at this point we should become better acquainted with the 'Aberites'.

ἀλλὰ καὶ οἱ Ἀβδηρῖται τέλος ὑπάρχειν διδάσκουσι, Δημόκριτος μὲν ἐν τῷ Περὶ τέλους τὴν εὐθυμίαν, ἣν καὶ εὐεστὼ προσηγόρευσεν [here he cites Democritus B188], Ἑκαταῖος δὲ αὐτάρκειαν, καὶ δὴ Ἀπολλόδοτος ὁ Κυζικηνὸς τὴν ψυχαγωγίαν, καθάπερ Ναυσιφάνης τὴν ἀκαταπληξίαν· ταύτην γὰρ ἔφη ὑπὸ Δημοκρίτου ἀθαμβίην λέγεσθαι. ἔτι πρὸς τούτοις Διότιμος τὴν παντέλειαν τῶν ἀγαθῶν, ἣν εὐεστὼ προσαγορεύεσθαι. (*Strom.* 2.130.4ff.)

---

[34] Ridings (1995) esp. 73ff.; Canfora (1994) suggests that Diogenes attacks this sort of project in his Prologue.

And the Abderites also teach that the following are the goal of life (*telos*). Democritus in his *On the Goal* identifies the *telos* as *euthymia*, which he also terms *euestō*... Hecataeus says that it is *autarkeia*, Apollodotos of Cyzicus *psychagōgia* – and similarly Nausiphanes says *akataplēxia*, which he claims is the same as what Democritus called *athambia*. Further, Diotimus [takes as the goal] the completeness of goods, which he said is termed *euestō*.

The sources for Clement's doxography are obscure.[35] But there is good reason to think that the choice of members for Clement's list is based on some account of the interrelationship of these various characters: Clement's choice of philosophers is not governed solely by place of birth.[36]

Clement elsewhere offers a version of the successional list found buried in Diogenes' *Lives*:

Δημοκρίτου δὲ ἀκουσταὶ Πρωταγόρας ὁ Ἀβδηρίτης, καὶ Μητρόδωρος ὁ Χῖος, οὗ Διογένης ὁ Σμυρναῖος, οὗ Ἀνάξαρχος, τούτου δὲ Πύρρων, οὗ Ναυσιφάνης. τούτου φασὶν ἔνιοι μαθητὴν Ἐπίκουρον γενέσθαι. (Clem. *Strom.* 1.64.4)

The pupils of Democritus are Protagoras of Abdera, and Metrodorus of Chios, who taught Diogenes of Smyrna, who taught Anaxarchus, who taught Pyrrho, who taught Nausiphanes. Some say that Epicurus was Nausiphanes' pupil.

So Clement was aware of the successional tradition, but when he was writing or copying his list of 'Abderite' *telē*, he was not following this successional list. He instead relied on other information. He chooses, for example in 2.130 not to list Metrodorus of Chios, although he is well aware that he was one of Democritus' followers. It is plausible that Metrodorus offered no ethical theory and was therefore not included in Clement's source περὶ τέλους. For that reason I can also exclude Metrodorus from my account of the Democritean ethical tradition. His major concerns were cosmological and epistemological and his contribution to the latter in particular has received some scholarly attention in recent years.[37]

---

35 Natorp (1893) 124–6 suggests that the source must be post-Epicurean, and that the many points of contact between Clement's doxography and the evidence of Cicero (especially in *Fin.* 5), Stobaeus, and Diogenes, point to a pre-Antiochean Academic source for all of these accounts. Cf. Usener (1887) lxviff. Philippson (1929) 352 (tentatively) suggests that they derive from Panaetius' περὶ αἱρέσεων (Panaetius is referred to by Clement at *Strom.* 2.129).

36 Hirzel (1882) 328.

37 See especially Brunschwig (1996) and (1999b), and also Shorey (1919) and Bicknell (1982).

Similarly, Protagoras is also from Abdera (Eupolis calls him a Tean, Teos being Abdera's metropolis,[38] at DL 9.50), but for all his doxographical assimilations to Democritus and despite his appearance at 1.64.4, he is not included as Hecataeus is in Clement's list. He too, like Metrodorus, might have been omitted from 2.130.6 since he was not felt to have proposed a goal of life (a *telos*).[39] Conversely, Nausiphanes is a Tean (DL 9.69, *PHerc.* 1005), and Diotimus is a Tyrian (Aët. 2.17.3 = DK 76 A1), but they are nevertheless listed among Clement's 'Abderites'.[40] There must be, therefore, more to this group of 'Abderites' than their simply all being residents of Abdera or its metropolis; they are a group of thinkers listed for their related ethical views.

If, as now seems likely, Clement has preserved in *Strom.* 2.130 an otherwise erased list of 'Abderite' philosophers and their ethical *telē*, how should we read that list? Two tactics have been suggested. The first, that of Hirzel,[41] proposes that we should read each of the 'Abderites' in 2.130 as offering a partial synonym or clarification of Democritus' ethical goal. The second, made first by Natorp,[42] suggests that the later Abderites each proposed their own ethical goal, thus allowing them some philosophical autonomy, but that these *telē* are related to the Democritean *moralia* insofar as they were inspired by, or originate in, certain themes in Democritus' work.

As I discuss each of the thinkers in these two collections (the 'Abderites' of *Strom.* 2.130, and the successional lists in Diogenes and Clement), it will be necessary to return to these sources and assess in each case the contribution which they can offer to the understanding of the various thinkers individually and as a tradition, and the plausibility of the relationship they propose between members of this group. At this stage, therefore, I suspend judgement between

---

[38] For the close relationship between these two *poleis*: Graham (1992). *Pace* Brunschwig (1999a) 1037 n. 3, Chios was not a colony of Abdera.

[39] Note also that Clement's successional list at 1.64 mirrors the traditions uncovered in Diogenes book nine insofar as Protagoras and Metrodorus are both listed as ἀκουσταί of Democritus, but the subsequent tradition stems only from Metrodorus.

[40] Cf. Alfieri (1979) 36, Bodnár (1997). Fraser (1972) vol. II, 718 n. 5 thinks that Strabo's designation of Hecataeus as a Tean (DK 73 A2) 'lies in a confusion... between the mother-city Teos and the colony Abdera. Protagoras the Abderite was called a Tean by Eupolis (DL 9.50ff.)'.

[41] Hirzel (1882) 327.   [42] Natorp (1893) 123.

the views of Hirzel and Natorp, while noting that neither provided sufficient backing for the acceptance of his respective thesis.

Democriteans, Abderites, Atomists: naming the Democritean tradition

Clement's list of *telē* at *Strom.* 2.130 is unique. Not only is it the sole source for many of these ethical ends, but it also unusually designates this group by the term 'Abderites', 'Αβδηρῖται.[43] This could be either a designation of a place of origin, or it could function as the denomination for a particular philosophical movement.[44] The latter is more probable. Although 'Αβδηρίτης does not appear as one of the stock examples of a philosophical movement named 'after a city' (ἀπὸ πόλεως),[45] it is clear that Clement has used it as such to encompass a group whose members do not, as tends to be the case for the 'Eleans', 'Megarians', or 'Cyrenaics', all originate in Abdera – the city of the founder of the school.

Another term, the periphrasis 'those around Democritus', οἱ περὶ Δημόκριτον, is commonly used by the Aristotelian commentators (e.g. Simpl. *in Phys.* 28.27) but this can hardly be regarded as evidence for a 'school' of Democriteans; it means perhaps no more than 'Democritus' or, at most, 'Democritus and Leucippus'. Simplicius himself is quite happy to talk about οἱ περὶ 'Αναξαγόραν (*in Phys.* 24.25), or οἱ περὶ Θαλήν (6.32).[46] Simplicius also uses Δημοκρίτειος (*De an.* 64.13: used of σφαιρία; 39.33 of ὑποθέσεις),[47] and Philoponus used the adjective 'Αβδηρικός to describe terminology specific to atomism (*in Phys.* 117.11: ῥυσμός, τροπή, διαθιγή).[48] All of these instances are concerned with the physical theories of Democritean atomism, and therefore

---

[43] Jacoby (1943) 31: 'als Sektnamme'. There is a parallel use at Simpl. *in de Caelo* 609.25.

[44] Democritus, of course, would qualify for both those designations, e.g. DL 9.34: 'Αβδηρίτης, ἤ, ὡς ἔνιοι, Μιλήσιος; *Suda* s.v. (DK 68 A2); Aët. 1.3.16 (DK A3), Arist. *Mete.* 365a17 (A7). Cf. Leucippus, DL 9.30: 'Ελεάτης, ὡς δὲ τινές, 'Αβδηρίτης, κατ' ἐνίους δὲ Μήλιος (BPFD, Marcovich prints Μιλήσιος).

[45] DL 1.17, ps.-Galen *Hist. phil.* 4. [46] Cf. Decleva Caizzi (1998) 343.

[47] Also of δόξα: Alex. *in De sensu* 24.12, Philop. *in Gen.* 159.16; 170.17; 186.17; 247.23; Philop. *in De an.* 67.5; 172.20; of ἀπόφασις: Philop. *in Gen.* 186.33; of the λόγος that there are atoms: Philop. *in Gen.* 38.27; of ἄτομα: Simpl. *in Phys.* 459.27; of δόγμα: Syr. *in Met.* 143.17.

[48] Asclepius *in Met.* 33.26 uses 'Αβδηριτικός.

mirror Aristotle's own concerns. The thought that such expressions might refer to an 'atomist' school is implausible, but there is no reason for us to privilege atomism as the criterion for assessing philosophical inheritance.[49] Neither Clement's list of Abderites, nor the successional lists, make reference to atomism.

Some sources prefer to use Δημοκρίτειος to denote a follower of Democritus.[50] Diotimus of Tyre is so called at Aët. 2.17.3 (DK 76 A1),[51] and there are references to a αἵρεσις denoted by οἱ Δημοκρίτειοι, but these too offer slim evidence for the historical existence of a specific group who were so named, or who identified themselves in this way. Little can be made of the plural -ειοι.[52] Moreover, that commentators could identify a Democritean αἵρεσις offers little support for the presence of a Democritean 'school'.[53]

More interesting for my purposes is the fact that other instances of the epithet 'Democritean' occur in polemical contexts, specifically those concerning Epicurus' relationship to these thinkers.[54] For example, Plutarch (*Adv. Col.* 1108E) uses Epicurean sources to 'prove' that Epicurus called himself Δημοκρίτειος in support of his claim that, by attacking Democritus, Colotes is attacking his master's master.[55] All such sources have some ulterior motive in attempting to show that Epicurus was himself a Democritean.

---

49 Cf. Stückelberger (1984) 13–15. Alfieri (1957) 149 prefers to refer to 'Abderites' rather than 'atomists' in order to avoid including Epicurus.

50 Anaxarchus is *Democriteus* at Cic. *ND* 3.82.

51 If we accept Diels' conjecture for the MSS διοκριτίος *vel sim.* Two other persons are designated Δημοκρίτειος in DK: Bion and Bolos. Bion is called an Ἀβδηρίτης at DL 4.58 and a homonym of Bion of Borysthenes, but we have no other evidence for his place of birth. He may be the Bion referred to at Strab. 1.2.21 (Posidonius fr. 137a EK). Bolos (DK 78) held some sort of agricultural theory. See DK 68 B300 vol. II, 210ff.; also Laurenti (1985), Salem (1996) 366–8.

52 Cf. Olympiodorus *in Plat. Alcibiadem* 92.6; Philop. *in De an.* 70.26; Schol. *in Euclidis Elementa* 10.26.2. Ammonius *in Cat.* 1.15 offers οἱ Δημοκρίτειοι as an example of how a αἵρεσις might derive its name from its founder. Compare Olymp. *Proleg.* 3.13, Aelian *VH* 12.25.

53 A Democritean αἵρεσις is mentioned in item λ' in the contents to Sextus *PH* 1. Even if the contents page is original (Mutschmann (1911) and (1912) xii–xiii), here αἵρεσις means little more than φιλοσοφία, the term which Sextus uses for the title of this section when it appears at 1.213. Cf. Glucker (1978) 166ff.

54 Also compare *ND* 1.93 (Haslam (1993) 44–5 discusses the text). Nausiphanes is called a Democritean at *ND* 1.73, and in the *Suda* s.v. Ἐπίκουρος.

55 See Westman (1955) 220–2, who also weakens the praise implied by the verbs ἅψασθαι and περιπεσεῖν.

They see instances where Epicurus or an Epicurean criticises Democritus and counter by pointing out that Epicurus is, despite his protestations to be self-taught and self-inspired (SE *M.* 1.3),[56] a Democritean himself.[57] Thus they put pressure on Epicurus' simultaneous desires to look directly back to Democritus for much of his physical and perhaps even ethical theory, and, insisting on his own originality nevertheless, to bypass the intervening 'sceptical' phase of the succession. Cicero and Plutarch insist that Epicurus cannot have it both ways. He cannot retain the required distance from his predecessors while his physical theory remains relevantly similar.

How one reads such exchanges depends on one's preferred view of Epicurus' attitude to his atomist predecessors, and my view will emerge more fully as I detail the Democritean tradition itself, but it is worth setting down some preliminary remarks at this stage even though they may pre-empt to some extent what will follow.[58] It has been argued that Epicurus was not so hostile to Democritus as once thought, but that he respectfully corrected Democritus' views on a number of subjects, principally the composition of atoms by minimal parts, the ontological status of secondary qualities, and above all, Democritus' determinism. More work on the exact expression of these disagreements would help

---

56 *Pace* Sedley (1976a) 135, this is a more radical claim than the thought that Nausiphanes taught him nothing. Epicurus claims complete originality and internal inspiration: cf. Lucr. *DRN* 1.62ff., 3.1ff., 5.1ff. See Laks (1976) 56, 68–70; Balaudé (1994) 23–8; Blank (1998a) 78 compares Heraclitus B101, and DL 9.5 (also Pl. *Theaet.* 180b9), Xen. *Mem.* 4.2.4.

57 E.g. Cic. *Tusc.* 1.82: Epicurus criticises Democritus' view that the soul might linger in a recently dead body. Cicero retorts: *nemo id quidem dicit, etsi Democritum insimulat Epicurus, Democritii negant.* There is no need to take the plural *Democritii* to imply an actual group. See also Proclus *in Pl. Rep.* II.1136ff. Kroll, on which: Gottschalk (1986).

58 Sedley (1976a) argues that Epicurus was notably hostile only towards Nausiphanes. Huby (1978) 85 cites Diog. Oin. fr. 7 Smith but cuts off the quotation before 7.II.10–12 in which Diogenes criticises Democritus' view of secondary qualities as making life impossible. Smith (1993) 443: Democritus is mentioned by Diogenes more than any other philosopher, usually critically (frr. 7; 9.VI.3ff., 10.IV.10ff., 43.I.12ff.; 54.II.3ff.). Huby (1978) 84 claims that 'Lucretius speaks of Democritus in the highest possible terms' (3.370, 1039; 5.621) but Smith (1993) 443 cites the same passages as criticisms of Democritus. The one reference to Democritus by name in Epicurus' extant writings comes in *PHerc.* 1148 (*On Nature* XIV Col. XXX Leone). Leone (1984) 83–4 considers the reference to indicate a positive attitude on Epicurus' part. Gigante and Indelli (1980) find Philodemus generally positive towards Democritus, although with some reservations (e.g. *PHerc.* 1457 X.4–12 = DK B 153). Cf. Morel (1996) 249–355.

the inquiry,[59] but it is clear both that Epicurean atomism undeniably derived to a great extent from Democritus and that Epicurus was far from happy to be seen as a mere follower of Democritus. I shall defer dealing with his criticisms in detail until my Conclusion, since they can fully be understood only by setting them against the background of the intervening Democritean tradition. Nevertheless, it should be clear even at this point that Epicurus' particular criticisms of Democritus, and the matters on which he is most keen to dissociate himself from his atomist predecessor are metaphysical or epistemological issues. Epicurus' relationship to Democritean ethics is not a concern of these sources. Indeed, and perhaps as a result, the link between Democritean and Epicurean ethics is often overlooked or even denied. Epicurus is often characterised in the ancient sources as deriving his physics from Democritus and his ethics from Cyrenaicism or some other tradition of hedonism. This claim is justified by the sort of evidence from anti-Epicurean sources, namely Cicero and Plutarch, whose attempts to force the Epicureans into proclaiming a Democritean heritage are in turn motivated by the Epicureans' own attempts to distance their (meta)physics from the earlier atomism. The very fact that the Epicureans differ vocally from Democritus on such issues offers support for the view that only in physics was there any degree of influence between these thinkers. If we look outside the Epicureans' own comments, however, further aspects of Democritean influence will emerge. But as I explained in my introduction (p. 7–9), the metaphysical questions posed by atomism will also play a part in the ethical story.

---

[59] Silvestre (1985) 19 and Morel (1996) 34 n. 51, 252 n. 18 argue that by the assessment of Epicurus' various philosophical positions in comparison to those of Democritus, rather than by point by point discussion of texts where Democritus is named, we might come to a more nuanced view of their relationship. The passage of Epicurus *On Nature* 25 (Arr. 34.30.7–15; now Laursen (1997) 41) is not conclusive. Laks (1981) 23 concludes that Epicurus did indeed locate a number of slips made by Democritus in his atomic theory, 'mais, pour nombreuses qu'elles soient, elles ne mettent jamais en question les fondements, parce que d'autres explications plus plausibles peuvent être élaborées, qui les respectent mieux'. Compare Arrighetti (1979), and Sedley (1998b) 142. A similar passage of mixed praise and criticism occurs in Philodemus *De lib. dic.* fr. 20: Konstan et al. (1998) 38.

Self-presentation of a tradition

So far I have been discussing these Democriteans as a tradition manufactured and identified by other writers. We have only a few indications of these philosophers being themselves conscious of such a tradition and concerned to place themselves within it. The form of Timon of Philus' satirical verses (*Silloi*) aimed at other philosophers is well designed for the assessment of the views of the various philosophers it encompasses and the relationships between them. His comments on the philosophers who appear in the same successional tradition as his mentor, Pyrrho, will be extremely important if we wish to see how Timon fashioned his own philosophy according to those around him.

Already evident from Clement's Abderite *telē* is the indication that Nausiphanes himself identified his *telos*, *akataplēxia*, with a Democritean term: *athambia*.[60] This indicates a desire to present himself as an heir to Democritus' ethical thought. Similarly, there is evidence that Nausiphanes also located his thought in relation to his other philosophical ancestor, Pyrrho: DL 9.64. Perhaps Nausiphanes was the first of our list of Abderites to see the successional tradition, and his place within it, in something like the form in which it appears in Clement and Diogenes. In this case, Epicurus' strong desire to deny the influence of Nausiphanes would serve a double rôle in his drive to appear 'self-taught': it denies his immediate tutor, but also distances Epicurus from the tradition to which both Democritus and Pyrrho belong. It is Nausiphanes whom Diogenes cites as claiming that Epicurus greatly admired Pyrrho's conduct and often asked for information about him (DL 9.64). So it is Nausiphanes who threatens to tie Epicurus closely to the elements of the philosophical succession about which he had the greatest reservations, namely those thinkers who were being increasingly viewed as sceptics, and therefore Nausiphanes is the target of Epicurus' harshest criticisms. In fact, Epicurus' desire to distance himself from Nausiphanes and deny any strong affiliation

---

[60] Alfieri (1979) 161 n. 2.

to Democritus is perhaps the best evidence we have for the notion that Democritus, Metrodorus, Nausiphanes and the others were seen as belonging to a particular tradition even in Epicurus' time. When this tradition was first proclaimed explicitly is impossible to know for sure, but there are already hints that Nausiphanes at least saw his place as a follower of Democritus and an admirer of Pyrrho.

2

DEMOCRITUS' ETHICS
AND ATOMIST PSYCHOLOGIES

Democritus as the source for a tradition

The discussion of the retrospective creation of a philosophical succession has already pointed to Democritus' metaphysics and its
accompanying epistemology as important criteria for the positioning of Democritus within a philosophical heritage. As I discuss the
various thinkers in that heritage those themes will recur. For now,
however, I wish to concentrate on Democritus' own ethical thought,
in order to show how that too provided a rich source for the later
tradition.

I shall not discuss at length any of the more 'social' or
'political' fragments – although I realise that this makes my picture of Democritean *moralia* incomplete – because my interest in
Democritus is precisely in his rôle as a source for later Democritean
and sceptical ethical traditions.[1] It is their concern with the definition and accomplishment of a personal *telos* of life (itself an
Aristotelian and post-Aristotelian concern) which therefore directs
and narrows my attention. With this end in view the possibility of
multiple interpretations of the Democritean fragments is particularly interesting, since they provided the source-material for the
divergent philosophical views which followed.[2]

It is important to recognise when considering the influence of
Democritus on these later thinkers that it is chronologically unlikely that any of the various 'Democriteans' had met and studied
with Democritus himself. Metrodorus of Chios alone might have

---

[1] There are useful treatments of Democritus' social and political thought in Nill (1985)
84–91, Farrar (1988), and Procopé (1989a–90).
[2] Democritus' ethics also had an influence on other thinkers. On Democritus and the Cynics:
Stewart (1958), Gigante (1992) 21–3.

had the opportunity.[3] This means that the Democriteans' encounter with Democritus was through his writings, although these were almost certainly not in the form that we read them in now.[4] Contrast this with what was the case for the various followers of Socrates, or the first generation of followers of Pyrrho, who met and knew the philosopher whose authority they invoked. Their encounter with the thoughts of their master was personal and oral – Socrates and Pyrrho left no writings of their own.

The study of Democritus himself presents a number of methodological problems. Although the majority of the 'B' fragments listed in Diels–Kranz are of an ethical nature and therefore of prime importance for this study, most of the doxography is centred around Democritus' physical, epistemological, and psychological thought. It is therefore difficult to secure any particular reading of the B fragments by reference to surrounding doxography.

Further, most of those B fragments derive from one of two sources, the 'Democrates' collection (B35–115), and Iohannes Stobaeus' collection of *gnōmai* (B169–297).[5] Those fragments not from these two collections, B1–34 and B116–68, come from

---

3 Brunschwig (1996) 27 n. 26 dates Metrodorus' birth to around 420 BC on the basis of a fragment of Antiphanes (DK A1a = Antiphanes 219 Kassel–Austin, *apud* Athen. 100D) dated *c*. 388. This refers to a Μητρᾶς ὁ Χῖος, interpreted as a shortened form of Μητρόδωρος. (This shortened form is used to justify the reconstruction by Crönert (1906a) 192 of a reference to Metrodorus in Philodemus' *Rhetoric* (DK A25), cf. Capasso (1987) 152 n. 204.) But the fragment of Antiphanes contains a lot of word-play: ἔμμητρον, μητρόπολις and Μητρᾶς. The comedy from which it comes is the Φιλομήτωρ. A 'Theocritos' (the name of Metrodorus' father) appears in the *Suda* (DK A2) as a pupil of 'Metrodorus the pupil of Isocrates'. Perhaps Theocritos named his son after his teacher, or Antiphanes refers to this elder Metrodorus. This Theocritos might be the author of an epigram on Aristotle preserved in DL 5.11, and/or the prominent Chian statesman: Plut. *QC* 633C, *Lib. educ.* 11A–C, Macrob. *Sat.* 7.3.12 (Teodorsson (1990), Flower (1994) 24). This latter Theocritos was executed by Antigonus Monophthalmos after 321 BC.

4 Alfieri (1979) 22.

5 Stewart (1958), on the basis of the strong resonances of Democritean material in a passage of Seneca *Ben.* 7.1.3ff. deriving from Demetrius the Cynic (first century AD), argues (184) 'that it was among the Cynics and their allies that his fragments were preserved during the period, and probably deformed for more convenient use'. He also suggests a Cynic origin for the tradition of the laughing Democritus (Cic. *De or.* 2.235, Hor. *Ep.* 2.1.194–200, Sen. *Tranq.* 15.2ff.), which was later teamed with the image of the weeping ('Stoic') Heraclitus. Further on this see the Hippocratic *Pseudepigrapha* letters 10–21 (esp. 17) in Littré vol. 9 and Smith (1990); discussion in Lutz (1953–4), Stewart (1958) 186–7, Buck (1963), Decleva Caizzi (1984b) 19 n. 44, Rütten (1992), Müller (1994), Padel (1995) 91–2, Salem (1996) 362ff., Ayache (1996).

a number of disparate sources, and are therefore generally considered to be the most secure. But most of the major ethical fragments do indeed come from Stobaeus or the Democrates collection, and are therefore subject to difficulties caused by the form of such works. Both are examples of later antiquity's practice of scouring the literary output of the past to pick out useful and educational citations.[6] The compilers of such works were not averse to altering the wording of the citation a little, and very rarely give any indication of the work from which it derives.

The 'Democrates' collection in particular has been suspected of inauthenticity. Reattributed to Democritus on the assumption that ΔΗΜΟΚΡΙΤΟΥ became corrupted to ΔΗΜΟΚΡΑΤΟΥΣ,[7] the fragments, although still in the Ionic dialect, tend to be shorter and more gnomic than the Stobaean quotations.[8] However, this is not necessarily evidence for their inauthenticity. Stobaeus himself used the Democrates collection.[9] Nevertheless, it is a generally accepted *modus operandi* not to base any interpretation on Democratean rather than Stobaean fragments.

The Stobaeus collection too is not without its difficulties.[10] This mammoth work was truncated sometime in the Byzantine period when the copying of its entirety became impractical and unpopular.[11] Still, from what we know of the practice of ancient *gnōmologoi* a number of considerations arise which affect our handling of the material. Stobaeus does not note where he found these *gnōmai*. He notes only the original author. He might, therefore, be copying from an earlier citation (which in turn might have contaminated the transmission of the original expression). Also, although the anthologist's input appears to be limited to the arrangement of the material within his anthology, there was no compulsion *not* to

---

[6] On this genre: Barns (1950–51).   [7] As in e.g. Porph. *De abst.* 4.21.6.

[8] On 'Democrates' see Welleman s.v. in *RE* 5.134, and Philippson (1924) 369–86. Voros (1973) provides a comprehensive analysis of the Democrates fragments, and has a generally optimistic view of their Democritean source.

[9] Stobaeus copies the final χρυσοῦ in B51 (= Stobaeus 2.4.12) on to the end of his version of B52 (= Stobaeus 3.10.42). See Procopé (1971) xvi–xvii.

[10] For Stobaeus' aims see Photius *Bibl.* 167 = 112a14ff. Also see Mansfeld and Runia (1997) ch. 4.

[11] After the first saying attributed to a certain author, following sayings are denoted by simply τοῦ αὐτοῦ. If, then, the first saying of a new author is omitted by a copyist, all the subsequent sayings will be misattributed.

alter the expression of the fragment. In addition, we know from Diogenes' biography that even by the time Diogenes was writing there were a number of compilations of Democritus' work in existence as well as some works which Diogenes claims are generally agreed to be mis-attributed (DL 9.49).[12] We have no idea how careful Stobaeus was in his collection of material.

In the face of these doubts, in order to make any progress it is prudent to set a number of methodological principles. It is preferable to use, where possible, fragments from authors other than Stobaeus and the Democrates collection, to prefer Stobaean to Democratean fragments, and to prefer longer Stobaean fragments which appear less subject to truncation and manipulation in order to produce a more memorable *gnōmē*.[13]

Naming the *telos*

Even in the case of the doxographical sources our view is clouded by later periods. But here the problems are not so much those of transmission as of intervening interpretation.[14]

Diogenes Laërtius 9.45

τέλος δὲ εἶναι τὴν εὐθυμίαν, οὐ τὴν αὐτὴν οὖσαν τῇ ἡδονῇ, ὡς ἔνιοι παρακούσαντες ἐξεδέξαντο, ἀλλὰ καθ᾽ ἣν γαληνῶς καὶ εὐσταθῶς ἡ ψυχὴ διάγει, ὑπὸ μηδενὸς

---

[12] This is good evidence against the suggestion of von der Mühll (1919) that Democritus himself composed a *gnomologium* which Epicurus then copied with his *Kyriai Doxai* (Philippson (1924) suggests this was the work of a pupil of Democritus). The evidence of Dionysius of Alexandria *apud* Eus. *PE* 14.27.5 (B119) for Democritean ὑποθῆκαι could easily refer to post-Democritean compilations: Procopé (1989a) 307–8 and n. 3. Nevertheless Epicurus' *KD* 16 is clearly modelled on B119: DK ad loc., Kahn (1985) 3, Clay (1972) 60–3.

[13] Compare Procopé (1971) xiii–xxxv, and Taylor (1999) 223–7.

[14] It has been thought reasonable to search through Plutarch *Tranq.* and Seneca *Tranq.* for extensive and substantial portions of the Democritean work. I cannot think this is at all profitable. Plutarch is clear that he is writing his piece from the various works he has with him at the time, not only the Democritean treatise (464F). For previous discussions see Hirzel (1879), Heinze (1890), Fowler (1890), and Siefert (1908). Herschbell (1982) argues that Plutarch had direct access to Democritean works, including the περὶ εὐθυμίης. Gill (1993) tries to reconstruct Panaetius' περὶ εὐθυμίας from Cicero's *De officiis* I (esp. 1.66–81, 92ff.), seeing in Panaetius' work a synthesis of Stoic and Democritean/Epicurean material. Abel (1987) is extremely sceptical about the possibilities for finding Panaetian material in Plutarch. Cf. Alesse (1994) 14–15 and n. 10; Van Straaten (1962) vii. On Seneca and Democritus: Laurenti (1980).

ταραττομένη φόβου ἢ δεισιδαιμονίας ἢ ἄλλου τινὸς πάθους. καλεῖ δ'αὐτὴν καὶ εὐεστὼ καὶ πολλοῖς ἄλλοις ὀνόμασι.

He says that *euthymia* is the goal of life – which is not identical with pleasure as some have mistakenly understood, but is the state in which the soul proceeds peacefully and well settled, disturbed by no fear or superstition or any other passion. He also calls this *euestō* and many other names.

This is often cited as the definitive description of what Democritus offered as the *telos* of human life. However, as a piece of doxography it is appropriately and instructively careful about how dogmatic an interpretation it claims. It notes first that many people have *mis*understood Democritus as a hedonist. This is a false interpretation, notes Diogenes, because *euthymia* and *hēdonē* are not identical. Second, it notes that Democritus was not overly worried about providing a single-word description of his *telos*. εὐθυμία, εὐεστὼ and 'many other names' are noted.[15] We too should similarly be reticent to state Democritus' *telos* in dogmatic terms. Diogenes resorts to a brief description: καθ' ἥν γαληνῶς καὶ εὐσταθῶς ἡ ψυχὴ διάγει. But this too has been suspected of Hellenistic influence. Compare a very similar Epicurean phrase retained in Plut. *Non posse* 1089D (Us. 68): τὸ γὰρ εὐσταθὲς σαρκὸς κατάστημα...[16]

There are also Latin sources which describe or explain Democritus' *telos*. Seneca provides this brief gloss, but this too has been thought to reflect the influence of later Hellenistic thoughts about *ataraxia*:

hanc stabilem animi sedem Graeci euthymiam vocant, de qua Democriti volumen egregium est, ego tranquillitatem voco. (*Tranq.* 2.3)

The Greeks call this settled state of the soul, about which there is an excellent book by Democritus, *euthymia*. I call it tranquillity.

This sentence comes only a few lines after an example of the – by then common – use of imagery of the sea to convey ideas of mental tranquillity (at 2.1).[17] In a similar vein, Cicero comments: *id enim summum bonum* εὐθυμίαν *et saepe* ἀθαμβίαν *appellat, id est animum terrore liberum* (*Fin.* 5.87). Perhaps Diogenes, Seneca, and

---

[15] Cf. Stob. 2.7.3 (DK A167).
[16] Cf. Philod. (*PHerc.* 1015/832) L.4 Sudhaus. Grilli (1983) 100–2. Procopé (1971) 125.
[17] Cf. Plut. *Virt. et vit.* 101B, *Tranq.* 466B.

Cicero have indeed all read what Democritus might have said about *euthymia* through Hellenistic eyes. We might have good reason to be suspicious when Diogenes sets up Democritus' *telos* as a kind of *galēnē*, in which the soul is 'disturbed by no fear, superstition, or any other affection', since this sounds very much like Epicurean *ataraxia*.[18]

However, we should not dismiss these sources too hastily. The image of *galēnē* is not confined to Epicurean and post-Epicurean thought (e.g. *Ep. Hdt.* 37.3, 83, Usener *Glossarium Epicureum* s.v.; cf. Cic. *Tusc.* 5.16, ps.-Pl. *Axioch.* 370d3).[19] It is at work in Diogenes' biography of Pyrrho (DL 9.64–6),[20] and has been detected in much earlier writings, notably those of Solon (frr. 12, 37 West). There are also interesting Platonic parallels.[21] This shows that there is no chronological reason why Democritus could not have used the image of *galēnē*, had he so wished.[22] Diogenes could well be responding to Democritean material without this response being coloured to the point of inaccuracy by Hellenistic concerns. Certainly, the pursuit of tranquillity was a concern of the Hellenistic era but there are plenty of pre-Hellenistic examples to show that this same image for a similar mental state was already available.

Let us, therefore, return to the Latin sources and see how much they can add to an understanding of Democritus' thought. Seneca defines *tranquillitas* as:

[18] εὐθυμία also appears in Diogenes of Oinoanda 113 Smith in what might be a paraphrase of Democritus B3/191. However, the authorship of this section of the inscription is unclear: Smith (1993) 533–4. This might be a citation of Democritus rather than a *bona fide* Epicurean use of the term. Cf. Procopé (1971) 3, 8–9, 27; Langerbeck (1935) 61.

[19] Cf. χειμών at *Ep. Men.* 128; Polyst. *De cont. irrat.* XX.26, XXXI.22. γαλήνη βίου at Luc. *Alex.* 61 seems to have Epicurean connotations: Clay (1992) 3439. Cf. Plut. *Tranq.* 477A, *Non posse* 1100E; Zacher (1982) 109–10. The Cyrenaics also used the image to describe not a state of pleasure, but an intermediate state between pleasure and pain (Aristoc. *apud* Eus. 14.18.32: see Tsouna (1998c) 11).

[20] For its use in early Pyrrhonism, see Timon frr. 63 and 64 (Diels) *apud* SE *M.* 11.141. Timon's models have been seen as primarily Homeric (*Od.* 5.391–2, 11.575: Long (1978) 69 and n. 15).

[21] *Phaedo* 84a2ff., *Symp.* 197c5, *Pol.* 273a6, *Tim.* 44b3, *Leg.* 791a3, pseudo-Plato *Axiochus* 370d3. Aristotle tends to restrict his use of the word to its primary significance as the state of a calm sea: *Met.* 1043a24, *Top.* 108b25, *Meteo.* 367b15, *Probl.* 931b20. At *Physiog.* 811b38 it refers to a particular facial expression. Padel (1992) 78–88 traces the image of flux and disturbance through Homeric epic and fifth-century tragedy.

[22] Aelian *VH* 12.17 (A152) reports Democritus' claim that some foetuses remain ἐν γαλήνῃ in the womb until the right time for delivery.

... quomodo animus semper aequali secundoque cursu eat propitiusque sibi sit et sua laetus aspiciat et hoc gaudium non interrumpat sed placido statu maneat nec attollens se umquam nec deprimens. id tranquillitas erit. (*Tranq.* 2.4)

... the state in which the soul proceeds always in a measured and untroubled course, and is well disposed to itself, and looks on its own affairs happily and never interrupts this joy. It remains in this peaceful state, never raising nor depressing itself. That will be 'tranquillity'.

This immediately follows Seneca's explanation of how he is rendering Democritus' *euthymia* with the Latin *tranquillitas* (cf. Cic. *Fin.* 5.23), which I quoted above, and confirms that *euthymia* has definite positive connotations. It also suggests that any understanding of *galēnē* as 'tranquillity' and *therefore* not a positive state such as *euthymia* is misguided. Latin authors were often quite careful about rendering Greek terms in their own language, and are often explicit about the methods they use. Seneca explains his own view as follows:

nec enim imitari et transferre verba ad illorum formam necesse est; res ipsa, de qua agitur, aliquando signanda nomine est, quod appellationis Graecae vim debet habere, non faciem. (*Tranq.* 2.3)

It is not necessary to mimic and adapt words in their [sc. Greeks] form. But the thing itself – about which we are thinking – sometimes should be denoted by a word which should have the force, not the form, of the Greek term.

Although *tranquillitas* is not a lexically exact rendering (*bono esse animo* would be closer), it captures what Seneca feels is the force of *euthymia*.[23] We can also find instances of *tranquillitas* standing for *ataraxia*: Cic. *Fin.* 1.43, 1.46, and especially 2.118, all in the context of discussions of Epicurean ethics. But this suggests only that the closest Latin can come both to *euthymia* and to *ataraxia* is the word *tranquillitas*. It does not, for example, provide any support for the view that *euthymia* is an earlier term for what came to be called *ataraxia* in the early Hellenistic period until *euthymia*

---

[23] Inwood (1995) 74. Striker (1990) 97: 'In fact, "tranquillitas" is probably closer in meaning to the Greek *ataraxia* ... a term which seems to have been used interchangeably with *euthymia* and which became the favoured technical term in early Hellenistic times.' Grimal (1992) 142 notes that *tranquillitas* might be related etymologically to the transparency of a calm sea, and therefore share some connotations of the Greek γαλήνη. Cf. Ernout and Meillet s.v. *tranquillus*.

was reclaimed by Panaetius.[24] However, some conclusions might
be drawn from this usage of *tranquillitas* by Seneca and Cicero.
If Seneca (*Tranq.* 2.3–4) is happy to use *tranquillitas* to capture
the positive connotations of *euthymia* and that same word is used
to render *ataraxia*, why should *ataraxia* not share similar positive
connotations?[25] This is still compatible with Diogenes' insistence
at 9.45 that Democritean *euthymia* is not 'pleasure' and that therefore Democritus does not directly anticipate Epicurean hedonism.
Both *euthymia* and *ataraxia* might still have positive connotations
without the Epicurean hedonistic conception of the *telos* necessarily being read back into Democritus.[26]

Removing fear

The absence of fear and of superstition, both of which are mentioned in Diogenes' characterisation of Democritus' preferred
soul-state, were also to be made prominent in the *tetrapharmakos*
of Epicureanism (see also *KD* 1 and 2). But again, that should not
compel us to see their inclusion here as anachronistic. Unfortunately for any more sophisticated understanding of Democritus'
view of superstitious beliefs, Democritus' theology is no clearer
than its Epicurean descendant.[27] The word *theios* or one of its
cognates is used in a number of fragments (B21, 37, 112), but may
prove nothing positive about Democritus' own views; he is entitled
to use the word to refer to 'how most people believe gods to be'.[28]

---

[24] Cf. Striker (1990) 97–8. The only clear evidence we have for the content of Panaetius'
περὶ εὐθυμίας is that it mentioned the attitude of Xenophanes and Anaxagoras to their
sons' deaths (DL 2.13, 9.20; Cic. *Tusc.* 3.30, 58; Plut. *Tranq.* 474D, *Cohib. ira* 463D:
Abel (1987) 152. There is no reason to think that Democritean material was unavailable
before Panaetius, through the Epicurean and Cynic traditions. See Gill (1993) esp. 343–4,
(1994); Annas (1993b) 361; and above p. 32, n. 14.

[25] Cp. Barnes (1979) vol. II, 231.

[26] Striker (1990) 109 n. 8 suggests that the ἔνιοι παρακούσαντες of DL 9.45 are Epicureans
who misunderstand Democritus.

[27] See esp. B30, B205, B234, B297 (on which cf. B160, A74–9, and Epic. *Ep. Men.* 126).
Cf. Bossu (1982). Often the doxographical sources conflate Democritean and Epicurean
theology. At Cic. *ND* 1.29 Velleius contrasts Democritus' theory with his own Epicureanism and suggests that Democritus had no mechanism in his atomist physics which
would explain the indestructibility of the immortal gods: cf. Vlastos (1945–6) 580 n. 24.
Compare SE *M.* 9.19 on Democritus' gods: δύσφθαρτα μέν, οὐκ ἄφθαρτα δέ.

[28] For arguments disarming the theist language of the fragments: Vlastos (1945–6) 579–81.
McGibbon (1965) responds. Later sources seem sure of Democritus' atheism: Apul.
Apol. 27, Eus. *PE* 14.3.7.

Although there is not a great deal of evidence for this, it is nevertheless reasonable to suggest that – like Epicurus – Democritus disapproved of the damaging psychological effects of superstition, and further argued that his cosmology left no room for demiurgic or interventionist deities.

Although Diogenes does not refer specifically to the fear of death in his paraphrase of Democritus' ideal state, there are extant fragments which seem to address this particular source of anxiety, and show that this is one species of fear which he was keen to remove.

B203 ἄνθρωποι τὸν θάνατον φεύγοντες διώκουσιν.
B205 ἀνοήμονες ζωῆς ὀρέγονται <καὶ> γήραος θάνατον δεδοικότες.[29]
B206 ἀνοήμονες θάνατον δεδοικότες γηράσκειν ἐθέλουσιν.

B203 In fleeing death men seek it.
B205 The unwise desire life and old age through fear of death.
B206 The unwise wish to grow old because they fear death.

These are part of a series of fragments in which Democritus gives examples of what the 'foolish' do (B197–206), and therefore might plausibly be interpreted as negative paradigms. One of the contrasts exposed is between the desire to live and a fear of death. Democritus claims that only because people are afraid of dying do they want to live on for as long as possible, postponing their demise and prolonging their old age.[30]

B203 is deliberately expressed as a paradox. Although men fear death, and therefore attempt to escape it, in fact the measures they take to ward off their demise hasten the end. So in their attempt at fleeing death they pursue it.[31] In the surrounding fragments the method employed to escape death is simply to try to live for as long as possible. It is hard to see this as a way of pursuing death. But Democritus appears to use 'life' and 'death' elsewhere in a normative sense. This next fragment refers to 'Democrates' rather than Democritus but I see no reason to regard it as spurious.[32]

---

[29] <καὶ> Taylor; γήραος del. Diels.
[30] Cf. Anon. Iamb. DK 89 5.2 (= Iambl. *Prot.* 20, 99.18–28 Pistelli).
[31] Note that B203 refers not to 'the foolish' specifically, but 'men' in general. However, Stobaeus places it in the middle of his compilation of Democritean saying about foolish men, and therefore clearly understood a more restricted reference. Meinke emends ἄνθρωποι to ἀνοήμονες.
[32] See Taylor (1999) 223–7 and 238.

B160 τὸ γὰρ κακῶς ζῆν καὶ μὴ φρονίμως καὶ σωφρόνως καὶ ὁσίως
Δημοκράτης ἔλεγεν οὐ κακῶς ζῆν εἶναι, ἀλλὰ πολὺν χρόνον ἀπο-
θνῄσκειν. (= Porph. De abst. 4.21)

B160 Living badly, and without understanding, temperance, and piety,
'Democrates' used to call not living a bad life, but dying a long
death.

Living badly, failing to achieve the good life which Democritus
recommends, is revealed as dying a long death. So the people
described in B203, since they do not achieve the human good,
instead of 'living a life' in this normative sense, pass their existence
as a long slow death. Democritus elsewhere asserts that to live in
fear of death is to live a miserable life.

B199 ἀνοήμονες τὸ ζῆν ὡς στυγέοντες ζῆν ἐθέλουσι δείματι ἀίδεω.
B200 ἀνοήμονες βιοῦσιν οὐ τερπόμενοι βιοτῆι.
B201 ἀνοήμονες δηναιότητος ὀρέγονται οὐ τερπόμενοι δηναιότητι.

B199 Fools want to live, but hate living through fear of Hades.
B200 Fools live without enjoying living.
B201 Fools desire a long life but do not enjoy living long.

A life worth living is a life of enjoyment. I will discuss further
the specific sort of pleasure recommended by Democritus below,
and will there suggest that *terpsis* is used to denote a particular kind
of objectively good pleasurable feeling. The people described here
take no such enjoyment from life because they are overwhelmed
by the fear of death. In contrast, someone who has conquered the
fear of death can enjoy what life he has. The divorce of the value
of a life from its duration can be paralleled in Epicureanism, and
was presumably derived in part from Democritus.[33]

It is important to recognise that both the fear of death, and
the anxiety caused by false religious suppositions are tackled by
Democritus and Epicurus on the basis of certain consequences of
their atomist and anti-teleological cosmology. This provides the
required basis from which they argue that the soul is mortal, and
death is annihilation, and that there is no need to posit interventionist or demiurgic gods. Later the question will arise to what
extent Democritus' ethical thought was derived from his physics.

[33] *Ep. Men.* 124, 126: χρόνον οὐ μήκιστον, ἀλλὰ τὸν ἥδιστον καρπίζεται; Lucr. *DRN*
3.952–71.; *KD* 20, 21. See also Warren (2000a).

Here already there is a link between the two which survives into Epicureanism. That is not, of course, to say that the arguments against fearing death or fearing the gods *require* an atomist cosmology. However, these arguments can be seen to stem from and contribute to a general picture of the world and man's place in it which is maintained by Democritus and Epicurus, however much they differ on other issues.

Euestō

From the evidence of Diogenes and Cicero we might be tempted to see an uncomplicated picture. Democritus had a general conception of the human good and he called it various different things in different contexts. This is perhaps what we expect as a result of Cicero's warnings about Democritus' lack of fixed terminology, and is confirmed by Clement's list of Abderite *telē* (cited above, pp. 20–1):

> And the Aberites also teach that the following are the goal of life (*telos*). Democritus in his *On the Goal* identifies the *telos* as *euthymia*, which he also terms *euestō*...Hecataeus says that it is *autarkeia*, Apollodotos of Cyzicus *psychagōgia* – and similarly Nausiphanes says *akataplēxia*, which he claims is the same as what Democritus called *athambia*. Further, Diotimus [takes as the goal] the completeness of goods, which he said is termed *euestō*. (*Strom.*2.130.4ff.)

There is no reference in Thrasyllus' list of Democritean works (DL 9.46) to an *On the Goal*, and we should not expect one; that terminology belongs to a period after Democritus. We should identify the work which Clement cites as the περὶ εὐθυμίας in Diogenes' list, or assume that Clement is referring to a non-existent work, having received his information second-hand about Democritus' ethical views and assuming that he *must* have written a work 'on the end of life'. Also, whereas Cicero identified *euthymia* and *athambia*, in Clement we find an implicit distinction. *Athambia* is not mentioned as a term for Democritus' *telos* but instead as something which Nausiphanes equated with his *akataplēxia*.[34] Did

---

34 The particle γάρ can be explained. Clement begins the citation with the assertion that the Abderite school all teach that there is a *telos*. He then gives Democritus' terms for his *telos*, then Hecataeus' and Apollodotos'. The καθάπερ continues the train of thought: 'similarly Nausiphanes [sc. taught that there was a *telos* which he called] ἀκαταπληξία', and then the report of Nausiphanes' identification of his *telos* with Democritus' ἀθαμβία

Democritus include *athambia* in *euthymia*? Further discussion of Nausiphanean *akataplēxia* will help, but it seems likely that *euthymia* is not to be entirely identified with *athambia*.[35]

More intriguing is *euestō*. Diogenes also refers to the 'Democritean *telos*' by this name at 9.45, but beyond these two references its nature is obscure. In his list of Democritus' ethical works Diogenes records the second of Thrasyllus' tetralogies thus (9.46):[36]

περὶ ἀνδραγαθίας ἢ περὶ ἀρετῆς·
'Αμαλθείης κέρας·
περὶ εὐθυμίης·
Ὑπομνημάτων ἠθικῶν· ἡ γὰρ Εὐεστὼ οὐχ εὑρίσκεται.

On manly goodness, or On virtue,
Amaltheia's horn,
On euthymia,
Ethical reminders (for the Euestō cannot be found).

Someone (Thrasyllus, or some earlier scribe) tried to find a work of Democritus by that title but failed. There must have been some reference to a Democritean work by that name which occasioned the search, and either the work was lost before the compilation of Thrasyllus' catalogue, or it was never a separate work.[37] Still, Diogenes was sure enough of the term's Democritean heritage that he included it in his description of the *telos* a chapter earlier.[38]

Only one Democritean fragment, B257, uses the term *euestō*, and there the connotations are not necessarily eudaimonistic: it means

is included as further evidence for (γάρ) this claim that the Abderites proposed ethical *telē*. Striker (1990) 98 suggests that the immediate predecessor of Epicurus' ἀταραξία was Democritus' ἀθαμβία. Clay (1992) 3444 n. 98 strangely claims a reference to Democritean ἀθαμβία at Luc. *Alex.* 17.

[35] Note B215 and 216. Cf. Bossu (1982) 298, and Gale (1994) 194 on *horror* at Lucr. *DRN* 3.29.
[36] On Thrasyllus' catalogue: Tarrant (1993) 85–9, Mansfeld (1994) 97ff., Morel (1996) 368–74.
[37] Mansfeld (1994) 102: '[Thrasyllus'] cautious remark proves that he possessed or at any rate had actually seen copies of all the other works listed in the catalogue, and gives one the impression of philological meticulousness.'
[38] *Suda* s.v. εὐεστώ cites DL 9.45.

simply 'prosperity'.[39] Diels–Kranz print another 'fragment', an entry from Hesychius' lexicon (s.v. εὐεστώ) as Democritean:

B140 εὐδαιμονία ἀπὸ τοῦ εὖ ἑστάναι τὸν οἶκον.

B140 Happiness from a good state of one's household.

Others commentators have already questioned the inclusion and relevance of this fragment.[40] There is no reason to assume that this is at all Democritean. Furthermore, Hesychius' etymology here is incorrect: *euestō* derives from εἶναι, not ἑστάναι.[41]

However, no commentator as far as I am aware has noticed that Hesychius' lexicon offers a number of other 'definitions' alongside that printed as B140:

εὐεστώ· εὐθηνία ἀπὸ τοῦ εὖ εἶναι.
        ἢ ἀπὸ τοῦ δαψιλεῖν τὰ πρὸς τὸ ἐσθίειν.
        εὐετηρία.

Euestō: 'Flourishing' from 'well-being'.
        or from having plenty to eat.
        'Prosperity'.

These, the first most obviously, derive more clearly from the root verb 'to be' (εἶναι), and together provide a consistent general picture. *Euestō* tends to refer to a prosperity of 'external goods'.[42] That is the impression from at least three of Hesychius' four derivations.[43] Now we might return to Clement's doxography, because there we find another important indication of the sense of *euestō*. Clement cites a later, obscure Democritean who picked up this term, and provides a useful gloss:

---

[39] Procopé (1971) 118 compares Antiphon B22. In (1990) 24 he suggests that 'more probably he is claiming that [the elimination of dangerous animals] should also enhance the private well-being of the killer', noting that B258 reads in this way. Cp. Bailey (1928) 192.

[40] Vlastos (1945–6) 583 n. 29, Procopé (1971) 123.

[41] Building on von Fritz (1938) 35, Vlastos (1945–6) 582 rests much of his insistence of the derivation of Democritus' ethics from his physics on this etymology: 'to an atomist ἐστώ (Doric for 'being') can mean only one thing: atoms and void'. His n. 30 cites Philolaus B6, and Antiphon B22 as parallels. Taylor (1967) 11 is rightly unconvinced.

[42] Taylor (1967) 12. Cf. Aesch. *Ag.* 647, 929; Hdt. 1.85.

[43] 1. that in B140 refers to the state of one's οἶκος; 2. ἢ ἀπὸ τοῦ δαψιλεῖν τὰ πρὸς τὸ ἐσθίειν; 3. εὐετηρία is standard Aristotelian terminology for external goods: *EN* 1098b26, 1155a8, *Pol.* 1306b11.

Further, Diotimus [takes as the goal] the completeness of goods, which he said is termed *euestō*. (*Strom.* 2.130)

For Diotimus, at least, *euestō* means the absolute completeness of goods. Perhaps he means 'external' goods; it is difficult to tell.[44]

Recall one of the ways of reading Clement's list of Abderite *telē*, which I introduced earlier (p. 22). Natorp sees each of the 'Democriteans' in Clement's doxography reacting to various areas of Democritus' thought, each emphasising one particular aspect.[45] So Nausiphanes picks on *athambia* as his emphasis.[46] Natorp's Diotimus is an acquisitive Democritean, convinced of the link between bodily and psychic well-being and his *euestō* is not a *mis*reading, but an interpretation which emphasises one facet of Democritus' ethics.[47]

Acquisitiveness is not a characteristic consonant with Democritus' ethics (see below). But rather than τὴν παντέλειαν τῶν ἀγαθῶν meaning 'as many goods as possible', it might mean 'the complete collection of goods', the total amount necessary. As B257 and the various parallel uses of *euestō* suggested, this is likely to be a reference to external goods, to the well-being of one's household, to having enough to eat, and the like. So if Democritus

---

44 All we know of Diotimus of Tyre is this one passage, and a piece from Aëtius (2.17.3 = DK 76 A1 = Stob. 1.24.3) where he is listed after Straton and Metrodorus of Chios as holding a particular astronomical theory. A further passage from Sextus (*M.* 7.140) in which a Diotimus is described assigning three 'criteria of truth' to Democritus has been cited as another reference to this character: Hirzel (1882) 327, Spinelli (1997) 163–5. Sedley (1992) 43–4 thinks this refers to the Stoic Diotimos (DL 10.3) and is a Stoic attack on the originality of Epicurus' criteria of truth. Hirzel (1882) 326 had noted an anti-Epicurean Θεότιμος at Athen. 611B and proposed emending to Διότιμος. Athenaeus claims that Zeno of Sidon responded to this Diotimos, so he can be dated to the early first century BC. There is a reference to a Diotimos in *PHerc.* 176 fr.5 Vogliano and in connection with Eudoxus at Philodemus ΠΡΑΓΜΑΤΕΙΑΙ (*PHerc.* 1418) XX.17 (see Militello (1997) 239). Sedley (1976b) 29–31 also thinks this is unlikely to be a reference to Diotimus of Tyre: the Diotimus here is probably a head of the Cyzican school. Gigante (1981) 85 retains the identification, suggesting that this Diotimus who advocated a life of εὐεστώ might well have been allied to a Eudoxan school in Cyzicus. Cf. Fowler (1984) 243.

45 Natorp (1893) 123.

46 Natorp goes on to suggest that Apollodotos' ψυχαγωγία is equivalent to τέρψις. Wigodsky (1995) 67 notes that ψυχαγωγία was often used in later literary criticism as a substitute for ἡδονή.

47 Natorp (1893) 123, cf. Langerbeck (1935) 119–20, Procopé (1971) 123 n. 1: 'Despite its vagueness, or perhaps because of it, Diotimus' paraphrase is probably the best, or the least misleading, one that we have for the Democritean term εὐεστώ.'

wrote about *euestō*, either in περὶ εὐθυμίης or in a separate work, perhaps these are the considerations which it contained.[48]

These difficulties should urge us to look for a much more complex set of relationships than the simple: Democritus' X is Nausiphanes' Y is Epicurus' Z. There are suggestions that some ancient readers were instructively reticent to attribute a simple and familiar (i.e. Hellenistic) *telos* to this earlier thinker.

Cicero gives the strongest indication of a more critical reading of the Democritean material, and offers a model which we would do well to follow.

id [i.e. bono esse animo] enim ille summum bonum εὐθυμίαν et saepe ἀθαμβίαν appellat, id est animum terrore liberum. sed haec etsi praeclare, nondum tandem perpolita; pauca enim, neque ea ipsa enucleate, ab hoc de virtute quidem dicta. (Cic. *Fin.* 5.87–8)

For he names that the highest good [sc. one's soul being in a good state] *euthymia* and often *athambia* – which is a soul free from fear. But even if he said these well, he did not say them in a very refined way – for little was said by him about virtue, and what he did say was not clear.

Democritus' method of expression was not that of the later schools who competed in the presentation of their *telos* and the criticism of others'. This agenda had not yet been set. Democritus sometimes uses *euthymia* and often he uses a different term, *athambia*, glossed by Cicero differently from the more general *euthymia*. *Athambia* (*id est animum terrore liberum*) appears to fit Diogenes' description at 9.45 (ὑπὸ μηδενὸς ταραττομένη φόβου ἢ δεισιδαιμονίας ἢ ἄλλου τινὸς πάθους). As we have seen, there are texts which show Democritus to be concerned with such

---

[48] B3 focuses on the 'external' requirements for well-being. If so, and if it comes from the περὶ εὐθυμίης then perhaps that work contained Democritus' thoughts on εὐεστώ. Thrasyllus' catalogue's second tetralogy lists an ethical work entitled Ἀμαλθείης κέρας. Already in the classical period this was identified as the 'horn of plenty' (Pherecydes of Athens *apud* [Apollod.] *Bibl.* 2.148 = *FGrH* 3.42). It provides, therefore, an apt title for a work on 'external goods' (cp. Tarrant (1993) 87 n. 5). Stewart (1958) n. 40, suggests that this is the name of a work composed of ethical *gnōmai*, a compilation probably Cynic in origin (cf. above, p. 30, n. 5). Pliny the Elder implies that this was not an uncommon title (*NH praef.* 24). Ibscher (1983) 229 compares Phocylides of Miletus fr. 7 Diehl (Stob. 4.15.6). Philodemus (*Rhet.* L.12 vol. 2 p. 53 Sudhaus) complains that young men are being drawn from 'Amaltheia's horn' of philosophy to the 'rhyton' of political sophistry. On Τριτογενεία: Hirzel (1883) vol. I, 132 n. I, Zeller and Mondolfo (1969) 258 n. 121. Cf. below p. 183, n. 56.

things as fear, superstition, and the removal of anxiety. But Cicero knows that this is not all Democritus means to set up as the goal of life. There is a positive side too: *bono esse animo*. Whether this positive state depends on, is identical with, or includes the absence of fear Cicero cannot say. Democritus was not a systematic ethicist in the vein of Aristotelian and post-Aristotelian eudaimonistic ethics.[49] That is not to say that he had no ethical views, but that the expression of those views was not in the form of a *telos*-centred eudaimonist theory.

An analysis of B191

The remainder of my treatment of Democritus' thoughts about *eudaimonia* will concentrate on one fragment. Although B191 has attracted some discussion, and although it is the longest continuous surviving piece of Democritean ethical thought, it has received only one – sadly unpublished – detailed and systematic analysis of its content, manner of expression, and interrelation with other ethical fragments.[50] I shall attempt to provide another such analysis, and will use that analysis to refer to other, shorter fragments which, if taken alone, might indeed appear as trite and uninteresting as some commentators have claimed.[51] I begin with an overview of the fragment, and then move on to the issues and difficulties which it raises.

Overview: form, content

(**A**) ἀνθρώποισι γὰρ εὐθυμίη γίνεται μετριότητι τέρψιος καὶ βίου συμμετρίη· (**B**) τὰ δ᾽ ἐλλείποντα καὶ ὑπερβάλλοντα μεταπίπτειν τε φιλεῖ καὶ μεγάλας κινήσιας ἐμποιεῖν τῇ ψυχῇ. αἱ δ᾽ ἐκ μεγάλων διαστημάτων κινούμεναι τῶν ψυχέων οὔτε εὐσταθέες εἰσὶν οὔτε εὔθυμοι. (**C**) ἐπὶ τοῖς δυνατοῖς οὖν δεῖ ἔχειν τὴν γνώμην καὶ τοῖς παρεοῦσιν ἀρκέεσθαι, τῶν μὲν ζηλουμένων καὶ θαυμαζομένων ὀλίγην μνήμην ἔχοντα καὶ τῇ διανοίᾳ μὴ προσεδρεύοντα, (**D**) τῶν δὲ ταλαιπωρεόντων τοὺς βίους θεωρέειν, ἐννοούμενον ἃ πάσχουσι κάρτα (?),[52]

[49] Cf. Kahn (1985) 25–8, (1998) 36; Striker (1990) 98; Annas (1993a) 17–18. Cp. Gosling and Taylor (1982) 29.

[50] Procopé (1971) 69–214.   [51] E.g. Barnes (1979) vol. II, 228.

[52] Jacobs emends to κακά which would be picked up by κακοπαθεῖν τῇ ψυχῇ in the following clause.

ὅκως ἂν τὰ παρεόντα σοι καὶ ὑπάρχοντα μεγάλα καὶ ζηλωτὰ φαίνηται, καὶ μηκέτι πλειόνων ἐπιθυμέοντι συμβαίνῃ κακοπαθεῖν τῇ ψυχῇ. ὁ γὰρ θαυμάζων τοὺς ἔχοντας καὶ μακαριζομένους ὑπὸ τῶν ἄλλων ἀνθρώπων καὶ τῇ μνήμῃ πᾶσαν ὥραν προσεδρεύων ἀεὶ ἐπικαινουργεῖν ἀναγκάζεται καὶ ἐπιβάλλεσθαι δι' ἐπιθυμίην τοῦ τι πρήσσειν ἀνήκεστον ὧν νόμοι κωλύουσιν. (E) διόπερ, τὰ μὲν μὴ δίζεσθαι χρέων, ἐπὶ δὲ τοῖς εὐθυμέεσθαι χρέων, παραβάλλοντα τὸν ἑαυτοῦ βίον πρὸς τὸν τῶν φαυλότερον πρησσόντων καὶ μακαρίζειν ἑωυτὸν ἐνθυμεύμενον ἃ πάσχουσιν, ὁκόσῳ αὐτέων βέλτιον πρήσσει τε καὶ διάγει. (F) ταύτης γὰρ ἐχόμενος τῆς γνώμης εὐθυμότερόν τε διάξεις καὶ οὐκ ὀλίγας κῆρας ἐν τῷ βίῳ διώσεαι φθόνον καὶ ζῆλον καὶ δυσμενίην.

(A) *Euthymia* arises in men through a moderation of joy and a good balance in life. (B) Deficiencies and excesses tend to change into one another and set up great motions in the soul. Souls moved out of large intervals are neither well settled nor *euthymoi*. (C) So you should pay attention to what is possible and be content with what is present, paying little heed to and not dwelling in thought on what is envied or marvelled at. (D) But you should consider the lives of people in trouble, thinking on what they suffer so that what you have at present appears great and enviable, and it no longer happens that you suffer in the soul through desire for more. For he who wonders at those who are rich and are thought blessed by other men and constantly dwells on it in his memory is always forced to find new things and is driven by desire to do something which cannot be put right, and which the laws forbid. (E) So you should not seek some things, but be happy with others, comparing your life with those who fare worse and consider yourself blessed when you consider what they suffer and by how much better your life is proceeding than theirs. (F) Clinging to this thought you will live your life a more *euthymos* person and will remove no few troubles from your life, namely envy, jealousy, and ill-will.

This fragment passes from a general statement of the conditions in which *euthymia* arises (A) to a description of the state of the soul of those who have not attained this *telos* (B). Then Democritus offers a set of recommendations for the attainment of the former and the avoidance of the latter, recommendations which involve the assessment of one's own capacities and the comparison of one's own lot with that of those worse off (C–D). He recommends a reassessment of the categories in which we normally assess success and failure, happiness and misery. He contends that by such a process of comparison we will be led to a more accurate view of our own state and be in a position to make progress towards what is truly desirable (E–F). There is little reason to think that B191 is an incomplete argumentative unit, although the γάρ at the beginning of the phrase suggests that it was preceded by some earlier discussion.[53]

The chiastic phrase which is used at the beginning of B191 tells us that *euthymia* depends on two 'moderations': a specific moderation of *terpsis* and a more general moderation of one's 'life'. It is likely that these are both necessary conditions for the attainment of *euthymia*. Perhaps they are severally necessary and jointly sufficient for *euthymia*. This phrase confirms that Democritus is no full-blooded hedonist since he does not characterise the best life as one in which the maximum amount of pleasure is enjoyed. Only a moderate amount of *terpsis* is advised, and even then simply to have correctly moderated one's *terpsis* is of itself insufficient to guarantee *euthymia*: it must be accompanied by a general moderation of one's life. I shall offer more general comments on the terminology of pleasure below (pp. 48–52).

The next phrase (**B**) is particularly difficult to interpret, since it might point to a link between Democritus' ethical thought and his physics – and his psychology in particular. I shall therefore defer comment on this particular phrase to a later more detailed discussion (pp. 58–72).

In section **C**, B191 proceeds from its descriptive model of the effects of excess and deficiency (however understood) to draw inferences (οὖν) based on that description. Democritus passes into a normative address (δεῖ) which prescribes the correct attitude to adopt in order to attain the favourable state previously described. The first suggestions have been prefigured already in our discussions of a 'moderate' life. Democritus prescribes a change of outlook and a rejection of the common modes of evaluation in favour of an appreciation of the sufficiency of what is at hand.

Section **D** contains our first indication of a method for achieving the correct reconsideration of values which other fragments suggest, perhaps the earliest example of the therapeutic arguments which will later be so extensively employed by Hellenistic schools.[54]

---

[53] Perhaps B191 is the 'summing up' of the work; its close seems to support this suggestion.
[54] Procopé (1971) 214 dubs this passage 'an exercise in practical psychotherapy'. Cf. B31.

First we are advised to consider and spend time contemplating the lives of those who are in pain.[55] The purpose is not self-gratifying *Schadenfreude*, but a reassessment of one's own relative well-being by drawing attention to otherwise unnoticed goods: 'so that what *you* have might appear great and enviable and so that you will not suffer psychic distress through desire for more'. Second, the realisation that what is great and enviable is not necessarily what qualifies for those terms in the eyes of most people should head off any potentially damaging desires for ever-greater fame or success. The final sentence of this section describes what happens to those who follow conventional modes of evaluation and aspiration.

The passage advocates a radical reassessment of and dissent from convention. The Democritean ideal is presented as unlike any contemporary view of success and prosperity. Lucretius is clearly drawing on this or similar passages for the proem to his second book. Here again the pleasure derives from a realisation of the absence of pain rather than positive delight in faring better than others. (Note also that Lucretius' borrowing of Democritus' suggestion is tied to the image of *galēnē* examined earlier.)[56] Lucretius dramatises this distinction by setting his Epicurean high on a cliff overlooking the sea, not only safe from the storms happening far below, but also now able to see and appreciate the fact that he is free from the highs and lows, peaks and troughs of the churning sea.

The close of Democritus' fragment B191 turns to examine the *pleonectic* character, someone always driven for a desire to possess more than he already has. *Pleonexia* ushers in a disregard for the limits of nature and those imposed by society. He is compelled 'always to do something new' (ἐπικαινουργεῖν). This desire will never result in stability, but always in the search for greater novelty

---

[55] Procopé (1989a) 330.

[56] Other parallels have been suggested for the Lucretian image, e.g. Archippus fr. 45 Kassel–Austin, Cic. *Ad Att.* 2.7.4, Hor. *Ep.*1.11.10. On the proem of *DRN* 2: Holtsmark (1967); Konstan (1973) 3–10; Fowler (1983) 4ff.; Hardie (1986) 200–2; Grilli (1992). (Cf. *DRN* 5.8–12: Gale (1994) 120–1, 124–6). This passage might be recalling part of Epicurus' own works, specifically the story of Epicurus' narrow escape from a shipwreck: Diogenes of Oinoanda fr. 72 Smith (revised in Smith (1996)). Clay (1972) discusses the Homeric parallels (*Od.* 5.367–463, 12.235–8) and the use made of this passage by Plutarch at *Non posse* 1090Eff., 1103D–E. For more on the shipwreck theme: Grilli (1978). Cf. Cic. *Tusc.* 5.16.

and greater excess. The achievement of *euthymia*, of *eustatheia* or *galēnē* must involve the rejection of this self-perpetuating process. The compulsion to commit acts which are contrary to the customs of the surrounding society is not simply the symptom of this *malaise*, but itself is the cause of yet more disturbance not only to that society but also and more importantly to the agent himself, since wrong-doing brings along with it the worries of being found out and the potential for being punished.[57]

B191 continues in E with a restatement of the need to compare various lives and evaluate each not on the basis of conventional wisdom, but in terms of the *euthymia* provided by each. There appears to be a gradated scale of lives. The fragment then concludes (**F**) with a positive evaluation of the reader's prospects. One can begin to approximate to *euthymia* by trying to adopt this attitude (the comparative again suggests a scale of improvement), and in the process one will rid oneself of various ills (κῆρες):[58] namely a preoccupation with the evaluation of oneself with regard to the (conventional) prosperity or otherwise of others.

Democritus on pleasure and moderation

The noun *terpsis*, which is introduced in B191 section **A**, appears elsewhere in the fragments, and it appears to be distinguished from *hēdonē*:

B69 ἀνθρώποις πᾶσι τωὐτὸν ἀγαθὸν καὶ ἀληθές· ἡδὺ δὲ ἄλλῳ ἄλλο.
B74 ἡδὺ μηδὲν ἀποδέχεσθαι, ἢν μὴ συμφέρῃ.
B207 ἡδονὴν οὐ πᾶσαν ἀλλὰ τὴν ἐπὶ τῷ καλῷ αἱρεῖσθαι χρεών.

B69 The same thing is good and true for all men. But what is pleasant differs from one to another.
B74 You should not accept anything pleasant unless it is beneficial.
B207 You must not choose every pleasure, but only that taken in what is good.

---

[57] The theme of obedience to the law is prominent in the *moralia*. It is well examined in Procopé (1989a–90). See B47, B62, B174, B181, and for the importance of correct and lawful social interaction to collective and individual well-being: B107, B124, B164, B237, B249, B250, B252. In an age of endemic political *stasis*, Democritus was a strong advocate of its avoidance. Cf. Farrar (1988) 254ff. He may have had personal experience of political management: Procopé (1989a) 309 examines numismatic evidence from Abdera.
[58] φθόνος is the στάσιος ἀρχήν in B245; cf. B88.

B69 notes that the objects which people find pleasant differ and vary, and contrasts this relativity with the positing of an objective good. What is pleasant (ἡδύ) is not to be identified immediately with what is good. Further, B74 is a normative statement, which requires its addressee to pursue only those things which he finds pleasant *and* are beneficial. This implies, as did B69, that there are objects which one finds pleasant which are not beneficial, and ought not to be pursued. Similarly B207 urges us only to pursue those pleasures whose object is indeed good.

Yet B4 – and B188, which is almost identical[59] – seem to make what produces *terpsis* in some way the criterion of choice and avoidance:

B4 τέρψις καὶ ἀτερπίη οὖρος τῶν συμφόρων καὶ τῶν ἀσυμφόρων.

B4 Joy and lack of joy are boundary-markers of what is and is not beneficial.

Although some things we find ἡδύ were not to be thought beneficial, it seems that things which produce *terpsis* are at least an indicator of what is beneficial.[60] There are a number of interpretations available at this point.

1 B74 and B188 were not written with a view to the provision of a theoretical consistency.
2 *Terpsis* and *hēdonē* are both feelings of pleasure, but B74 and B188 are dealing with different stretches of time, or are from different perspectives.[61]
3 *Terpsis* and *hēdonē* are feelings distinguished by some characteristic of the object of the pleasure.

Procopé offers reading 1, claiming that B74 offers an assertion for general practice, and B4 and B188 are offering advice to be used in cases where the agent is unsure.[62] But there is no evidence to support this view of the purpose of B4 and B188.

Taylor advocates 2, claiming that while B74 deals with particular occasions of and objects of pleasure, B188 is looking at an agent's

---

[59] B188: ὅρος συμφόρων καὶ ἀσυμφόρων τέρψις καὶ ἀτερπίη.
[60] On οὖρος: Vlastos (1945–6) 587, cf. Kullmann (1969) 133–4. Cf. Epic. *Ep. Men.* 129: pleasure is the κανών.
[61] Suggested by Gosling and Taylor (1982) 32.   [62] Procopé (1971) 177.

life as a whole.[63] While some things might be pleasant but not beneficial (B74), pleasantness overall (B4 and B188) is more closely linked with what is beneficial. Therefore, a good life, one lived in accordance with what is beneficial, is not to be identified with the accumulation of particular experiences of *hēdonē*, but if one leads a good life this should be marked by *terpsis*. *Terpsis* is a pleasant on-going state, the pleasure of a life lived well, whereas *hēdonai* are one-off pleasures.

However, other fragments count against this particular reading. For example:

B194   αἱ μεγάλαι τέρψεις ἀπὸ τοῦ θεᾶσθαι τὰ καλὰ τῶν ἔργων γίνονται.

B194   Great joys come from considering the beauties of deeds.

Here the plural (τέρψεις) rather implies that *terpsis* too is produced on particular occasions.

B232   τῶν ἡδέων τὰ σπανιώτατα γινόμενα μάλιστα τέρπει.

B232   The rarer pleasures cause special joy.

Here *terpsis* appears as episodic as *hēdonē*; moreover the objects of pleasure (ἡδέα?) can cause *terpsis*.

I prefer a version of 3, which attempts to distinguish *hēdonē* as a feeling of pleasure which might or might not be beneficial, from *terpsis* which is a feeling we can accept as *objectively* good. They are both pleasant feelings, which can be felt at any particular instant, so we need not restrict *terpsis* as Taylor does to 'an overall tenor and approach to life'.[64] Instead, we can allow *hēdonē*'s relativity to be caused by an element of preference and opinion. Some things bring me *hēdonē* because I like them. In this case B69 marks an insistence by Democritus that I might not find *hēdonē* in

---

[63] Taylor (1967) 17.

[64] Taylor (1967) 17. My preference for 3 is not to be thought to be support for another version of 3, namely the interpretation which identifies τέρψις and ἡδονή as 'spiritual' and 'bodily' pleasure respectively. See for this view: Philippson (1924) 393ff., Mesiano (1951) 79–87, Kullmann (1969) 138. This is often linked with a Natorpian view of the *moralia*, which relies heavily on B112, B194, and Cic. *Fin.* 5.23 to give a picture in which Democritus makes cosmological inquiry the highest and most 'pleasant' human activity. For a convincing refutation of this view: Taylor (1967) 6–8.

things which are good for me, whereas B188 notes that I *do* tend to receive *terpsis* from things which are beneficial.

What is beneficial must in some way be identified with the objective good of B69, and is generally marked by *terpsis*. The normative statements of B74 and B207 may thus be interpreted as an injunction to arrange our opinions so that what we enjoy is identical with what we objectively ought to pursue. In this case, whatever brings *terpsis* will also produce *hēdonē* but not *vice versa*. *Terpsis* and *hēdonē* both belong to a unitary conception of pleasure but are distinguished by extrinsic factors: *hēdonai* form a larger class of pleasures which may or may not have unwanted concomitants; *terpseis* are *hēdonai* which have no such drawbacks.[65] I am tempted to see in this interpretation the seeds of the later Epicurean distinction between natural, necessary and unnecessary desires, and the introspective method of determining which pleasures to pursue.[66]

This interpretation may be supported to some extent by the following:

B200 ἀνοήμονες βιοῦσιν οὐ τερπόμενοι βιοτῇ.
B201 ἀνοήμονες δηναιότητος ὀρέγονται οὐ τερπόμενοι δηναιότητι.

B200 Fools live without feeling joy in life.
B201 Fools desire luxury but feel no joy in it.

The foolish in B200 and 201 experience no *terpsis* even if they achieve what they desire since what they do in fact desire is at odds with what they should desire.[67]

However, at the very beginning of B191 *euthymia* is said to be brought about by a moderation of *terpsis* (μετριότητι τέρψιος), but if we wish to identify *terpsis* with the feeling which arises when one attains the objectively good and beneficial state, why would it have to be moderated? Surely one would wish for as much *terpsis* as possible. Either one must suggest that Democritus has misused

---

[65] Cf. Nill (1985) 79–80.
[66] Cf. B235, B233: Democritus distinguishes the natural desires of the σκῆνος from those of ἡ τῆς γνώμης †κακοθιγίη†: Spinelli (1991) 305 and n. 71.
[67] Vlastos (1945–6) 587ff. argues that B188's ὅρος should be read as an indication that one cannot see the objective underlying atomic pattern which constitutes pleasure, but can infer it from the supervening emotion. Thus B69 refers to the feeling of pleasure which can be affected by external environmental factors and so might not always correspond with the objectively good atomic configuration.

some of his own terminology, or that his terminology was never particularly fixed. *Terpsis* and *hēdonē* tend to be used in different contexts, and *in general* we might be able to sustain the sort of reading just outlined, but no interpretation which insists on fixing a particular theoretical significance to different items of vocabulary will be able to embrace all the surviving evidence.[68]

At the least, we should see in these fragments positive evidence against any 'mere tranquillity' view of Democritus' preferred life. His life of *euthymia* was filled with pleasant experiences.[69] These pleasures are nevertheless to be found in a life of balance and moderation. The very first sentence of B191 introduces the notion of 'balance', *symmetria*, in the good life. (συμμετρίη looks forward to the following sentence where ἐλλείποντα and ὑπερβάλλοντα are its negative counterparts.) *Symmetria* might function in two ways. It might be relational and denote (e.g.) 'commensurateness' with something, or absolute, and mean (e.g.) 'balanced', contrasting with the excess and deficiency in the following phrase.[70]

Other fragments might help to decide between these alternatives, for example, B3 and B235.

B3: τὸν εὐθυμεῖσθαι μέλλοντα χρὴ μὴ πολλὰ πρήσσειν μήτε ἰδίῃ μήτε ξυνῇ, μηδὲ ἄσσ' ἂν πράσσῃ ὑπέρ τε δύναμιν αἱρεῖσθαι τὴν ἑαυτοῦ καὶ φύσιν· ἀλλὰ τοσαύτην ἔχειν φυλακὴν ὥστε καὶ τῆς τύχης ἐπιβαλλούσης καὶ ἐς τὸ πλέον ὑπηγεομένης τῷ δοκεῖν, κατατίθεσθαι καὶ μὴ πλέω προσάπτεσθαι τῶν δυνατῶν. ἡ γὰρ εὐογκίη ἀσφαλέστερον τῆς μεγαλογκίης.

He who is going to be *euthymos* should not be a busy-body – neither in private nor in public. Nor should he choose what he does in excess of his ability and nature. But he should take such great care that even when good fortune strikes and urges him to think he can aim higher, he sets this aside, and only attempts what he is capable of. For a good amount is safer than a large one.

---

[68] Cf. Alfieri (1936) 254 n. 640.   [69] As recognised by Taylor (1967) 17–18.

[70] See Viano (1993) 436 on συμμετρία in Theoph. *De sensibus*. Cf. Fränkel (1955) 175, Silvestre-Pinto (1983) 46 n. 39, Laks (1990) 15. Compare Galen *QAM* 821: ἔμπαλιν δ' οἱ σύμμετροι ταῖς κράσεσι συμμέτρους τὰς τῆς ψυχῆς κινήσεις ἔχοντες εἰς εὐθυμίαν ὠφελοῦνται. This may be a conscious reference to Democritean material. συμμετρία and its cognates are common ways of describing a 'balanced' bodily composition, or a 'balanced' diet, in which the various elements are σύμμετρα with *each other*. See Alcmaeon B4, Critias B6, Empedocles A70. It is common in medical texts: Hippoc. *Acut.* 18, *Aph.* 5.62, *Vict.* 1.2 and 4.89, *Gland.* 7. Cf. Xen. *Hipp.* 1.16.

It is generally thought that this was the opening passage of Democritus' work *On Euthymia*.[71] It recalls the advice to avoid deficiency and excess found in B191, but in B3 the view is *extroverted*, turned towards external trappings, in contrast to B191's more introverted tone.[72] This might provide a clue to the *external* measure of συμμετρίη, to which B191 can therefore provide an internal counterpart: 'don't try to do more than you are able' (μή πλέω προσάπτεσθαι τῶν δυνατῶν). There is no symmetrical precept not to do *less* than one is able, which fits the general thrust of the passage towards risk avoidance. It is dangerous to *over*stretch one's capabilities and resources in a way in which it is certainly *not* dangerous to *under*-use them. B3 maintains this one-sided view throughout: ὑπερ, μὴ πλέω, ἀσφαλέστερον τῆς μεγαλογκίης. B191 adds to B3, offering an alternative, introverted perspective. From the point of view of external goods, 'to try to do too much is risky', but on the internal view, doing too little is also to be avoided.

B235 also sheds light on these issues.

B235 (first part): ὅσοι ἀπὸ γαστρὸς τὰς ἡδονὰς ποιέονται ὑπερβεβληκότες τὸν καιρὸν ἐπὶ βρώσεσιν ἢ πόσεσιν ἢ ἀφροδισίοισιν, τοῖσι πᾶσιν αἱ μὲν ἡδοναὶ βραχεῖαί τε καὶ δι' ὀλίγου γίνονται, ὁκόσον ἂν χρόνον ἐσθίωσιν ἢ πίνωσιν, αἱ δὲ λῦπαι πολλαί.

All those who make pleasures come from the belly, having overlooked what is appropriate as far as food, drink, and sex are concerned, all their pleasures are short-lived, and arise only for as long as the short time when they are eating or drinking. But their pains are many.

The important word here is 'the appropriate' (καιρός), an idea which will find greater elaboration in the thought of Anaxarchus,[73] and which certainly is not restricted to temporal appropriateness. The thrust of B235 is that indulging beyond what is appropriate is bad for one. Not only are the pleasures to be gained from such over-indulgence short-lived, but they are followed by pains.[74]

---

[71] Primarily on the basis of Sen. *Tranq.* 13.1: *hoc secutum puto Democritum ita coepisse: 'qui tranquille volet vivere, nec privatim agat multa nec publice'*. The MSS read *cepisse* for *coepisse*. Still, the phrase τὸν εὐθυμεῖσθαι μέλλοντα χρή . . . sounds plausible as the beginning of a piece of ethical advice. This same gnomic thought is repeated by Seneca at *De ira* 3.6.3, and Plutarch *Tranq.* 465c.

[72] Cf. Procopé (1971) 10.   [73] Cf. Tortora (1983).

[74] Cf. B219 and Porph. *De abst.* 1.54.

Again we might notice a distinction between *hēdonē* and *terpsis*. Some *hēdonai* certainly are not identical with, nor even efficient guides to, what is beneficial. Again Epicurean parallels spring to mind, and B235 might be viewed not only as an intimation of the Epicurean 'hedonic calculus' (*Ep. Men.* 129–30), but also of Epicurean criticism of profligate hedonism, specifically its resignation to inevitable pains.[75]

The openings of B191 and B235 could profitably be read as elaborations of the two Delphic maxims: 'nothing to excess', and 'know thyself'. The latter becomes an injunction to be aware of and be happy with one's own capabilities. The former is elaborated in B235: excess leads to painful after-effects; excess leads to deficiency. Here I shall note parallel Democritean examples of this suggestion. I have already discussed B3 (above pp. 52–3).

B283 πενίη πλοῦτος ὀνόματα ἐνδείης καὶ κόρου· οὔτε οὖν πλούσιος <ὁ> ἐνδέων οὔτε πένης ὁ μὴ ἐνδέων.

B283 Poverty and wealth are words for need and sufficiency. Hence the needy is not rich, nor is the man not in need poor.

Wealth and poverty are not objectively defined, but are merely names given to relative states. If someone has less than he needs, we should call him poor, even if he is already very wealthy. If someone has more than he needs we call him rich, even if he does not have much. The force of this fragment is to drive people away from the thought that they should strive to be 'called rich', say, but should rather reassess *how much they need* (a theme restated in B284). There are a number of problems and risks associated with striving for anything greater than what one already has. The first of these is the thought that this very acquisitiveness might devalue and destroy what one already has:

---

[75] Cf. Kahn (1985) 17, Warren (2001). Lucretius dramatises this picture of indulging beyond what is necessary or appropriate by the allegory of the Danaids: 3.1003ff. For criticism of those who always aim at this sort of indulgence, see *KD* 10. Also note *SV* 14, where I would retain χαῖρον with the Vatican codex rather than Stobaeus' καιρόν. The former is supported by the version of *SV* 14 in *PBerol*. inv. 21312 fr. a, and the version found on a mosaic floor at Autun. See Bouquiaux-Simon (1992), and Bouquiaux-Simon and Rutten (1992); Blanchard (1991), and Blanchard-Lemée and Blanchard (1993).

B224 ἡ τοῦ πλέονος ἐπιθυμίη τὸ παρεὸν ἀπόλλυσι τῇ Αἰσωπείῃ κυνὶ ἰκέλη γινομένη [cf. B219].

B224 The desire for more destroys what is present – like in Aesop's story of the dog.

Pleonexia[76] destroys what has already been won, just as in Aesop's story about the dog who loses the meat it is carrying because it pursues the reflection of that food in some water (133 Perry).[77] The constant search for 'more' jeopardises already hard-won gains. Further, the 'more' for which one is searching may be no more certain or substantial than a reflection. Democritus' advice is to strive only for *enough*, and to value the present over the contingent future, or the irrecoverable past:

B202 ἀνοήμονες τῶν ἀπεόντων ὀρέγονται, τὰ δὲ παρεόντα καὶ παρῳχημένων κερδαλεώτερα ἐόντα ἀμαλδύνουσιν.

B202 Fools desire what is absent, but they overlook what is present and more profitable than what is past.

Only fools would disregard the security of the present for what is out of reach (cf. B77). The objects of this vain desire are vaguely defined (they are 'what I do not have') and thus the desire for them is directionless. To reach out for these vague goals I must make myself vulnerable to the contingencies of chance. The fragments on the effects of τύχη make this clear:

B119 ἄνθρωποι τύχης εἴδωλον ἐπλάσσαντο πρόφασιν ἰδίης ἀβουλίης. βαιὰ γὰρ φρονήσει τύχη μάχεται, τὰ δὲ πλεῖστα ἐν βίῳ εὐξύνετος ὀξυδερκείη κατιθύνει.[78]

B119 Men fashioned an image of chance as an excuse for their own lack of thought. For on rare occasions chance fights against prudence, but the understanding of clear sight sets straight most things in life.

---

[76] Cf. MacIntyre (1984) 137.

[77] Stewart (1958) 190 n. 26 notes that Democritus is linked with Aesop also at Arist. *Meteo.* 356b10ff., and Plut. *An. an corp. aff.* 500D–E.

[78] As also in B222: ἡ τέκνοις ἄγαν χρημάτων συναγωγὴ πρόφασίς ἐστι φιλαργυρίης τρόπον ἴδιον ἐλέγχουσα. The sense of 'pretext, or excuse' seems strongest here: ἐπλάσσαντο in B119 makes this clear. With B119 compare Epicurus *KD* 16, and see Clay (1972) 60–1.

The first phrase might suggest that chance is merely a human creation, that it is an *eidōlon* fashioned as an excuse for a lack of foresight. It is merely 'the absence of thought', mismanagement. However, the next sentence qualifies this: τύχη is the subject, actively fighting against our reasoning capacities. Only the final phrase makes clear on what basis Democritus could make his grand declaration at the beginning of this fragment: *for the most part* our lives are quite amenable to reasoned management. Only on rare occasions will such management be unable to guard against the effects of fortune.

Also relevant is the following:

B176 τύχη μεγαλόδωρος, ἀλλ᾽ ἀβέβαιος, φύσις δὲ αὐτάρκης· διόπερ νικᾷ τῷ ἥσσονι καὶ βεβαίῳ τὸ μεῖζον τῆς ἐλπίδος.

B176 Chance gives great gifts, but is unreliable. Nature is self-sufficient. So with its smaller and reliable gift it beats the greater gift of hope.[79]

Here there are two contrasts: between generous chance and self-sufficient, economical nature, and between the great gift of hope and the smaller but reliable gift of nature. I am therefore inclined to read 'nature', φύσις as something which contrasts with chance, τύχη: it is the way in which things *normally and naturally* work in a self-maintaining way. There is a constancy in natural processes which, while it is not going to bestow any huge fortunes, can nevertheless be counted on. If a farmer pinned all of his hopes on some unreliable chance occurrence, rather than being content with the reliable workings of nature, he might well come unstuck. The reliable φύσις does not command our imagination and aspirations in the way that hope for a great munificent occurrence might, but it *should* always win out in our deliberations.[80]

These musings on the security and desirability of moderate desires have much in common with Epicurean discussions of the same theme. They urge us to do away with all desires which are neither natural nor necessary; only these natural necessary desires must be

---

[79] For this understanding: Procopé (1971) 32 n. 1.
[80] B185 suggests that aspirations can be 'trained' to what is more reliable and likely. On wealth and poverty in Democritus: Spinelli (1991).

fulfilled in order to attain *eudaimonia* and their fulfilment is easily guaranteed (*Ep. Men.* 127–8, 130).[81] Epicurean texts continue
the diatribe against *pleonexia* and ambition, and the praise of self-
sufficiency. Of course, the Epicureans claim that this is the route
to the greatest possible pleasure, but nevertheless, it is clear that
many of these Democritean statements find an echo in Epicurean
discussions of the desires.[82]

One final Democritean fragment should be mentioned here.
It suggests that in order to understand which things really are
necessary, and to see the limits of self-sufficiency, one should go
travelling, and become a stranger to one's surroundings.

B246 ξενιτείη βίου αὐτάρκειαν διδάσκει· μᾶζα γὰρ καὶ στιβὰς λιμοῦ καὶ
κόπου γλυκύτατα ἰάματα.

B246 Being a foreigner teaches you self-sufficiency in life. Bread and
straw are the sweetest releases from hunger and tiredness.

'*Maza*' (μᾶζα) is a kind of barley cake, a plain and simple food.[83]
Poor food is the most pleasant cure for hunger since, when one
is *truly* hungry, any food will satisfy this hunger, and if one is
not truly hungry then if all that is available is unappetising, one's
'hunger' will rapidly disappear. The Epicureans retain this example
to make their claim that the type of food one eats is irrelevant to
the attainment of happiness, which they identified as the absence
of pain. Bread and water (μᾶζα καὶ ὕδωρ) occur at *Ep. Men.* 131,

---

[81] Cf. Cooper (1999) 498ff.

[82] Irwin (1986) 102–4 cites B284 and B191 in his discussion of Socrates' 'adaptive' account
of one's desires for external goods. He notes (103) that 'while the Cynics interpret
this ascetically, Aristippus points out that self-sufficiency and independence does not
require abstention from pleasures when they are available'. Compare the practice of
Anaxarchus: below pp. 79–81. Irwin goes on to claim (104) that 'Epicurus' advice sounds
quite similar to Democritus'; but, unlike Democritus he rejects the ascetic influence
supporting Cynicism'. I see no clear distinction. Democritus does not strongly advocate
asceticism for its own sake (B284 is expressed as a conditional and B191 refers to looking
ἐπὶ τοῖς δυνατοῖς). If Democritus seems rather Cynic at times, then perhaps this is due
to the transmission of his *moralia*: Stewart (1958).

[83] Aesch. *Ag.* 1041 (the text is debatable), Aristoph. *Ra.* 1068–73, Hdt. 1.200, Pl.
Rep. 372b3; Brumfield (1997) esp. 152–3. Note esp. Porph. *De abst.* 1.48.3: τῶν
γὰρ Ἐπικουρείων οἱ πλείους ἀπ' αὐτοῦ τοῦ κορυφαίου ἀρξάμενοι μάζῃ καὶ τοῖς
ἀκροδρύοις ἀρκούμενοι φαίνονται; cf. Timon fr. 3 Diels and Di Marco (1989)
117–20.

and in Aelian's version of *SV* 33.[84] It is not implausible that B246 was the inspiration for this.

It is tempting to speculate that Democritus is speaking from personal experience when recommending foreign travel, even though it was something of a commonplace to tell stories of philosophers wandering about the known world and acquiring wisdom. Such stories were certainly told about Democritus' own life, whether or not they were based in any historical fact.[85] In his biography of Democritus, Diogenes Laërtius refers to comments made by Demetrius (of Magnesia) in his work *On men who share the same name* (DL 9.37). Demetrius assumes (δοκεῖ δέ) that Democritus went to Athens and kept a deliberately low profile, because while he knew Socrates, Socrates did not know him (perhaps referring to Plato's infamous failure to mention Democritus).[86]

Psychological implications of B191 – ethics and physics

I turn now to the implications of B191 for other areas of Democritus' thought, his psychology in particular. But in doing so I do not leave ethics behind entirely. It might be possible to speculate on the basis of the fragment about possible connections between Democritean psychology and physics and Democritean ethics. These questions also will lead into a further area of disagreement between the Epicureans and Democritus.

B191 (**B**) τὰ δ᾽ ἐλλείποντα καὶ ὑπερβάλλοντα μεταπίπτειν τε φιλεῖ καὶ μεγάλας κινήσιας ἐμποιεῖν τῇ ψυχῇ. αἱ δ᾽ ἐκ μεγάλων διαστημάτων κινούμεναι τῶν ψυχέων οὔτε εὐσταθέες εἰσὶν οὔτε εὔθυμοι.

Deficiencies and excesses tend to change into one another and set up great motions in the soul. Souls moved out of large intervals are neither well settled nor *euthymoi.*

---

[84] Ael. *VH* 4.13, cf. Us. 602.

[85] See Montiglio (2000) 89.

[86] B116 probably sparked off this biographical speculation: ἦλθον γὰρ εἰς ᾿Αθήνας καὶ οὔτις με ἔγνωκεν. There are also the standard stories of the philosopher travelling to study with wise men in Egypt and Asia: B299, A12, A13, A16, A20, A40. (Thrams (1986) 2–5, 16–21 is keen to make a close connection between Democritean and Egyptian ethics.) Stewart (1958) 191 n. 38 notes that Democritus' oriental journey might be an example of his being fitted retrospectively into a tradition of which Anaxarchus and Pyrrho were also thought to be part. Also see B247 ἀνδρὶ σοφῷ πᾶσα γῆ βατή· ψυχῆς γὰρ ἀγαθῆς πατρὶς ὁ ξύμπας κόσμος.

This is perhaps the most tantalising phrase in the fragment.[87] The first few words form a clear link with the preceding phrase (**A**), by presenting what happens when the preferred moderation is not achieved. No neuter noun has appeared in the fragment so far and there is no reason to suppose that anything crucial preceded what we have as the beginning of this text. Therefore we should read the τά here with as general application as possible. Democritus is evoking 'excess' and 'deficiency' in all their possible reference.[88]

Excess and deficiency tend (φιλεῖ) to do two things. They are themselves unstable (μεταπίπτειν), and they cause instability in the soul. The first of these characteristics confirms my interpretation of the link between **A** and **B**: excess and deficiency are not only the two extremes on either side of moderation, but they are also in a sense mutually entailing. One tends to lead directly to the other. B235 similarly suggested that excessive pleasures bring on terrible pains.[89] There, the excess pleasure is *temporally* unstable; it persists only as long as the input of food or drink persists. When it terminates, pain results.

The soul is elsewhere identified as the seat of *euthymia* (B170, 171), and it is also known from doxography to have been conceived by Democritus as a material soul, made of atoms. The question asked by many commentators on this passage is, therefore, whether the disturbance here described is meant to be understood as a physical and atomic, or merely metaphorical, movement away from the mean.[90] If a physical interpretation of this phrase can be secured, then it gives considerable support to any attempt to argue for a close connection between Democritus' ethics and physics – namely the identification of a certain physical arrangement of atoms as the ideal state of *euthymia* (hereafter: E/Ph):

E/Ph: Democritus conceived of and gave, perhaps in a rather vague formulation, some kind of physical (and therefore atomic) analysis of psychic states of well- and ill-being.[91]

---

[87] Bailey (1928) 199 strangely omits this from his translation of B191.
[88] Cf. Procopé (1971) 84, 91.
[89] Procopé (1971) 87 compares Heraclitus B88. Also cf. Pl. *Rep.* 563a9–564a1.
[90] On the literal/metaphorical distinction and its application to Greek texts: Lloyd (1987): 172–214.
[91] Contrast Natorp (1893) 88–121 who suggested that B112 and B194 imply that the greatest pleasure is to be gained from the contemplation of the universe as revealed in atomic

The first piece of evidence often offered by proponents of E/Ph is the reference to 'large motions' (μεγάλας κινήσιας). They ask whether it is credible that a thinker whose renown was built on his physical system of atoms moving within a void could have referred to such 'motions' *without* intending it to describe real, physical, atomic motion. This argument is not compelling.[92]

A better tactic in favour of E/Ph is to stress not this first phrase but the second: αἱ δ' ἐκ μεγάλων διαστημάτων κινούμεναι τῶν ψυχέων οὔτε εὐσταθέες εἰσὶν οὔτε εὔθυμοι. Kirk, Raven, and Schofield translate: 'Such souls as are in large-scale motion are neither in good balance, nor in good spirits.' But this requires a rather strained understanding of the preposition ἐκ ('from', 'out of'), making it function in this instance as an equivalent of διά ('through', 'over') – which Democritus could perfectly well have written had he wished.[93] However, I think that more justice is done to Democritus' Greek in fragment B191 if we understand that the souls are moved/move *out of* or *from* large 'intervals' and *for this reason* are no longer well balanced or enjoying *euthymia*, and that is how I have translated this phrase.[94]

Let me now outline the consequences of such an understanding. When applied to the phrase in B191, this reading offers an image quite the opposite of that of Kirk, Raven, and Schofield's understanding; rather than the large motions occurring when the soul is disturbed, the soul experiencing *euthymia* is characterised by these large intervals. By being moved out of this arrangement, the soul is disturbed. Does this offer additional support for a version of E/Ph?

---

theory; cf. Taylor (1967) 8. Varieties of E/Ph are to be found in von Fritz (1938) 33–6, Vlastos (1945–6), Luria (1964) 13–15, Müller (1980a) 330–4, (1980b) 4. Cf. Stella (1942) 234, Thrams (1986) 22ff., Farrar (1988) 222–3. For an extreme reaction to Vlastos' (1945–6) account, see Barnes (1979) vol. II, 232. Cf. Taylor (1967) 10, (1999) 232.

92 For such an objection see Taylor (1967) 13.

93 Kirk, Raven, Schofield (1983) 430. Freeman (1948) translates the relevant phrase from B191: 'Souls when stirred by great divergences are neither stable nor cheerful.' Farrar (1988) 223: 'moved from large intervals', citing Procopé (1971) 92, who also observes that B191 reads ἐκ and not διά. However he translates ἐκ 'modally' as 'in accordance with' (LSJ s.v. III.7) and then the whole phrase as 'motions on a large scale'.

94 Compare Theoph. *De sensibus* 65: τὸν δὲ γλυκὺν ... · τοὺς <δ'> ἄλλους ταράττειν, ὅτι διαδύνων πλανᾷ τὰ ἄλλα καὶ ὑγραίνει· ὑγραινόμενα δὲ καὶ ἐκ τῆς τάξεως κινούμενα συρρεῖν εἰς τὴν κοιλίαν. Also cf. Arist. *De caelo* 277a4 (and *Met.* 1063a18; *Phys.* 219a10, 224b1, 239a23; *De sensu* 496a30; Pl. *Parm.* 156e1); Xen. *HG* 2.1.22; Eur. *Ba.* 690.

The expression can still be understood in a *metaphorical* rather than physical manner, but I think this is now a little more difficult. One cannot interpret the phrase simply as claiming that souls 'thrown out of harmony' no longer experience *euthymia* without disregarding the force of the qualification that these intervals are large. If Democritus wishes to convey the impression of metaphorical harmony, there is no reason for the metaphorical intervals of that harmony to be large.

Even so, the reference to 'large intervals' in B191 can be used to explain the existence of evidence linking Democritus with Pythagoreanism and with views which liken the soul to a harmony.[95] In musical theory, the correct conjunction of intervals (διαστήματα) produces a harmony.[96] So Democritus was certainly read by later commentators as promoting something akin to a 'soul as harmony' thesis.

Comparison with Epicurean psychology is illuminating. It might confirm the interpretation offered for this clause of B191, and introduce a discussion of the Epicurean reception of Democritean psychology.

A possible Latin equivalent for διάστημα is *intervallum*.[97] This is the word which Lucretius uses to denote the distance between atoms.[98] At *DRN* 2.95–111 he explains how the nature of

[95] The *Pythagoras* is the first of the 'ethical works' listed at DL 9.46. Also see 9.38 where Diogenes cites Glaucus of Rhegium, a contemporary of Democritus, who had claimed that Democritus was taught by a Pythagorean. He also mentions that Apollodorus of Cyzicus thought that Democritus lived with Philolaus. This is perhaps the Apollodorus of DL 8.12 who wrote an epigram on Pythagoras and/or the Apollodorus of Clement's list of Abderites, whose *telos* is ψυχαγωγία (Burkert (1972) 180 and n. 110, 229 and n. 51). Burkert (1972) 110 n. 2 notes the presence of Abderan coins *c.* 430 BC which show Pythagoras. On ψυχαγωγία in rhetoric see below: pp. 181–3. On Democritus and Philolaus: below pp. 67–71.

[96] Archytas B2. Michaelides (1978) s.v. διάστημα. Aristoxenus also uses this term, e.g. *Harm.* 1.20, 14–15.

[97] The word originally denoted the divide between the two palisade walls of an army camp, and later extended to mean 'distance' more generally, both spatially (Cic. *ND* 2.53, Lucr. *DRN* 4.187, 198) and temporally (Cic. *Ad fam.* 1.7, *Fin.* 2.94). It functions in musical theory as the word for an 'interval': *ND* 2.146. Cicero *Tusc.* 1.41 uses *intervallum* in his objection to Aristoxenus' thesis that the soul is nothing but the harmony of bodily parts (cf. *Tusc.* 1.19–20). Aristoxenus uses διάστημα for an interval in his musical works, and perhaps also in his psychological writing. (For this use in music cf. Archyt. B1.2; Pl. *Rep.* 531a7, *Phlb.* 17c11–e6; ps.-Arist. *Prob.* 922b6; DL 3.68). On non-musical uses of διάστημα: Barker (1989) 194 n. 9, 474 n. 91.

[98] *DRN* 2.726 (= 2.1020 Bailey *secl.*), 5.438. Epicurus uses the noun διάστημα to designate the spaces between *kosmoi*, the *intermundia*. Simplicius *in Phys.* 571.22ff. uses

a compound is in part related to the density of its atomic structure. Small 'intervals' are characteristic of dense substances such as rock and iron. Sometimes atoms bounce far apart on collision (98) and sometimes their motion is restricted by collision from other, closely packed atoms (101). Atoms are in constant motion, but their relative 'intervals' vary according to the number of atoms in a specified area of void.

If the atoms of iron and rock display small relative 'intervals', then the atoms of the soul, which are exceedingly small, light, and mobile (3.177–230) and form a soul which is characterised as a mixture of *vapor, aer, calor,* and the 'fourth element' (3.231–40) should display 'intervals' as large as possible (3.394, cf. 3.566ff.).[99] Only the constraining force of the body prevents them from flying far apart. So Lucretius, as Democritus, would contend that the atoms of the soul are positioned relative to one another at 'large intervals'.

Lucretius also offers some support for my interpretation of the ἐκ-construction in B191. In book two, he shows that the atoms themselves do not possess qualities proper to macroscopic objects (for example, colour: 2.730ff.). As part of this, he argues that the atoms themselves are not 'alive', but that certain complexes of atoms are (2.934ff.). He then passes from a discussion of death and unconsciousness which occur when the atomic complex is disturbed (943–53) to a discussion of pleasure and pain.

> ... dolor est ubi materiai
> corpora vi quadam per viscera viva per artus
> sollicitata suis trepidant in sedibus intus,
> inque locum quando *re*migrant, fit blanda voluptas ... (2.963–6)

> Pain occurs when the particles of matter are by a certain force disturbed through the living organs and limbs, and shudder deep in their positions. When they return to their places there arises sweet pleasure.

διάστημα to denote what οἱ περὶ Δημόκριτον καὶ Ἐπίκουρον call κενόν. Sedley (1982) argues for a distinction between Democritus' and Epicurus' conceptions of void. Grilli (1983) 101 suggests that διάστημα means 'l'intervallo di quel παλμός atomico, che entro certi limiti contribuisce al mantenimento dell' εὐστάθεια'.

[99] Furley (1967) 230.

Here we see a thought similar to B191: pain is the disturbance of a certain arrangement of atoms. Moving *out of* this arrangement generates pain. Returning to this arrangement produces the converse process: pleasure.[100]

Lucretius is also keen to dissociate the Epicurean from the Democritean theory on the issue of the number and position of the soul atoms. In doing so, he provides a picture of the arrangement of Democritean soul atoms which might appear incompatible with B191. Lucretius claims that Democritus thought that atoms of body and soul alternated throughout the organism (3.372–3).[101] If this is indeed Democritus' view, how can B191 maintain that soul atoms should ideally display 'large intervals'? How can the intervals be large if there is only ever one body atom between any two soul atoms? Perhaps although each pair of soul atoms is only separated by one body atom, the interval of *void* between them should be large. But in that case, of course, the intervals between body atoms would be just as large.

However, it has been claimed that Lucretius' interpretation and the picture of alternating soul and body atoms which he paints is an Epicurean interpretation of Theophrastus *De sensibus* 58, which claims that Democritus described a συμμετρία of soul and body. This was taken by the Epicureans to mean a numerical and spatial one-to-one correspondence, and produces the view outlined by Lucretius here, although Theophrastus – and Democritus himself – perhaps intended no such view.[102] If so, then perhaps Lucretius' picture can be passed over as not accurately representing a *bona fide* Democritean position. In any case, Lucretius proceeds to reject the 'Democritean' model he has just outlined, and offers some empirical observations in support (3.374–80). Some things are so small or so fine that when they brush against our bodies they do not cause

---

[100] Cf. *DRN* 4.858–76, deleted by some editors, where pain is described as caused by the erosion and destruction of the *natura* as *rarescit corpus*.

[101] Cf. Alfieri (1979) 149ff., Farrar (1988) 223–4, Luria (1970) *ad* §§454, 460 (= *DRN* 3.372–3 and Theoph. *De sensibus* 58). Salem (1996) 195–6. Democritus does seem to allow that soul atoms would be sloughed from the surface in the form of *eidōla*. This perhaps underlies his strange insistence on the existence of 'living' dream images: SE *M*. 9.19, Plut. *QC* 734F, Diog. Oin. 10.v.2–6 Smith. Cf. Morel (1996) 295–332, Sedley (1998b) 149 n. 28.

[102] Silvestre (1985) 175ff., compare Taylor (1999) 202. Cf. Diog. Oin. 37.1.1ff. Smith.

us to sense them. Lucretius concludes that they did not come into contact with an atom of the *anima*, and therefore these soul atoms are more rarely distributed through the body than Democritus, on his reading, suggested.

If, on the other hand, Lucretius' report is accurate then we must make a further decision. Either we can choose to accept that it poses an unavoidable obstacle to a strict physical reading of the 'large intervals' phrase from B191 – which can then be understood in a more metaphorical manner – or we might have to think that Democritus saw no incompatibility between a model of alternating soul and body atoms, and the view that it is best if the soul atoms are spread as far apart as possible. Without any more detailed evidence to provide a more detailed picture of Democritus' view of the position of soul atoms throughout the body, it is difficult to come to any more definite conclusions.[103]

The evidence of Theophrastus *De sensibus*

We might find some corroboration of the general picture which is beginning to take shape in Theophrastus' description of Democritean perception. Theophrastus does not, of course, specifically deal here with Democritean ethics, or psychic well-being. But at *De sensibus* 58 he does offer a description of perception and thought which includes remarks about how these processes affect the physical composition of the soul. It is possible that this is a parallel process to that envisaged by B191.

General character of the treatise

Theophrastus' description of various earlier philosophers' thoughts on perception follows a clear pattern.[104] In the first chapter he distinguishes two groups of theories about sense-perception: that it occurs by 'likes' and that it occurs 'by opposites'. To the

---

[103] SE *M.* 7.349 says that Democritus placed the soul throughout the body. Theoph. *De sensibus* 57 complains that Democritus makes the *whole body* see, hear, etc. because sensory information enters the body and διαχεῖσθαι κατὰ πᾶν [τὸ σῶμα].

[104] Mansfeld (1996) esp. the table on 188.

former side he assigns Parmenides and Empedocles, to the latter Anaxagoras and Heraclitus. Democritus, who takes up much of the extant work, is not mentioned in this early programmatic statement. When he is introduced, it is after the delineation of these two 'schools of thought' and with the comment that he does not make clear whether perception arises through opposites or through 'likes' (49). This impels Theophrastus to explicate Democritus' theory more fully, and sense by sense, beginning with sight.

Two concepts, 'mixture' and 'symmetry' (κρᾶσις and συμμετρία), which will become crucial to our understanding of *De sensibus* 58, are introduced in the earlier discussion.[105] First, Theophrastus examines Parmenides fragment B16 and sees his theory of perception as based on the understanding that the mixture of the body (understood in terms of the hot and cold, Light and Night) affects perception and that the best state is a *preponderance* of heat (3).[106] Empedocles treats perception similarly as a 'like to like' relation (12–13).

Alcmaion (25) and Anaxagoras (27) define perception as a reaction of opposites. Theophrastus, in an interlude, considers this to be somewhat more plausible (31–5). Then Cleidemus (38) and Diogenes of Apollonia (39) are fitted into this scheme of thinking in terms of mixture and 'symmetry'.

Theophrastus on Democritus on thought

περὶ δὲ τοῦ φρονεῖν ἐπὶ τοσοῦτον εἴρηκεν, ὅτι γίνεται συμμέτρως ἐχούσης τῆς ψυχῆς μετὰ τὴν κίνησιν· ἐὰν δὲ περίθερμός τις ἢ περίψυχρος γένηται, μεταλλάττειν φησί. διὸ καὶ τοὺς παλαιοὺς καλῶς τοῦθ' ὑπολαβεῖν, ὅτι ἐστὶν 'ἀλλοφρονεῖν'. ὥστε φανερόν, ὅτι τῇ κράσει τοῦ σώματος ποιεῖ τὸ φρονεῖν, ὅπερ ἴσως αὐτῷ καὶ κατὰ λόγον ἐστὶ σῶμα ποιοῦντι τὴν ψυχήν. (*De sensibus* 58)[107]

---

[105] Cf. Sassi (1978) 166–74. Generally on Democritus in the *De sensibus*: Morel (1996) 201–40.

[106] Theophrastus assumes, I think, that Parmenides endorses this position although it probably comes from the *Doxa* section of his poem. See Laks (1990).

[107] On this text, specifically the emendation by Diels of κατὰ τὴν κρᾶσιν for the MSS μετὰ τὴν κίνησιν, see Sassi (1978) 161–90, esp. 187–90. κρᾶσις occurs again in 58, and also in 64. Sassi argues against the emendation. Cf. Silvestre-Pinto (1983) 46 n. 39, Taylor (1999) 111 n. 105. Morel (1996) 221 argues for the emendation, although I think his general understanding of the passage is similar to mine. Luria (1964) 24 n. 73 argues that the MSS reading is non-sensical.

He said this much about thought – that it arises when the soul is in a symmetrical state after the motion/change. But if someone becomes too hot or too cold,[108] he says that they alter. And hence the ancients were right to suppose that it is possible to 'think differently'.[109] So it is clear that he makes thinking dependent on the mixture of the body – which is perhaps also reasonable for him, as he makes the soul a body.

If this is introduced as evidence for E/Ph, since it seems to allow that a soul-state can be altered by physical circumstances, on what level are we to understand the mixture? The atoms themselves are neither hot nor cold (B9). It is the macroscopic atomic compound of the body which is affected by environmental factors and in turn affects cognition. But on this account, no reference to atoms is required at all; the argument is simply that the body's state and temperature affect the soul. This gives no possibility of inferring the nature of the soul from the fact that it can be affected by the body. Even Plato would allow that; it is consistent with, but does not entail a materialist conception of the soul.[110]

However, a little later in the treatise Theophrastus gives a brief description of how we should understand 'heating' and 'cooling' in Democritean atomic terms. Heating is the introduction of more void into the macroscopic body, which therefore rarefies (*De sensibus* 65). When the body is over-heated, or over-cooled, this is expressed at the atomic level by a change in the admixture of void among the constituent atoms of the body.[111] Such a change would presumably prevent the soul from maintaining the desired arrangement of soul and body atoms suggested by B191. Any motion or change (κίνησις) which adversely altered the arrangement

---

[108] On περι- compounds denoting excess: Sassi (1978) 180.

[109] The reference to οἱ παλαιοί suggests that we should think of Hom. *Il.* 23.698. This is confirmed by the reference in Aristotle *Met.* 1009b30 to Hektor ἀλλοφρονέοντα (although the Homeric reference does not describe Hektor). Cf. Hdt. 5.85, Hippoc. *Morb.* 2.16, *Mul.* 1.41. Aristotle reuses this illustration at *DA* 404a29–30. Mansfeld (1986) 17–18 suggests that Theophrastus remembers Aristotle's use, which itself comes from some further source. Cf. Mansfeld (1996).

[110] Vlastos (1945–6) 579 distinguishes between Democritus' and Plato's conception of *how* the body affects the soul. For Democritus, 'in so-called bodily excesses soul, not body, is to blame. Drunkenness and voluptuousness are foisted on the body by the soul, not the reverse': B159, B223.

[111] Compare Luria (1970) ad loc. (§ 460) (similar to Diller (1934) 63, cp. Guthrie (1965) 452–3).

of the soul atoms would compromise one's psychic well-being, just as it can alter one's power of cognition.[112]

A further parallel comes from Aelian, reporting Democritus' views about pregnancy (V*H* 12.17). He claims that in excessively warm climates the bodies of the mothers, their veins and joints, undergo expansion.[113] The verb διίστασθαι is repeated. Although the discussion here is focused on macroscopic bodies, I am tempted to see an echo in this verb of the intervals, διαστήματα, of B191 and the explanation of differing cognitive states in Theophrastus. This paragraph of Aelian seems concerned to retain recognisably Democritean vocabulary – it ends with a reference to the *galēne* enjoyed by some fortunate foetuses.[114]

Soul and mixture

Theophrastus concludes his discussion of Democritus on thought by adding that making thinking dependent on the body's 'mixture' is natural for someone who considers the soul to be itself a body. It is no revelation that Democritus' soul is material, but Theophrastus has offered a link between the metaphorical and the physical understandings of 'interval' (διάστημα). He has noted that Democritus' soul is involved in a mixture (κρᾶσις).

There are two ways of understanding the relationship between the soul and this mixture.

1 The soul is the mixture of different elements or substances. Without the correct mixing each of the elements remains, but there is no soul.
2 The soul is one of the elements or substances within the mixture. The exact mixing, however, affects the state of that soul, and its ability to think, perceive, and induce movement.

The first alternative makes the soul the harmony of non-psychic elements; the second makes the soul's effectiveness and state dependent on its harmony with these elements. The first is the sort of

---

[112] Cf. Sassi (1978) 187. Compare Leucippus' explanation of sleep and death (DK 67 A34): ὕπνον σώματος γίνεσθαι ἀποκρίσει τοῦ λεπτομεροῦς πλείονι τῆς εἰσκρίσεως τοῦ ψυχικοῦ θερμοῦ· <ἧς> τὸν πλεονασμὸν αἴτιον θανάτου. Cf. Lucr. *DRN* 2.944–62.

[113] Also see Epic. *Ep. Hdt* 43.

[114] Cf. Vlastos (1945–6) 583. Also note Philodemus *De morte* VIII. 6–10 and Gigante (1983) 152–3.

theory outlined in Simmias' objection at Plato *Phaedo* 85e3ff.;[115] the second would be more consonant with a conception which describes specifically psychic atoms arranged among other types of atom, and is the position ascribed to Democritus by Theophrastus at the end of *De sensibus* 58. Still it is important to note how subtle this distinction becomes when we consider the mechanism of body–soul interaction.

Democritus allows that in some sense thinking and perception are affected by bodily change, by heating, cooling, and other physiological alteration. Once this, and the mortality of the soul (B297), have been granted it becomes less obvious how he can sustain a strict division between body and soul atoms. Since:

- The soul [the complex of soul atoms] thinks and perceives only when it is within a body.
- The soul's thought and perception are affected by bodily change.
- Given certain bodily changes [e.g. extreme heat or cold], the soul is destroyed.

The soul *atoms* are not destroyed at death, but the soul [complex] is. The soul, if considered in terms of either the complex of soul atoms or the power to think and perceive, is dependent for its continued functioning as a soul on a certain mixture of the atoms in an animal's body, and is affected by changes in the specific composition of that mixture. So we see both how Democritus could be assimilated by Thrasyllus to the Pythagoreans as a result of a possible slide from version 2 to version 1,[116] (since the version of the harmony thesis found in Plato's *Phaedo* has often been identified as Pythagorean or Philolaan),[117] and how Democritus' particular

---

[115] NB: κρᾶσιν... τῶν ἐν τῷ σώματι 86d2. Cf. Arist. *DA* 407b30: ἁρμονίαν γάρ τινα αὐτὴν [ψυχὴν] λέγουσι· καὶ γὰρ τὴν ἁρμονίαν κρᾶσιν καὶ σύνθεσιν ἐναντίων εἶναι καὶ τὸ σῶμα συγκεῖσθαι ἐξ ἐναντίων. This is not offered as the position of any particular school.

[116] Tarrant (1993) 84–8 suggests this might offer a link between Thrasyllus' interest in Democritus and Plato. Note also that if, with Usener (1887) Index s.v. Ἀβδηρῖται we identify the Apollodotos of Clem. *Strom.* 2.130.4ff. whose *telos* is listed as ψυχαγωγία with the Apollodorus of DL 9.38, who claimed that Democritus spent some time with Philolaus, then we might have some evidence for a Pythagorean assimilation or use of Democritean material. Cf. Natorp (1893) 123.

[117] Bostock (1986) 11–12. Echecrates might be the Pythagorean and pupil of Philolaus of that name (DL 8.46). 61d6: Cebes and Simmias had studied under Philolaus. Huffman (1993) 326–7 is sceptical about finding anything 'Pythagorean' or 'Philolaan' in the

version of this harmony theory would provide for a mortal soul, composed of soul atoms.[118]

In the *Phaedo*, Simmias argues that the conception of the soul as a harmony can fulfil the requirements of the preceding 'Affinity Argument' (77e–80b), i.e. be invisible, incorporeal, beautiful, and divine (85e4), but nevertheless be perishable.[119] He concludes, therefore, that Socrates must reject the soul as harmony thesis, or he cannot conclude that the soul is immortal on the grounds produced in the dialogue thus far. We have good reason to think that the Epicureans were interested in this theory. Epicurus provided an explicit version of one of Socrates' arguments against the *Phaedo*'s harmony thesis (Epicurus *apud* Philop. *in De an.* 143.1–10), and Lucretius offers a number of arguments against harmony theorists (*DRN* 3.94–135).[120] The Epicurean distaste for this theory centres around its inability to explain localised psychic phenomena (3.106–29), and its epiphenomenalist tendencies. It is difficult to see how a harmony of this sort can independently produce any effects on the body, since it owes its own very existence to a particular arrangement of bodily material. This latter is not explicitly stated by Lucretius, but can be inferred from the Epicurean insistence that soul must be physical in order to be bring about bodily effects (3.161ff.), and the resultant theory of a soul constructed from four types of atom.

It has been wondered why the Epicureans felt the need to include such soul atoms. They sometimes seem happy to talk as if living things were composed of the same sort of atoms that constitute (and have constituted) inanimate objects, and inanimate objects gave rise to living beings as the result of atomic rearrangement. This is the picture of Lucretius' second book (2.865–990). Why take the extra step of insisting that one of the four types of atom

dialogue. Cf. Sedley (1996) 22–6 and (1995) 11, Burkert (1972) 292 n. 75. Philolaus' psychology remains obscure: Huffman (1993) 328–32. Gottschalk (1971) 195 concludes that Simmias' theory was a Platonic invention drawing on current (perhaps medical) theories.

[118] Arist. *DA* 403b28ff., 405a5ff.: Democritus likened soul atoms to fire atoms. Morel (1996) 136ff. has a good discussion of the doxography.

[119] *Phaed.* 86c3–6. Gallop (1975) ad loc.: 'The attunement theory of the soul is not merely consistent with its destruction at death but actually entails it.' Gottschalk (1971) 182. Cf. Sedley (1995) 12.

[120] See Gottschalk (1971).

required to produce a soul is a specific nameless 'soul atom', the *anima animae* (*DRN* 3.241–5, 273–81)?[121]

The insistence on specific soul atoms is more perplexing if we are inclined to see in Epicureanism an insistence on the emergence of genuinely novel characteristics out of more basic physical constituents. As I will explain at greater length in the Conclusion, they had a particular interpretation of Democritus B9 (see above pp. 7–9) and took Democritus to task for his eliminativist atomism, perhaps offering instead the view that once atoms are arranged in particular complex ways new properties and qualities – which are no less real although they are not fundamental in the way atoms and void are – come into being. The Epicureans were keen to maintain the reality of macroscopic objects and qualities (and therefore reject Democritus B9) despite agreeing with Democritus that atoms and void are the fundamental constituents of the world. If so, why did they on this occasion feel tempted to posit a different sort of atom to explain a difference between things which are alive and things which are not? There is no similar temptation to posit a different sort of atom to explain why some things are, for example, green and some things are not. There is also clear Epicurean criticism of Democritus on the metaphysics of mixture. On the Epicurean view, Democritus understood mixture as little more than a collocation of the constituent ingredients, whereas Epicurus appears to have insisted that each ingredient is broken into its constituent atoms, from which a new compound is then formed.[122] This elaboration again reveals a concern to underline the unity and uniqueness of the soul-complex. It is not merely a combination of various elemental characteristics.[123]

Epicurus seems unwilling to rest his explanation of the distinction between animate and inanimate compounds solely on the emergence theory, and so the Epicureans retain the Democritean

---

[121] A complaint voiced by Annas (1992) 139–43.

[122] Alex. Aphrod. *De mixtione* 214.16–215.8. Kerferd (1971) 90–2. Todd (1976) 184 compares Arist. *GC* 328a8–16 and doubts whether Alexander is reporting genuine Democritean theory. Morel (1996) 86–8 is less sceptical. The Epicurean theory of κρᾶσις lies behind Lucretius' description of the combination of the four atom-types in the soul at 3.258–65, esp. 265: *quasi multae vis unius corporis exstant.* See Kerferd (1971) 90–1.

[123] Cf. Sedley (1983b).

view of soul atoms. They too insist on a particular kind of atom constituting the soul, although they embellish Democritus' account by distinguishing four types of soul atom: fire-like, air-like, *pneuma*-like, and the nameless 'fourth nature'. Epicurus offers his fourth element since, Lucretius says, the others are insufficient to account for the soul's ability as an atomic complex to function in a characteristically soul-like manner: *DRN* 3.236–40.[124] This overdetermines Epicurus' psychology. He offers two explanations for the soul's new abilities over and above those of other atomic composites. The soul is both generated by the emergence of certain new characteristics from particular atomic arrangements, and also made of certain 'soul' atoms.

The 'tension' sometimes found in Epicurean accounts of soul–body relations,[125] is equally present in, and probably originated in, Democritus' position. The Epicurean argument that soul must have a physical basis and that therefore there must be certain atoms which somehow explain the difference between animate and inanimate things, betrays a Democritean hangover which they should perhaps have resisted. This same tension in Democritean psychology gave rise to doxographical links with Pythagoreanism on the one hand, and Epicurean criticism on the other.

Democritean psychologies: interim conclusions

I conclude this chapter by returning to the question of a link between Democritus' ethics and physics along the lines of E/Ph (above, p. 59). However many links one might suggest between the language of the ethical fragments and physical theories, the deduction of the former from the latter will remain conjectural.[126]

---

[124] See Sharples (1991–3) 189, Annas (1992) 139. Also note esp. the scholion to *Ep. Hdt.* 66, presumably a criticism of Democritus and his 'fiery' soul atoms, perhaps motivated by earlier Peripatetic criticisms, as suggested by Kerferd (1971) 83, Silvestre (1985) 89, 93 n. 17.

[125] Found e.g. by Annas (1992) 147, 187.

[126] Linguistic resonances between ethics and physics have been detected in a number of fragments. B33 contains the participle μεταρυσμοῦσα to describe the action of teaching (cf. Tortora (1984)); cf. B197. ῥυσμός is one of the terms used for differences of atomic configuration at Arist. *Met.* 985b15ff. Thrasyllus' catalogue at DL 9.47 contains the titles of physical works περὶ τῶν διαφερόντων ῥυσμῶν and περὶ ἀμειψιρυσμιῶν. (See

Nothing in the fragments themselves compels us to argue that there was such an account of *euthymia* in Democritus' ethics. Conversely, there is nothing in the *moralia* which precludes such a connection, and my exploration of interpretations of the reference to 'large intervals' in fragment B191 has shown that a consideration of the atomist psychology which might underlie the moral psychology of the *moralia* can provide such interesting connections. I am inclined to see the modern debate as irresolvable; we simply do not have the required evidence either to affirm or conclusively to deny E/Ph.

A more interesting question for the purposes of the present study is the availability of such differing interpretations to ancient readers of Democritus. Anaxarchus and Pyrrho both react to and accept parts of the Democritean *moralia*, but as far as we can tell neither based such acceptance on an atomist psychology. Pyrrho was not an atomist at all. Anaxarchus was in all likelihood an atomist, but – as we shall see – there is no indication at all that his view of the good life made any reference to the atomic state of the soul. Therefore if E/Ph was true for Democritus himself it was not the case for many of his successors; it is not an essential component of a 'Democritean' ethics. Of the subsequent philosophers in this tradition, perhaps only Nausiphanes proposed anything like a systematic 'bottom up' ethical programme, beginning with the identification of the ideal physical state of the soul. Only in his case is there any suggestion that ethics could begin with and be encompassed by natural philosophy. For this claim Nausiphanes was savagely attacked by the eventual heirs of Democritus' atomism and *moralia* – the Epicureans. That particular story will be the focus of my chapter 7.

also Hesychius' glosses on such terms in B138 and B139.) Vlastos (1945–6) 54 and n. 78 is convinced that a strict theoretical link is implied between the action of teaching and the rearrangement of soul atoms. Cf. Luria (1964) 13–14, Farrar (1988) 229, Spinelli (1991) 301. Taylor (1967) 14–15 responds critically. The reprint of Vlastos' 1945–6 article in his (1995) *Studies in Greek Philosophy* vol. I, 342 contains a rejoinder after n. 79, and Taylor (1999) 233 is now inclined to agree with Vlastos to a degree. B266 refers to the ῥυθμός of a society. See Spinelli (1991) 301. Thrasyllus also notes the book title περὶ τῆς τοῦ σοφοῦ διαθέσεως (DL 9.46). Is this physical atomic arrangement? For διάθεσις in Epicureanism: Grilli (1983).

3

ANAXARCHUS' MORAL STAGE

The first of the followers of Democritus listed in the doxographical tradition is Anaxarchus of Abdera. He is notable not only for the stories told about his life but also because he is a direct link to the sceptical tradition of Pyrrhonism. Although Aristocles of Messene complains that another Democritean, Metrodorus of Chios, provided the unfortunate impulse for Pyrrhonian scepticism (*apud* Eus. *PE* 14.19.9), Anaxarchus is more commonly regarded as Pyrrho's mentor.[1]

Much of our information about Anaxarchus comes from sources such as Arrian or Plutarch's *Lives*, which are more concerned with the biography of Alexander the Great than the detailed presentation of philosophical positions. Our picture of Anaxarchus is concentrated on his conduct rather than his thought, and it was this very conduct and attitude which – it is said – so impressed Pyrrho. To such an extent do the sources concentrate on Anaxarchus' conduct and attitude, that there is little suggestion of the arguments which provided their foundation. We see the instantiation of the theories rather than the theories themselves, a situation repeated in the presentation of Pyrrho.

There is little direct evidence for the conclusion that Anaxarchus was an atomist, although there are one or two indirect clues. He is reported to have thought that there was an infinite number of *kosmoi* (causing Alexander to despair that he had not yet conquered even one),[2] a conclusion which Valerius Maximus says he advanced 'on Democritus' authority' (8.14). However, whether Anaxarchus held other Democritean theories and whether this particular cosmological thesis was held as a consequence of atomic physics is still

---

[1] E.g. ps.-Galen *Hist. phil.* 3.4 (Diels *Dox.* 601.13).
[2] Cf. Plut. *Tranq.* 466D.

uncertain. The infinite *kosmoi* thesis, coupled with his appearance in the successional lists of the Democritean tradition, nevertheless makes it a plausible–if unproven – assumption that Anaxarchus indeed was an atomist.[3] Anaxarchus is most renowned, however, for his moral outlook.

οὗτος διὰ τὴν ἀπάθειαν καὶ εὐκολίαν τοῦ βίου Εὐδαιμονικὸς ἐκαλεῖτο. (DL 9.60)[4]

Because of the absence of passions and the ease of his life he was called the 'Happy Man'.

The reference to an absence of passions, ἀπάθεια, immediately recalls the most widely known and widely related story about Anaxarchus: that of his death at the hands of the tyrant Nicocreon.[5] When tortured, Anaxarchus cried out, 'Strike the bag of Anaxarchus, you do not strike Anaxarchus himself' (πτίσσε τὸν Ἀναξάρχου θύλακον Ἀνάξαρχον δὲ οὐ πλήττεις, DL 9.59).[6] Whether someone can be *eudaimōn* under torture was a question which would occupy the Hellenistic schools, and even the Epicureans argued that a wise man would still be happy on the rack – although he might let out the odd groan.[7] In the case of Anaxarchus this attitude is probably related to the notion of *indifference*, which not only recalls Cynicism, but also looks forward to Pyrrho and his renowned *adiaphoria*. This is a topic to which I will turn in due course, but first it is necessary to pause to consider another facet of Anaxarchus' thought, namely his supposed view of the illusory nature of sense-impressions.

In Sextus Empiricus' review of previous epistemologies, which he classifies according to whether they accepted or rejected the 'criterion of truth', Anaxarchus' entry makes use of the striking simile of scene-painting.

---

[3] Anaxarchus' reported success in dissuading Alexander from believing in the efficacy of prophecy is another sign of possible Democritean influence: Diod. Sic. 17.112.4–5, Just. 12.13.5.

[4] Cf. DL 1.17, ps.-Galen *Hist. phil.* 4 (Diels *Dox.* 602).

[5] T30–63 Dorandi (34 of only 70 *testimonia* and fragments). For a detailed discussion of Anaxarchus' dealings with the tyrant, and diagrams of the particular torture-implements involved: Bernard (1984).

[6] πλήττεις MSS, πτίσσεις Menagius.

[7] Epicurus at DL 10.118; Cicero *Fin.* 1.62; *Tusc.* 2.17, 5.31, 5.74–5.

οὐκ ὀλίγοι δὲ ἦσαν, ὡς προεῖπον, οἱ καὶ τοὺς περὶ Μητρόδωρον καὶ 'Ανάξαρχον ἔτι δὲ Μόνιμον φήσαντες ἀνηρηκέναι τὸ κριτήριον, ἀλλὰ... [here Sextus gives a version of Metrodorus Β1], Ανάξαρχον δὲ καὶ Μόνιμον ὅτι σκηνογραφίᾳ ἀπείκασαν τὰ ὄντα τοῖς τε κατὰ ὕπνους ἢ μανίαν προσπίπτουσι ταῦτα ὡμοιῶσθαι ὑπέλαβον. (SE M.7.88)

There were not a few, as I said before, who claimed that also Metrodorus, Anaxarchus, and even Monimus removed the criterion – they included Anaxarchus and Monimus because these likened what is to a scene-painting and held it to resemble dreams and manic delusions.

Anaxarchus likens the phenomenal world to a scene-painting.[8] He argues that rather than accepting what our senses tell us, we should think of our sense-impressions as like the two-dimensional renderings of perspective placed behind the stage to create the deceptive impression of a large palace or temple. What we perceive is not 'real', just as when we sit in the theatre the action does not take place in front of a 'real' temple. Anaxarchus wishes us to realise in the case of every perception, as we do when we see this kind of artistic technique, that perceptions can be illusory. What we think are 'real' are instead scene-paintings. That, at least, is the epistemological story which Sextus wishes to tell, and it is a story consistent with Anaxarchus' allegiance to Democritean (meta)physics.[9]

Perhaps Anaxarchus was indeed an atomist, and perhaps he did hold such a thesis about the reality of the phenomenal world. After all, the metaphor of *trompe-l'oeil* painting is common in other epistemological writing, especially in Platonic texts, and a Democritean might well believe that there is a gulf between the reality

---

[8] Sextus does also mention the analogies of dreams or manic illusions, but this is more likely to be a commonplace characterisation of any sceptical position from the post-Academic period (see M.7.245; 8.18, 57).

[9] Von Fritz (1963) 94. Cf. Decleva Caizzi (1984b) 9 n. 16; Dal Pra (1989) 54 n. 23; Görler (1994) 751. Democritus did write a treatise on ζωγραφίη (DL 9.48), and Vitruvius includes a story of Democritus and Anaxagoras writing treatises on perspective after the innovative commentary of Agatharchus (*De arch.* 7 praef.11). Perhaps this was the content of Democritus' work ἀκτινογραφία (one of Thrasyllus' Μαθηματικά: DL 9.48). SE M.7.140 also suggests a Democritean approval of Anaxagoras' dictum: ὄψις τῶν ἀδήλων τὰ φαινόμενα which perhaps underlies Vitruvius' remarks. This is argued in an unpublished paper by Myles Burnyeat, 'All the world's a stage painting'; cf. Morel (1996) 458, 465–6. Sedley (1992) 43–4 thinks SE M.7.140 derives from an anti-Epicurean source, perhaps via Posidonius. Vitruvius certainly knew of Posidonius (8.27), and some Posidonian sources link Anaxagoras and Democritus, notably for their theory that comets are optical illusions caused by conjunctions of planets: frr. 130–2 EK.

of atoms and void and the phenomenal world of colours, tastes, and so on.[10] (This is one possible interpretation of Democritus B9, see above pp. 7–9). But there is no evidence to corroborate this suggestion. Indeed, as my observations on the general forces of sceptical doxography have shown (see above pp. 13ff.), later sources are often too keen to read sceptical epistemologies into the remarks of earlier thinkers – including those in this Democritean tradition. Similar forces will also appear at work in the reports of Pyrrho. Moreover, Diogenes' biography of Monimus (DL 6.82–3), the philosopher whom Sextus combines with Anaxarchus here, reveals no epistemology at all. Instead he is a most serious man (ἐμβριθέσ-τατος) whose major works were an ethical treatise on impulses and a *Protrepticus*.[11] In the absence of other evidence from which to infer that Anaxarchus had a generally sceptical outlook, therefore, I am wary of accepting the attribution of this epistemological theory to Anaxarchus and Monimus. It should be noted that Sextus himself does not attribute this theory to Anaxarchus. Instead some unidentified commentators are introduced to make this point.

I prefer to concentrate on Anaxarchus' moral outlook. In fact, the very simile of scene-painting used as the major piece of evidence for the picture of a sceptical Anaxarchus, can be given a moral dimension.[12] Anaxarchus' original thesis perhaps resembled the thesis of Ariston of Chios.

τέλος ἔφησεν εἶναι τὸ ἀδιαφόρως ἔχοντα ζῆν πρὸς τὰ μεταξὺ ἀρετῆς καὶ κακίας μηδ' ἡντινοῦν ἐν αὐτοῖς παραλλαγὴν ἀπολείποντα, ἀλλ' ἐπίσης ἐπὶ πάντων

[10] See Pollitt (1974) 237–54 on σκηνο- and σκιαγραφία, terms which became identified in later antiquity. The perspective drawing of *skenographia* is thought to have developed first: Apollodorus (fl. 425–400 BC) is credited with the development of *skiagraphia* (Plut. *De glor. Ath.* 346A). On the meaning of *skiagraphia*: Keuls (1975) and (1978), Pemberton (1976), Pollitt (1974) 251. For full references to uses in Platonic texts: Keuls (1978) 76. Aristotle uses the term much less, but see e.g. *Rhet.* 1414a9, and Trimpi (1978).

[11] On Monimus cf. Stob. 2.31.88 (cited below, n. 20), 4.31.89. Hankinson (1995) 54 advocates a strictly epistemological interpretation of Anaxarchus' original thought. Brunschwig (1984) 117 notes that Sextus introduces Xeniades' declaration that 'nothing is true' immediately before Monimus' definition of τῦφος, but that should not lead us to conclude that Monimus himself was offering an epistemological thesis. Sextus is stretching things in order to include Monimus at all: τάχα δὲ καὶ Μόνιμος. Timon's Xenophanes is ὑπάτυφος (60.1 Diels), and Pyrrho is ἄτυφος (9.1 Diels, Aristoc. *apud* Eus. *PE* 14.18.18). On τῦφος generally: Decleva Caizzi (1980a).

[12] Cf. Decleva Caizzi (1981a) 158; Bett (1999) 143–4 or (2000) 162–5.

ἔχοντα· εἶναι γὰρ ὅμοιον τὸν σοφὸν τῷ ἀγαθῷ ὑποκριτῇ, ὃς ἄν τε Θερσίτου ἄν τε Ἀγαμέμνονος πρόσωπον ἀναλάβῃ, ἑκάτερον ὑποκρινεῖται προσηκόντως. (DL 7.160)[13]

[Ariston] said that the goal of life was living indifferently to those things between virtue and vice – not allowing any distinctions at all within them, but being disposed equally to all. For he said that the wise man is like a good actor, who, whether he takes on the role of Thersites or of Agamemnon, will play each part appropriately.

Other Stoics hold that although virtue is the only good and vice the only bad, within those things which have no real ethical value, which they termed the 'indifferents', some are preferred and some dispreferred.[14] Ariston takes the radical line of recognising no such distinctions within the 'indifferents'. For him only virtue and vice were of value; anything else was entirely without value in respect of one's *eudaimonia*. Now, there is no need to attribute to Anaxarchus anything like a Stoic conception of virtue, but this passage reporting Ariston's view does use once again a theatrical metaphor. In the face of such indifferents, the wise man is told to act his assigned rôle. One might play the rôle of Agamemnon or Thersites, one might be rich and powerful or poor, ugly and despised, but what is of value is the virtue of the actor underneath. All else is mask and costume.

In a similar way, Anaxarchus may have turned to a theatrical metaphor. It would be entirely appropriate to compare those things which most people value or disvalue, pursue or avoid, with stage-scenery: the constructions and illusions which serve as the world in which the actors play out their rôles.[15] The Cynic flavour of the philosophies of Ariston and Anaxarchus has been noticed before, and we have already seen how Anaxarchus appears in Sextus as a partner of the Cynic Monimus, but a version of Democriteanism would also be a plausible candidate for the motivation for such an assertion.[16]

---

[13] On this passage see Ioppolo (1980a) 27, 189ff. and compare Cic. *Fin.* 3.24, Epict. *Diss.* 4.2.10. The Cynics also used a similar metaphor to show the sage's immunity from external τύχη; cf. Porter (1996) 157–8.

[14] See e.g. DL 7.102–7.

[15] For a similar suggestion see Bett (2000) 163.

[16] Cf. Brancacci (1980) 415 n.12 and (1981) 217 n. 5.

The denial of moral realism is a less radical thesis than the full eliminativist metaphysical position which Epicurean criticism unearthed in the Democritean outlook. If atoms and void are the only true existents, then the atomic compounds and their macroscopic qualities which form the perceptible around us lose their *value* along with their claims on true existence. (There can, for example, be no value in wealth if money, jewels, and the like do not – strictly speaking – even exist.) So the denial of moral realism is a consequence of this extremely economical ontology. But a more generous ontology can also leave room for denying moral realism. One can also insist that ethical qualities are not part of the fabric of the world while leaving perceptible qualities intact, whereas if one has eliminated perceptible qualities to leave only atoms and void, *a fortiori* one has eliminated ethical qualities.[17] I will claim in chapter 4 that Pyrrho originally expounded the less radical position (see DL 9.61), and it is possible that Anaxarchus did also. Sextus, however, evidently read Anaxarchus as proposing the more radical thesis – making all perceptible qualities like mere 'scene-painting'. However, if Anaxarchus' thought as revealed in the biographical anecdotes and the few fragments of *On Kingship* reveal mainly ethical concerns, then perhaps we would do well to stress his moral anti-realism and leave the extension of this train of thought into full eliminativist atomism as a mere possibility. And in fact the relevant evidence does indeed reveal a picture of someone who emphasised *moral* anti-realism, by claiming that nothing is good or bad 'by nature'.[18]

Democritus himself, as we have seen, is quite happy to make pronouncements about the human good, presumably basing it on some sort of implicit moral realism. After all, he seems prepared to recommend a life of moderate pleasure and provides the outline of a recipe for attaining a happy life. To glance ahead a little, after Pyrrho, Nausiphanes is even prepared to offer a vision in which

---

[17] Williams (1995), on Mackie (1977), discusses the parallels and differences between denying the reality of secondary and ethical qualities. Cf. below, p. 81 n. 25 and Williams (1985) 169 and 221 n. 13.

[18] Compare Democrates B115: ὁ κόσμος σκηνή, ὁ βίος πάροδος· ἦλθες, εἶδες, ἀπῆλθες. Thrasyllus lists a Democritean work κοσμογραφίη (one of the φυσικά, DL 9.46), but this is likely to mean something like 'a description of the *kosmos*': see Clem. *Strom.* 6.36; cf. οὐρανογραφίη at 9.48.

physical and psychological knowledge can provide the basis for incontrovertible ethical advice. Epicurus also had difficulties with this position – as we will see later. Still, it is interesting to observe that the tendency within the Democritean tradition to eliminate moral properties, or to make them merely conventional, seems to have been inspired not by any of Democritus' own ethical writings. Rather, this position takes its cue from Democritus' epistemology – which was, it appears, inspired by his metaphysics. Somewhat ironically, Anaxarchus' position was then in turn made more of an epistemological view – perhaps by the very sceptical descendants of Anaxarchus' own pupil, Pyrrho.

Let us look, then, at the evidence for Anaxarchus' moral position. Consider another anecdote often thought to describe an epistemological position. Anaxarchus appears in the biography of Pyrrho as a travelling companion on Alexander's conquests (DL 9.61). When Anaxarchus falls into a pond and is ignored by Pyrrho, Anaxarchus praises Pyrrho's indifference (αὐτὸς Ἀνάξαρχος ἐπῄνει τὸ ἀδιάφορον καὶ ἄστοργον αὐτοῦ, DL 9.63).[19] There is no suggestion at all in this anecdote that Anaxarchus' fall was the result of distrusting his senses. Rather, the question at hand is whether it is a bad thing and something worth worrying about whether one receives such an injury. Not only does falling down holes not matter to Pyrrho, it does not matter to him whether or not his friends fall down holes! So he wins this 'indifference contest', and is praised by Anaxarchus.[20]

Yet Anaxarchus did not always win in return the approval of Pyrrho. Immediately before the 'indifference contest' we read that Pyrrho withdrew from the world and appeared rarely to family and friends.

τοῦτο δὲ ποιεῖν ἀκούσαντα Ἰνδοῦ τινος ὀνειδίζοντος Ἀναξάρχῳ ὡς οὐκ ἂν ἕτερόν τινα διδάξαι οὗτος ἀγαθόν, αὐτὸς αὐλὰς βασιλικὰς θεραπεύων. (DL 9.63)

---

[19] ἀστοργία denotes (LSJ) a 'want of natural affection': Aeschines 2.146; Theoc. 2.112; Dem. Lac. *PHerc.* 1012 LXVI, LXVIII Puglia.

[20] Stobaeus preserves a fragment of Monimus which dramatises the Cynic commitment to the indifference of anything but philosophy (2.31.88): Μόνιμος ὁ Κυνικὸς φιλόσοφος ἔφη κρεῖττον εἶναι τυφλὸν <εἶναι> ἢ ἀπαίδευτον· τὸν μὲν γὰρ εἰς τὸν βόθρον, τὸν δὲ εἰς τὸ βάραθρον ἐμπίπτειν.

He did this having heard an Indian reproach Anaxarchus, saying that he could not teach anyone else to be good while paying court in a royal palace.

No one is likely to take advice on the subject of the indifference of external goods from a man who lives luxuriously in the retinue of a great conqueror. A contradiction threatens between Anaxarchus' practice and preaching, a contradiction excluded in the picture of the poor Pyrrho, washing a lowly pig as a sign of indifference (DL 9.66; see below pp. 113–21). Pyrrho himself, we might say, recognises the apparent contradiction in Anaxarchus' stance, and adjusts his own indifference to suit, taking steps to avoid being misunderstood. However, the accusation of a contradiction is mistaken, and the anonymous Indian of DL 9.63 is correct in his emphasis: you will never *teach* anyone indifference if you are seen in the company of the rich and famous. Being indifferent to external goods does not entail that I should eschew them, since to enjoin the rejection of external goods would be to assign them a (negative) value. Rather, indifference to external objects is just that; have them or not, they are valueless. So Pyrrho and Anaxarchus can both be indifferent, but Pyrrho's indifference is unquestionable to the outside observer. He starts with little and covets nothing.

We should note how Anaxarchus' version of the Democritean position advanced in B283–4 and B191 might relate to the later Epicurean position (*Ep. Men.* 127–8, 130). There, Democritus advised us to pay attention to what we are capable of and what is present (B191, my section **C**). Anaxarchus does just that; he has adapted his desires to his current situation. Asceticism is not the inevitable conclusion to the thought that external things are unnecessary for the attainment of happiness; that they are not good *per se* does not require that I must do without them.[21] Anaxarchus' position is consistent with the understanding that all possible external objects of choice are not good 'in truth' (ἐτεῇ) but, if they appear good, they are so only 'by convention' (νόμῳ). The Epicurean position too might be interpreted as not preventing us from

---

[21] Irwin (1986) 103: 'If I can easily afford a steak, and would prefer it over a bowl of porridge, an adaptive account of happiness does not require me to pick the porridge; it simply requires me to give up the desire for steak if I cannot satisfy it.' Similarly, if I have no preference for steak or porridge, but each is equally available, then I might choose steak.

desiring any particular object, so long as it is regularly available and the desire easily and quickly satisfiable. Any asceticism is instrumental; the world being as it is, we are better advised not to have any extravagant desires, even if at this moment they are quite satisfiable. Anaxarchus seems to have felt his luxury to be assured. The Indian's observation, thus misunderstood, led to an early conception of Anaxarchus as an *akratic*. On this picture he would dearly *like* to be a Cynic, who sees no particular good in various externals and therefore does without them, but simply cannot manage it. Our earliest source for Anaxarchus, Pyrrho's pupil Timon, offers this perception in his *Silloi*:

ἐν δὲ τὸ θαρσαλέον καὶ ἐμμενὲς ὅπτῃ ὀρούσαι
φαίνετ' Ἀναξάρχου κύνεον μένος, ὅς ῥα καὶ εἰδώς
ὡς φάσαν, ἄθλιος ἔσχε φύσις δέ μιν ἔμπαλιν ἦγεν
ἡδονοπλήξ, ἣν πλεῖστοι ὑποτρείουσι σοφιστῶν. (fr. 58 Diels)[22]

Then there appeared the brave and persistent, fiery and keen, dogged strength of Anaxarchus, who was miserable, although he knew better – so they say. His pleasure-struck nature seized and dragged him back. Most sophists tremble at it.

Although he knows better (καὶ εἰδώς), Anaxarchus cannot help himself; his nature drags him back against the dictates of reason.[23] Timon has an ambivalent evaluation of Anaxarchus. He was a flawed Cynic (κύνεον μένος is not *just* a Homeric borrowing),[24] and a flawed Pyrrho: someone who knew what he should have done, but could not reconcile his desires with his reason.

Once Anaxarchus has attained this total indifference to externals, he can claim that all judgements must now be based on internal criteria. The objective indifference of the external things leaves it to the agent himself to decide what to value, all the time recognising the subjectivity and arbitrary nature of such decisions.[25]

---

[22] Di Marco (1989) 245–6 suggests that calling Anaxarchus ἄθλιος is part of a strategy to undermine his usual epithet εὐδαιμονικός. Ioppolo (1980b) 503: similar accusations were levelled against Ariston (Athen. 281C–D).

[23] Robin (1944) 6 is keen to link Anaxarchus with Cyrenaicism.

[24] Nor is ὅς ῥα καὶ εἰδώς (cf. Hom. *Il.* 13.665): Brunschwig (1992a) 72 n. 27.

[25] Cf. Ioppolo (1980b) 563. Annas (1986) 24–5 claims that there is no ancient equivalent of the modern position of 'inventing right and wrong' (as Mackie (1977)). Concentrating on Sextan Pyrrhonism she sees the ancient sceptic as passive and detached, the modern sceptic as active and creative. Anaxarchus and Pyrrho (as I interpret him), are closer to Mackie's 'scepticism' (the dogmatic claim that things are neither good nor bad φύσει)

Confirmation of this suggestion is found in one of Anaxarchus' retorts to Alexander. The Macedonian king finds himself distraught after the death (at his orders) of Cleitus. Anaxarchus offers the following advice:

οὗτός ἐστιν Ἀλέξανδρος,... ὁ δὲ ἔρριπται κλαίων ὥσπερ ἀνδράποδον, ἀνθρώπων νόμον καὶ ψόγον δεδοικώς, οἷς αὐτὸν προσήκει νόμον εἶναι καὶ ὅρον τῶν δικαίων, ἐπείπερ ἄρχειν καὶ κρατεῖν νενίκηκεν, ἀλλὰ μὴ δουλεύειν ὑπὸ κενῆς δόξης κεκρατημένον. οὐκ οἶσθ'... ὅτι τὴν Δίκην ἔχει πάρεδρον ὁ Ζεὺς καὶ τὴν Θέμιν, ἵνα πᾶν τὸ πραχθὲν ὑπὸ τοῦ κρατοῦντος θεμιτὸν ᾖ καὶ δίκαιον; (Plut. *Alex.* 52 (DK A3))

This is Alexander, who cast himself down crying like a slave, fearing the law and censure of men. He should be their law and marker of justice, if he has won the right to rule and hold sway – and not be enslaved, worsted by empty opinion. Do you not know that Zeus keeps Justice and Right by him, so that all that is done by the ruler should be right and just?

Alexander is afraid of censure, but Anaxarchus reminds him that as the king he creates the law. Indeed, Alexander may be said to be Anaxarchus' indifferent man writ large. Just as there are no external constraints to Anaxarchus' decision that some thing is or is not 'just', so (thanks to his unique position of power) Alexander is able to impose his own particular decisions on the world.[26] To allow external considerations to colour one's attitude is to be enslaved (δουλεύειν) to empty opinion (κενῆς δόξης), whereas the truly free man, presumably, is liberated from external constraints. His *eudaimonia* depends on him alone, and can be guaranteed under any circumstances, even under extreme torture. Alexander is therefore the arbiter (ὅρος) of justice and injustice in a political sense, and his arbitration becomes the construction of these very values; if 'justice' and 'injustice' are merely pieces of scenery, then they need someone to construct them. Anaxarchus' indifference to the external world is complemented by his becoming the arbiter for himself of various values.

This 'internal criterion' can therefore explain what appear to be inconsistencies in the pictures of Anaxarchus we receive in the

than to Sextan scepticism (although Bett (1997) reads *M*.11 as negatively dogmatic; cf. Striker (1990) 104 on *PH* 3.235–8). Cf. Burnyeat (1979) 72–3, 96–8. Annas does not mention Anaxarchus. More reaction to Annas (1986): Bett (1988).

[26] Cf. Goukowsky (1978–81) vol.1, 46.

sources. He might well have appeared to be inconsistent, preaching indifference and enjoying immense luxury, but, if pressed, Anaxarchus can claim that he has no objective commitment to the value of riches. He would not be pained were he to lose them. The anecdotal evidence about Anaxarchus displays a remarkable range and variety, which some commentators have even called an 'ambiguity',[27] but perhaps the various rôles played by Anaxarchus, flatterer, teacher, indicator of vanity are just that: rôles or *personae*.[28] They are united by the constancy of the actor behind these masks. So we might return to his attitude under torture and the apparently radical distancing of himself from the object of that torture (DL 9.59). He can retreat behind another mask; the 'real' Anaxarchus, what matters to Anaxarchus, is unaffected by the pounding; nothing essential to Anaxarchus' *eudaimonia* is under threat.[29]

The only surviving fragments of Anaxarchus' own works come from his *On Kingship*. From the various citations and paraphrases collected by Dorandi (65A–E, 66), three thoughts emerge:[30]

1 πολυμαθίη κάρτα μὲν ὠφελεῖ, κάρτα δὲ βλάπτει τὸν ἔχοντα.
2 χρὴ δὲ καιροῦ μέτρα εἰδέναι· σοφίης γὰρ οὗτος ὅρος.
3 χαλεπὸν χρήματα συναγείρασθαι, χαλεπώτερον δὲ φυλακὴν τούτοις περιθεῖναι.

1 Much learning can especially benefit, and especially harm him who has it.
2 You should know the bounds of what is appropriate, for this is the marker of wisdom.
3 It is difficult to amass wealth and harder to keep it safe.

1 and 2 distinguish *polumathiē* and *sophiē*. In a number of other philosophers, including 'Democrates' (B64–5) and Heraclitus (B40), this distinction involves a negative appraisal of polymathy. For Anaxarchus, the accumulation of factual knowledge has no determinate value, negative or positive, for the goodness of one's life. Much learning can be useful and beneficial, but it can

---

[27] See Decleva Caizzi (1981a) 158, Brunschwig (1992) 65.
[28] For the irony of some of Anaxarchus' advice to Alexander: Brunschwig (1992a) 75–6.
[29] Philodemus *De morte* XXXV.11–14 Kuiper praises Anaxarchus.
[30] The different sources retain surprisingly similar wording: Gigante and Dorandi (1980) 482.

also cause distress and misfortune.[31] More important than learning is understanding (σοφίη), and the sign (ὄρος) of this particular skill is the ability to discern what is 'appropriate' (καιρός).[32] I doubt that the meaning of καιρός must be restricted to a temporal sense ('the appropriate moment'),[33] excluding any other normative meaning ('the right amount', 'the right attitude' ...).[34] It seems to be important for the understanding of 2 as a general observation that the scope of καιρός is kept as wide as possible. In that case, the ability which is of worth for the promotion of a good life is the ability to discern from particular circumstances the best course of action, or the most appropriate attitude to take. Alexander, we have seen, decrees the law. He is the legislator and arbiter of what is right and what is just (πᾶν τὸ πραχθὲν ὑπὸ τοῦ κρατοῦντος θεμιτὸν ᾖ καὶ δίκαιον).[35] In order to be a good king, presumably, one's decisions must be made with the kind of understanding described in 1 and 2; the decisions must be taken with a view to what is appropriate in the given circumstances. This flexibility is positively demanded in a system which equates the moral judgements we make to pieces of scenery.

Someone in power constructs the set on which all his subjects act out their rôles. In this case that person happens to be Alexander. There can, however, be better and worse constructions, the quality of which depends on the wisdom and understanding (σοφίη) of whoever makes the decisions. Further, whatever is said here about kingship can also apply in a derivative manner to other agents. Not all moral judgements are concerned with the codification of a set of laws, or the adjudication of a legal dispute, but all actions and attitudes must be guided by one's conception of what is good, or beneficial, or harmful, and so on. When making a decision to act,

---

[31] Cf. Stob. 2.21.116.

[32] There are antecedents of this idea in Democritus, especially B226: οἰκήιον ἐλευθερίης παρρησίη, κίνδυνος δὲ ἡ τοῦ καιροῦ διάγνωσις. Cf. B87, 94, 235; Tortora (1983).

[33] As in Aristotle: EN 1096a26.

[34] See Wilson (1980), Race (1981).

[35] Plutarch uses this phrase at Alex. 52 and Ad princ. iner. 781A–B. Cf. Arrian Anab. 4.9.7: τὰ ἐκ βασιλέως μεγάλου γιγνόμενα δίκαια χρῆναι νομίζεσθαι. Görler (1994) 752 contrasts this with Pyrrho's apparent dogmatism over the nature of the divine and the good, and the report of DL 9.61.

each agent must employ her/his own wisdom to discern what is or is not appropriate.[36]

The bare indifference of the world, however, will affect one's decisions. Anaxarchus' third proposition suggests as much. Anaxarchus does not say that wealth is to be avoided, nor that one should pursue it. Whether and to what degree one pursues wealth is dependent rather on whether it is thought appropriate to do so in those particular circumstances. A correct understanding of the world, based perhaps on an atomist cosmology, but including at least a total removal of 'vain opinion' (Plut. *Alex.* 52) will lead to these conclusions, and these conclusions will result in the kind of conduct presumably represented best by Anaxarchus himself. In those anecdotes where he reprimands, or flatters, or satirises Alexander, perhaps his actions were motivated by what he saw at the time as being appropriate.

---

[36] Gigante and Dorandi (1980) 482: 'Il filosofo invita il saggio ad estraniarsi dal mondo dell' azione e gli presenta un criterio interno che lo guida nel suo cammino.'

4

PYRRHO AND TIMON: INHUMAN
INDIFFERENCE

Pyrrho of Elis is a tantalising and frustrating figure, who left no writings and around whom grew up a powerful set of anecdotal myths designed to capture his charismatic equipoise. It is therefore difficult to penetrate the layers of appropriation and interpretation made by later schools and doxographers and produce a definitive picture of Pyrrho himself.[1] These later commentators felt the urge to claim Pyrrho for themselves and manipulate his image to ground their own theories (at least in origin) in an earlier time.[2] But these are enlightening difficulties. Timon's Pyrrho, and Sextus Empiricus' Pyrrho tell us much about Timon and Sextus, and the distance (chronological and philosophical) between them.

But first things first. Pyrrho was not a Pyrrhonist. Even the Pyrrhonists say (it appears) so.[3] Sextus Empiricus is keen to point out that although Pyrrho is the founder of the school of thought to which he belongs, he did not pre-empt all of the ideas to be found in the *Outlines of Pyrrhonism*. Sextus explains the choice of the school's name as 'because it appears to us that Pyrrho anticipated this scepticism in a more substantial and evident manner than those before him' (*PH.* 1.7).[4] Pyrrhonists resemble Pyrrho (or, rather, 'Pyrrho' as he appears to them) without claiming strictly to follow his instruction.

It is therefore foolhardy to claim that Pyrrho should be read as a Sextan sceptic. Not only do the Sextan sceptics tell us not

---

[1] Robin (1944) 12. Reale (1981) 247ff. provides eight substantially different interpretations of the same evidence.

[2] Ferrari (1981) 341.

[3] *Contra* Stopper (1983) 275. Decleva Caizzi (1981b) 123: in Sextus 'oἱ Πυρρώνειοι sono equivalenti a oἱ ἀπὸ Πύρρωνος ed indicano i filosofi recenti che a Pirrone in qualche misura si ispirano; quando occorra, Pirrone o Timone vengono citati per nome, così da evitare confusione con i Pirroniani'. Cf. Decleva Caizzi (1992a) 295.

[4] The same point is made more explicitly by one Theodosius cited at DL 9.70. On this Theodosius see Tsouna (1998a) 176, (1998b) esp. 267; von Fritz (1934); Barnes (1986a) 420 n. 57; Deichgräber (1930) 41, 219; Sedley (1983a) 20–1.

to do this, but it creates further unnecessary interpretative problems in the resulting need to flatten out the history of Pyrrhonism into a single monolithic philosophical position which persisted from the last quarter of the fourth century BC until it was described by Sextus in the second century AD. This homogenisation ought to be avoided, despite the historical accident that the writings of the two earlier major figures in the Pyrrhonian tradition, Timon and Aenesidemus, are almost entirely lost. There is no need to assume that, since we have so much of Sextus, he must be representative of the entire history of the school.[5]

It has been generally agreed for some time that the best piece of extant evidence for Pyrrho's thought is a section of Eusebius' *Praeparatio* (14.18.1–4 = T53 Decleva Caizzi). In this section Eusebius cites Aristocles of Messene's *On Philosophy* book eight, where Aristocles cites Timon on Pyrrho. The wealth of recent writing on this very short passage provides evidence of its difficulty. My interpretation of Pyrrho does not turn on this passage alone, since I shall discuss below how I think some of the biographical information might profitably be read. But it still should be noted that nothing in the Aristocles passage presents an insuperable obstacle to my reading.[6] So here is that difficult passage. I have translated the text as it appears in the manuscripts, but note the crucial emendation proposed by Zeller.

ἀλλ' αὐτὸς μὲν οὐδὲν ἐν γραφῇ καταλέλοιπεν, ὁ δὲ μαθητὴς αὐτοῦ Τίμων φησὶ δεῖν τὸν μέλλοντα εὐδαιμονήσειν εἰς τρία ταῦτα βλέπειν· πρῶτον μέν, ὁποῖα πέφυκε τὰ πράγματα· δεύτερον δέ, τίνα χρὴ τρόπον ἡμᾶς πρὸς αὐτὰ διακεῖσθαι· τελευταῖον δέ, τί περιέσται τοῖς οὕτως ἔχουσι. τὰ μὲν οὖν πράγματα φησιν αὐτὸν ἀποφαίνειν ἐπ' ἴσης ἀδιάφορα καὶ ἀστάθμητα καὶ ἀνεπίκριτα, διὰ τοῦτο* μήτε τὰς αἰσθήσεις ἡμῶν μήτε τὰς δόξας ἀληθεύειν ἢ ψεύδεσθαι· διὰ τοῦτο οὖν μηδὲ πιστεύειν αὐταῖς δεῖν, ἀλλ' ἀδοξάστους καὶ ἀκλινεῖς καὶ ἀκραδάντους εἶναι, περὶ ἑνὸς ἑκάστου λέγοντας ὅτι οὐ μᾶλλον ἔστιν ἢ οὐκ ἔστιν ἢ καὶ ἔστιν καὶ οὐκ ἔστιν ἢ οὔτε ἔστιν οὔτε οὐκ ἔστιν. (14.18.1–4)
*διὰ τοῦτο MSS, διὰ τὸ Zeller

[Pyrrho of Elis] himself has left nothing in writing, but his pupil, Timon says that someone who is going to be happy must look to these three things. First, how

---

[5] Cf. Decleva Caizzi (1998) 337.
[6] For a more extended discussion of Aristocles' treatment of Pyrrhonism see Warren (2000b), where some of the following material also appears.

things are by nature. Second, what attitude we should adopt in respect of them. Finally, what the result will be for people thus disposed. He says that Pyrrho declared all things to be equally indifferent, indeterminate, and unjudged, and [Timon says] that for that reason neither our senses nor our opinions are reliably true or false. And so we ought not to trust them but should be without opinion, unbiased, and unshaken, saying about each thing that it no more is than is not, or both is and is not, or neither is nor is not.

Aristocles introduces the section of his work as being 'about our knowledge of things'.[7] However, this epistemological introduction contrasts with Timon's exposition which begins with a distinctly ethical feel: 'he who is going to be happy should attend to these three things' (δεῖν τὸν μέλλοντα εὐδαιμονήσειν εἰς τρία ταῦτα βλέπειν). This is then mixed with metaphysical speculation since in searching for happiness, we are told to ask three things, of which the first is how 'things' are by nature and the second how one should behave as a result of the answer to the first question.

The answer to the first question is that things are 'equally indifferent, unweighed and unjudged' (ἐπ' ἴσης ἀδιάφορα καὶ ἀστάθμητα καὶ ἀνεπίκριτα).[8] Whether they are indifferent because of the objective nature of things or our sensory capacities is determined by whether one accepts the manuscript reading of διὰ τοῦτο or agrees to emend this with Zeller to διὰ τό.[9] This is a crucial interpretative decision. The manuscript reading gives a

---

[7] See Moraux (1984) 124–7, Chiesara (2001) xxiv–xxxv, Brennan (1998) 426–30, and the Appendix to Warren (2000b) on the probable original arrangement of the Aristoclean material. Cf. Eus. *PE* 14.2.4. Moraux (1984) 83–207 has a general discussion of Aristocles and (124ff.) his *On Philosophy*. Aristocles was not the tutor of Alexander of Aphrodisias (that was Aristotle of Mytilene: Moraux (1967), (1985); Gottschalk (1987)), and so should be dated to somewhere between the late first century BC and mid-first century AD. He refers to Apellicon, who died in 88–84 BC (*PE* 15.2.3), and to Aenesidemus who ἐχθὲς καὶ πρώην revived Pyrrhonism (*PE* 14.18.29): Moraux (1984) 83–9, Chiesara (2001) xviii–xix, 134–5. On the phrase ἐχθὲς καὶ πρώην, Russell (1990) 294 concludes that it is often used to refer to a rather remote period (cf. Plut. *Amat.* 715F).

[8] Dal Pra (1989) 62 and Stopper (1983) 292 n. 50 both agree that the adjectives should be read as subjective ('undifferentiable'), although Dal Pra retains the MSS reading in his translation on p. 61 and Stopper accepts the emendation. Ferrari (1981) 363, Decleva Caizzi (1981a) 223–4, and Frede (1999) 261–2 prefer an objective reading. Cf. Ausland (1989) 373 nn. 34 and 35. He also provides (391ff.) a detailed investigation of the connotations of these adjectives. The issue cannot be conclusively resolved solely on these grounds, but what evidence there is is in favour of non-modality: below p. 90 n. 16.

[9] A possible corruption given the διὰ τοῦτο in the following line. Stopper (1983) 273, n. 53 accepts the emendation and claims it restores sense and syntax. Cf. Annas (1993a) 203 n. 8, 204. Bett (1994b) 142 and (2000) 25–6 argues that the MSS reading is not impossible Greek, nor is the lack of a connecting particle to this clause a sign of textual

Pyrrho who was prepared to make a dogmatic statement about the way the 'things' are which entails a reconsideration of our reliance on sense-perception. The emendation gives a more familiarly sceptical Pyrrho.

But the emendation is unnecessary. The alpha-privative adjectives have no fixed technical force,[10] and only ἀνεπίκριτος is regularly used in Sextus.[11] More tellingly, if one accepts Zeller's emendation then the passage still gives no argument for its major premise.[12] It simply states the fact that (διὰ τό) the senses and our opinions provide no information of determinable truth-value and uses this to show that we cannot make any determinate pronouncement about the nature of things.[13] The argument is summarised at *PE* 14.18.5.2 and 7.1 with the same direction of inference as before:

5.2 ἐπεὶ τοίνυν ἐπ' ἴσης ἀδιάφορα πάντα φασὶν εἶναι, καὶ διὰ τοῦτο κελεύουσι μηδενὶ προστίθεσθαι . . .
7.1 εἰ ἐπ' ἴσης ἐστὶν ἀδιάφορα πάντα καὶ διὰ τοῦτο χρὴ μηδὲν δοξάζειν . . .

5.2 Since, then, they say that all things are equally indifferent and for this reason tell us not to incline towards anything . . .
7.1 If all things are equally indifferent and for this reason it is necessary to form no opinion . . .

Brunschwig notes that διὰ τοῦτο in these two phrases refers not to the disputed inference (3.2) but to the following one: διὰ τοῦτο [that our senses do not tell the truth or lie] οὖν μηδὲ πιστεύειν αὐταῖς δεῖν, ἀλλ' ἀδοξάστους [εἶναι] (3.3–4).[14]

If we accept Zeller's emendation, in his summaries at 5.2 and 7.1, Aristocles omits the first (unargued) assertion 'that our senses provide no definite information' from which ἀδιαφορία was derived and merely repeats the second inference. It seems more likely to

---

corruption. For parallel examples, see Brunschwig (1994a) 201 n.19, and Bett (2000) 26 n. 25.
[10] Ausland (1989) 390ff.
[11] See Long and Sedley (1987) vol. II, 6; Ausland (1989) 373 n. 36, 374 n. 37. On ἀδοξάστος here and in Sextus: Barnes (1983a) 28 n. 7.
[12] Conversely, if one accepts διὰ τοῦτο, the passage fails to explain why the πράγματα are ἀδιάφορα κτλ: Görler (1994) 739.
[13] Cf. Ausland (1989) 375 n. 39, Brunschwig (1994a) 196.
[14] Brunschwig (1994a) 196 n. 12.

me, however, that he would omit the intermediate than the starting premise, and this would be the case if the MSS reading is
retained. On Zeller's suggestion, the weak point in the argument
is the unargued premise 'that our senses neither tell the truth nor
lie'. But Aristocles does not attack this point. Rather, he focuses
on the assertion of indifference in his critique at 6.1 (καὶ μὴν εἰ
καὶ δῷημεν αὐτοῖς ἐπ' ἴσης ἀδιάφορα πάντα εἶναι...), at 7.1
(τ53 Decleva Caizzi), and at 16–17 (τ57 Decleva Caizzi): πῶς
οὖν ἐπ' ἴσης ἀδιάφορα τὰ πράγματα... δύναιτ' ἂν εἶναι; So this
is what Aristocles saw as the major premise of Pyrrho/Timon's
argument.[15] From this the uselessness of the senses is inferred.

Proponents of the emendation are not beaten by these objections.
They must in response claim that on each occasion in his refutations when Aristocles uses the premise ἐπ' ἴσης ἐστὶν ἀδιάφορα
πάντα, he does so not because he omits the primary premise, but
because the phrase stands as shorthand for the original inference
from the inability of senses and opinions to act as criteria of truth to
the undifferentiability of things. So Aristocles is said generally to
perform a *modus tollens* attack in his refutations; he demonstrates
the absurdity of the conclusion 'that things are undifferentiable',
and takes this as a refutation of the starting position from which
this undifferentiability is inferred.

A consequence of this approach is that the adjective ἀδιάφορα
in all of this section of the text must be read modally ('undifferentiable'), which was noted above as the 'subjective' reading of
the three adjectives at 14.18.1 (see n. 8), since this is all that can
be inferred from the premise of the senses' unreliability. There
is no basis for inferring anything about the nature of the 'things'
themselves, independently of our uncertain access to them. This
modal understanding may be possible for the instances which
I have noted so far, since they all use the adjective ἀδιάφορα.[16]
But it is not clear to me that such a modal force can be carried by the
bare positive verb διαφέρειν. Yet Aristocles is quite happy to use

[15] Trabucco (1960) 125–7, Ferrari (1968) 203ff., and Moraux (1984) 159–63 discuss
Aristocles' critique. See also Chiesara (2001) 109–34.
[16] Barnes (1990a) 101–2 investigates the use of ἀνεπίκριτος in Sextus, and concludes that
its significance is *non*-modal. Cf. Barnes (1990b) 17–20.

this form in his attempts to show the self-refutation of the Timonian thesis.[17]

At 14.18.5ff. he offers the first attempt.

If Pyrrho and Timon wish to show	1	that the many are wrong to think that the *onta diapherei*	
Then A:			
Pyrrho and Timon must say	2	that there are people who think falsely about *ta onta*	
and	3	that they themselves tell the truth about *ta onta*	
but if 2 and 3,	4	there will be truth and falsity.[18]	
And if 4,	5	they are themselves wrong to think that *ta onta* do not *diapherei* (i.e. not 1).	
Or, if not A, then B:			
If not 1, then	6	on what grounds do they reproach us?	

This offers a dilemma to Pyrrho and Timon. Either they are sure that we the majority are wrong, in which case they seem to allow some distinction among the ὄντα (1–5), or they are not, in which case they have no cause to rebuke us (6). In either case they cannot sustain their thesis in a dialectical exchange.

If Aristocles thinks that this amounts to a refutation of Timon's thesis (namely ἐπ' ἴσης ἀδιάφορα τὰ πράγματα), then regardless of the force of this refutation, it is clear that the proposition contained in 5 (namely μή διαφέρειν τὰ ὄντα) is offered as an equivalent to that thesis. This equivalent proposition seems clearly to be metaphysical, not epistemological, and to carry no modal significance. οὐ διαφέρει τὰ ὄντα cannot tolerably mean 'the things which are are undifferenti*able*'. Rather than a *modus tollens* attack focused on the conclusion of the Pyrrhonists' argument, Aristocles produces a series of *peritropē* attacks on the Pyrrhonians' opening thesis of indifference. Unless Aristocles is to be convicted of

---

[17] Compare Aristocles' refutations of Protagoras, which take a similar line and also use both Plato's *Theaetetus* (14.20.3) and Aristotle *Metaphysics* Γ. See Trabucco (1958–9) 48ff., and Tsouna (1998c) 64–72 for the similar tactics he uses against the Cyrenaics.

[18] Note that Aristocles does not infer: 'so truth and falsity are *differentiable*'.

ignoratio elenchi we must assume that he does indeed consider the above argument to counter the exposition of Pyrrho's and Timon's thought which precedes it.[19] He therefore wrote διὰ τοῦτο and not διὰ τό in the disputed inference.

But if that is how the argument proceeds, what did Pyrrho mean by it, particularly by his assertion about the nature of things? Things are 'indifferent' not (at least in Pyrrho's original formulation) in the sense of being metaphysically indistinct, but in the moral sense of having no intrinsic value, a sense already seen in the discussion of Anaxarchus and Ariston. In keeping with the ethical motivation behind the question 'How are things by nature?', 'things' (πράγματα) could have a narrow implication, referring rather to 'things which one does' (πράττειν), or just to things which are generally thought to have some kind of *moral* value.[20] The following report from Diogenes Laërtius offers strong support for this sort of view.

οὐδὲν γὰρ ἔφασκεν οὔτε καλὸν, οὔτ' αἰσχρὸν οὔτε δίκαιον οὔτ' ἄδικον· καὶ ὁμοίως ἐπὶ πάντων μηδὲν εἶναι τῇ ἀληθείᾳ, νόμῳ δὲ καὶ ἔθει πάντα τοὺς ἀνθρώπους πράττειν· (DL 9.61)

[Pyrrho] said that nothing was fine or foul or just or unjust, and generally for all things that nothing is in truth, but that men do everything through custom and habit.

The contrast here in DL 9.61 between what is 'in truth' good or bad (in fact, nothing turns out to be either) and what merely 'by convention' is again a metaphysical one. Pyrrho offers a claim about moral properties which parallels closely – and is probably intended to echo – Democritus' claim about phenomenal qualities in his B9 (see above, pp. 7–9).[21] The elimination of ethical qualities was also present in Anaxarchus' analogy of scene-painting,

---

[19] Aristocles repeatedly uses cognates of διαφέρειν in his refutations, e.g. 14.18.5.5, 5.10, 6.2, 7.2. See Warren (2000b).

[20] Cf. SE *M*. 11.3: τὰ κατὰ τὸν βίον πράγματα; *PH* 3.235; Frede (1999) 261, Brunschwig (1999b) 248. Brennan (1998) 432 suggests that the reference to πράγματα here is itself evidence of Aristoclean contamination, and closely related to his investigation of opinions concerning ἡ γνῶσις τῶν ἔξω πραγμάτων (*PE* 14.18.21.1). This does not prove contamination of the Timonian evidence, but instead suggests why Aristocles lighted on this particular section of text.

[21] For Pyrrho's approval of Democritus see DL 9.67, and Aristoc. *apud* Eus. *PE* 14.18.27, and see Decleva Caizzi (1984b). Decleva Caizzi (1981a) 171–2 conjectures that both

and although in Anaxarchus' case it was evident that later interpretations had understood him to be making a wider and more
general epistemological claim (above pp. 74–7), here in Pyrrho's
thesis at DL 9.61 we have clear evidence of the claim's restric-
tion to ethical qualities only. It is not implausible, therefore, to
think that Democritus' influence on Pyrrho was exerted via this
proposal of Anaxarchus, and that Pyrrho accepted the ethical an-
tirealism implied by Democritean metaphysics without accepting
atomism itself. Pyrrho claims that, if one recognises that things
which we consider to be good or bad are not so *by nature*, a state
of calm will result with respect to them, a state much like that
ascribed to him by the anecdotal evidence (which I shall discuss
below).

Other traces of this view can be found in the evidence about
Pyrrho. At Stobaeus 4.53.28, Pyrrho says that living and dying 'do
not differ' (μηδὲν διαφέρειν). This surely cannot mean that being
alive and being dead cannot be distinguished by the senses, but
rather that there is no intrinsic value either to being alive or being
dead. This position would account for the Ciceronian testimony
which links Pyrrho closely with the unorthodox Stoic Ariston who
denied any moral difference in anything other than virtue and vice.
Pyrrho, it is said, did not allow even virtue and vice to have intrinsic
value.[22]

Similarly in *M*. 11, the later Pyrrhonist Sextus Empiricus regis-
ters the impression that nothing is (morally) 'good or bad by nature'
(*M*. 11.78, 140)[23] and that a realisation of this truth will prevent
one being troubled in the avoidance of perceived bads and pursuit
of perceived goods. In this respect Sextus himself – on some readings of *M*. 11 – even retains echoes of a negative dogmatic view

Diogenes and Aristocles took this information from Antigonus. Bett (1999) and (2000)
132–40 argues for a Platonic background to Pyrrho's assertion of 'indifference'. I can
see no clear evidence for such an influence.

[22] Cicero *Acad*. 2.130, *Fin*. 2.43, 3.11, 4.43, 4.49, 4.60, *Tusc*. 2.15, *Off*. 1.6. Cf. Lévy (1980)
and contrast Bett (2000) 102–5. On Pyrrho and Cynicism: Brancacci (1981). Further on
Ariston: Ioppolo (1980a), Porter (1996), esp. 157 on DL 7.160. Ausland (1989) 379–89
(esp. 384 n. 66) argues for a close correspondence between Ariston's indifferents and
the phrase ἐπ' ἴσης ἀδιάφορα τὰ πράγματα (compare DL 7.130). Bett (1994b) 144–51
disagrees.

[23] *M*. 11.78 is Sextus' own impression. 11.140: Timon is cited with Sextus' approval.

much like that of Pyrrho (cf. DL 9.61).[24] He cites in support of his position a verse from Timon. The sort of things to which we attribute value are not so by nature, φύσει, 'but these are judged by the mind of men' (ἀλλὰ πρὸς ἀνθρώπων ταῦτα νόῳ κέκριται, Timon fr. 70 Diels *apud* SE *M.* 11.140).[25]

When Aristocles comes to attack Pyrrho's position, he happily points out the amorality of such a person, and strongly echoes the wording of DL 9.61:

ποῖος γὰρ ἂν γένοιτο πολίτης . . . ἢ ἁπλῶς εἰπεῖν ἄνθρωπος ὅ γε τοιοῦτος; ἢ τί τῶν κακῶν οὐ τολμήσειεν ἂν ὁ μηδὲν ὡς ἀληθῶς οἰόμενος εἶναι κακὸν[26] ἢ αἰσχρὸν ἢ δίκαιον ἢ ἄδικον; (Aristocles *apud* Eusebius *PE* 14.18.18)

For what sort of citizen would such a man be . . . or generally what sort of human? Or what evil would a man who truly thought that nothing was bad or foul or just or unjust not dare to commit?

He then cites Timon (fr. 9 Diels) extolling Pyrrho as just such a man. That Aristocles saw Pyrrho's moral scepticism as his main point of attack does not, of course, entail that Pyrrho was not sceptical about anything else, but he significantly picks on this particular area of Pyrrho's doubt. It is reasonable to conclude that the overwhelming picture of Pyrrho is of a moral sceptic who based his scepticism on the dogmatic claim that things are not good or bad by nature.

But the Aristocles passage is not unequivocal. One must not only explain why it has been so often interpreted in a radically epistemological sceptical manner, but also account for the passages of the text which clearly point in that way. Above all, why, if the 'things' are things accorded moral value, are we told not only that our opinions neither lie nor tell the truth (which is perfectly in line with the

[24] *Suda* s.v. Πύρρων (1B Decleva Caizzi): [Π.] ἐδόξασε δὲ μηδὲν φύσει αἰσχρὸν ἢ καλὸν ἀλλὰ ἔθει καὶ νόμῳ. Cf. Democritus B125. Bett (1997) xxiv–xxxi claims that *M.* 11 is earlier than *PH* and contains a dogmatic claim eradicated in later works: that nothing is good or bad φύσει (xiv–xix, 137–9). See esp. *M.* 11.112–18. Compare: Striker (1983) 110–11, (1990) 103–5, and Annas (1986) 9–10.

[25] Unsurprisingly, given the similarity to Democritus B9 and DL 9.61, νόῳ in this fragment of Timon was emended by Hirzel to νόμῳ. The emendation is unnecessary, however: see Bett (1997) 159.

[26] The parallel with DL 9.61 is so close that I am tempted to follow Ferrari (1968) 207 n. 2 and emend κακόν to καλόν to complete the equivalence and to produce, as in Diogenes, two pairs of contrary qualities.

interpretation suggested above) but also that our perceptions are unable to provide reliable information? Here we see a scepticism of a wider scope, where the 'things' are all sensible objects. The thesis now amounts to a wide ranging metaphysical claim that nothing in the world is determinate to the extent that we can perceive it with any security in the content of our sense-impressions.

We have already seen a similar process at work in the later understanding of Anaxarchus' simile of scene-painting. What seems originally to have been intended as a moral claim about what is truly of value and what a mere construction was taken up by later commentators and interpreted as a sceptical claim about our sense-impressions (above, pp. 74–7). Pyrrho originally made a moral claim which again was later viewed as a statement of a more general sceptical position. Stories of painting and painters are also found in sources about Pyrrho and from the work of later Pyrrhonists. Interestingly, in the biographical tradition Pyrrho himself is said to have been a painter (DL 9.61, 62; *Suda* s.v. Πύρρων, Aristoc. *apud* Eus. *PE* 14.18.27). This has been plausibly linked to the use made of the image of stage painting in epistemological contexts. *Trompe-l'oeil* painting has a clear connection with scepticism of various sorts. The sources also imply that Pyrrho gave up painting when he became a sceptic, and perhaps understandably so.[27] If it is a matter of fact that the world is objectively 'indifferent', then it would be appropriate for Pyrrho to be said to have given up painting. To engage in such painting – namely the depiction of what we perceive in paint – is to acknowledge that the world can be so depicted, and is to imply that the world is as we perceive it to be. This is an implication which this earlier phase of Pyrrhonism, with its dogmatic stance on the unreality of sense-impressions, would be keen to avoid.[28]

---

[27] E.g. *Suda* s.v. Πύρρων· πρότερον μὲν ἦν ζωγράφος, ὕστερον δὲ ὥρμησεν ἐπὶ φιλοσοφίαν.

[28] Note that DL 9.61 is a report from Antigonus, who was himself a sculptor, and besides philosophical biographies wrote works on art history which Diogenes consulted for homonyms (DL 2.15, 9.49). (See Dorandi (1994b), (1995a), (1999) ci–cxix.) He was probably the source of Quintilian's (12.10.3–9) and Pliny the Elder's (35.79–97) information on Apelles. If so, perhaps Sextus found his anecdote about Apelles in a work by the author of a *Life* of Pyrrho (cf. Aristocles *apud* Eus. *PE* 14.18.26 – which Brunschwig (1999b) 242 n. 40 insists should be read as implying that Anaxarchus too was formerly a painter before his philosophical career).

By the time of Sextus Empiricus' version of Pyrrhonism, however, things have changed such that Sextus can use a simile of the painter Apelles attempting to depict accurately the foam formed around a horse's mouth as a model for the sceptical life (*PH* 1.28–9). This divergence derives from the divergence between Pyrrho's scepticism and Sextan Pyrrhonism. In the latter it is unclear whether our senses allow us true access to the world, and whether the world is such that consistent and true judgements can be made of it. So we are content to live by and accept for practical purposes the *phainomena*. For earlier Pyrrhonism, the world is definitely not as we perceive it. So these sense-impressions must be rejected entirely.

The quest for a thoroughly sceptical Pyrrho who proposed a scepticism more or less like that later described by Sextus Empiricus not only requires Zeller's textual emendation in the famous passage of Aristocles, but has also led to a reconsideration of two fragments from Timon of Phlius' poetic work, *Indalmoi* (67, 68 Diels). I shall discuss these fragments further below in the context of Timon's representation of Pyrrho (pp. 103–6), but the interest in these fragments at this point is their apparent dogmatism. In 67, someone (often thought to be Timon) asks Pyrrho the secret of his success in attaining such a tranquil disposition. In 68, the response reads:

> ἦ γὰρ ἐγὼν ἐρέω, ὥς μοι καταφαίνεται εἶναι,
> μῦθον ἀληθείης ὀρθὸν ἔχων κανόνα,
> ὡς ἡ τοῦ θείου τε φύσις καὶ τἀγαθοῦ ἀεί,
> ἐξ ὧν ἰσότατος γίνεται ἀνδρὶ βίος.

For I shall tell you how it is evident to me, having this story as a right measure of truth, how the nature of god and the good are always, from which arises the most balanced life for a man.

If indeed Pyrrho is speaking here then the fragment promises a definitive statement on the 'nature of the divine and the good'. If it is assumed that this would contravene the image of Pyrrhonian scepticism which emerges elsewhere then the fragment must be explained away or modified.[29] However, it has not yet been demonstrated that our interpretation should understand Pyrrho in such a

---

[29] Burnyeat (1980a) removes the comma from Timon fr. 68.3 Diels to remove the dogmatic statement concerning the nature of the divine and the good, but recognises that Pyrrho

way as to preclude his having a teachable conception of the 'nature of the divine and the good'.

An instructive note of caution is sounded by Sextus' own reaction to the fragment. It is cited at *M.* 11.20 as a corroboration of Sextus' statement that:

κατὰ δὲ τὸ φαινόμενον τούτων ἕκαστον ἔχομεν ἔθος ἀγαθὸν ἢ κακὸν ἢ ἀδιάφορον προσαγορεύειν, καθάπερ καὶ ὁ Τίμων ἐν τοῖς Ἰνδαλμοῖς ἔοικε δηλοῦν, ὅταν φῇ...

We are accustomed to declare each of these things good or bad or indifferent according to its appearance. Just so Timon too in his *Indalmoi* seems to make clear, when he says...

Fragment 68 is intended to be an example of the Pyrrhonist practice of describing the moral value of each thing simply 'as it appears' without any commitment to the object in question having such a value φύσει. However, Sextus' phrasing sounds a note of caution: 'he *seems* to make clear' (ἔοικε δηλοῦν).[30] Understandably so. Although Timon *seems* to be agreeing with Sextus' proposal by using the verb 'it is evident' (καταφαίνεται), the reference to the nature of the divine and good is distinctly un-Sextan.[31] There is a palpable discord here between the demands of Sextan avoidance of assertion (ἀφασία) and the mode of expression in Timon.

Timon *philosophus*

We can explain the ambiguity of the Aristocles passage, and begin the story of the transformation of Pyrrho from moralist to sceptic, by elevating the importance of Timon from a mere reporter of Pyrrho's teaching to an independent thinker who had his own interpretation of Pyrrho.[32] When Timon moved to Athens some

might have held a 'meta-dogmatic' claim that tranquillity is good (allowing for the apparent dogmatism of fr. 71 Diels and here in Eusebius). Stopper (1983) 270 posits a lacuna between 68.3 and 4. Ausland (1989) 429ff rejects this suggestion. Bett (2000) 97–101 suggests that fr. 68 is spoken by an as yet not fully initiated Timon. Cf. Görler (1994) 740–3, Brennan (1999) 49–50.

[30] Noted by Burnyeat (1980a) 87, Decleva Caizzi (1981a) 256, Ausland (1989) 431.

[31] καταφαίνεται is not a word used by Sextus himself and is probably to be translated dogmatically: 'it is evident': Decleva Caizzi (1981a) 256; Brunschwig (1994b) 222–3; Bett (1994a) 314, (1997) 61, (2000) 95–6.

[32] A move also made by Brunschwig (1994a) 203.

time in the 260s BC the current hot debate was the epistemological discussion between Arcesilaus and the Stoics.[33] Timon seems to have entered this epistemological debate, perhaps claiming Pyrrho as the originator of his own brand of scepticism in a move designed to undercut the Academy's claims to the mantle of 'original sceptics'.[34] Timon's literary output included a work *On the funeral banquet of Arcesilaus*, and Diogenes' *Life* retains stories of rivalries between Timon and Arcesilaus (9.114–15).[35]

This interpretation may be supported by attempting to date the period at which Pyrrho becomes associated with an epistemological doctrine. Timon's reworking must have had an impact by the time of Ariston (mid third century) since the latter declares a Pyrrhonian influence on Arcesilaus (DL 4.33), whose interests were epistemological.[36] Note also at 4.33 the Timonian verses showing a 'Pyrrhonian' Arcesilaus. Again this might be designed to show Pyrrho as the true originator of scepticism, rather than Arcesilaus and his professed Socratic heritage. Arcesilaus must borrow his scepticism from the true originator, Pyrrho.[37] Decleva Caizzi also notes that there is no trace of Epicurean polemic against any sort of 'Pyrrhonian' scepticism in the Epicurean Colotes' work *That it is impossible even to live according to other philosophers* (at least as evidenced by Plutarch's retort *Adversus Colotem*), and considers this to be further evidence that Pyrrho was not perceived to be an important figure in philosophical circles until Timon's arrival in Athens.[38] Indeed Diogenes retains notices which trace a philosophical lineage (DL 9.115) from Timon (rather than Pyrrho)

---

[33] Dal Pra (1989) 109ff. draws attention to the Pyrrho/Timon divide by noting the transfer of the philosophy from Elis to Athens, where Timon had to engage in competition with other schools.

[34] See Robin (1944) 29; Decleva Caizzi (1986) 167.

[35] See Decleva Caizzi (1986) esp. 172ff., Brunschwig (1994a) 206–7.

[36] *SVF* 1.343–4 *apud* SE *PH* 1.232–4, DL 4.33, Numen. *apud* Eus. *PE* 14.5.11–14. See Ioppolo (1980a) 26–7, and (1986) 37 on the intention of these verses. Decleva Caizzi (1986) 164ff. notes that this Aristonian verse would make little sense if it were intended to suggest the picture of the *indifferent* philosopher from the earlier biographical tradition.

[37] Cf. Numenius *apud* Eus. *PE* 14.6.5ff. (Timon fr. 55 Diels); cf. Ioppolo (1986) 36–7, Pratesi (1988) 135–6, Di Marco (1989) 238–9.

[38] Cf. Decleva Caizzi (1986) 161–3. She sees the effects of Timon's epistemological reworking in Ascanius of Abdera's insistence on Pyrrho as τὸ τῆς ἀκαταληψίας καὶ ἐποχῆς εἶδος εἰσαγαγών (DL 9.61). The terminology used here postdates the Zeno–Arcesilaus debate (cf. Ioppolo (1986) 37 n. 51). She further conjectures that this report derives ultimately from the work of Hieronymus the Peripatetic περὶ ἐποχῆς (DL 2.105; cf. DL

through Aenesidemus to Sextus (9.116). Timon was perceived as the fountainhead of Pyrrhonism as a philosophical movement.[39] We have evidence of Timon's epistemological interests. He wrote an *On Senses*, from which Diogenes quotes:

τὸ μέλι ὅτι ἐστὶ γλυκὺ οὐ τίθημι, τὸ δ' ὅτι φαίνεται ὁμολογῶ. (DL 9.105)

That honey is sweet I do not posit, but I agree it appears so.

Perhaps, therefore, Aristocles is citing a Timonian reworking of an originally Pyrrhonian argument. Timon extends the scope of the term πράγματα in line with his own rather more extended scepticism, turning Pyrrho's claim of ethical anti-realism into a general metaphysical thesis. Nevertheless, he retains Pyrrho's *telos* and in his verses extols Pyrrho as a model of conduct for us to follow, while bequeathing to the rest of his 'school' a Pyrrho reworked in an epistemological vein. Aristocles has therefore preserved an important piece of evidence for a very early construction of 'Pyrrho', by his own pupil.

Pyrrho, the Oracle, the Python and the 'prophet'

Further evidence that we should expect a distinction between Pyrrho and Timon, master and pupil, can be drawn from the manner in which Timon himself has decided to portray their relationship. In his prose work, the *Python*, Timon encounters Pyrrho as the latter is travelling to Delphi (Aristoc. *apud* Eus. *PE* 14.18.14).[40] The title

4.41–2 and 9.112). Gigante (1986) 57–61 and (1997) 257–60 notes that in *POxy.* 3656 Hieronymus is given a work περὶ συνοχῆς and thinks that the reading at DL 2.105 is a corruption. Decleva Caizzi (1986) 166 n. 33 replies. Di Marco (1989) 4–5, n. 16 questions Decleva Caizzi's dating, based as it is on the hypothesis that the *Silloi* must have been published after the death of Cleanthes (232 BC) who appears in the *Silloi* at fr. 41 Diels. But it is not clear from fr. 41 that Cleanthes is part of the *nekyia*; Di Marco (1989) 30 thinks that the fragment suggests that Cleanthes is still alive, and even questions the insistence that those who appear during the *nekyia* must have been dead at the time of composition.

[39] E.g. DL 9.112. On the 'successions' of 9.115–16, Moraux (1984) 177 n. 327 notes that Menodotus claimed that the ἀγωγή had lapsed after Timon and was revived by Ptolemy of Cyrene (probably a first-century BC Empiricist: Deichgräber (1930) 20, 172). Aristocles *apud* Eus. *PE* 14.18.29 implies a similar story. The evidence for a 'school' of any sort between Timon and Aenesidemus is thin. Cf. Glucker (1978) 352–4.

[40] It is not certain that the conversation takes place next to the shrine of Apollo at Delphi, as is apparently assumed by Ferrari (1981) 345.

99

of the work, and its setting are therefore both intimately connected with the theme of Apolline prophecy, of self-knowledge, and of riddling oracular utterance.[41] Untersteiner has offered some intriguing speculations on the setting of the dialogue next to a shrine of Amphiaraus, not only a hero whose cult was associated with prophecy, but one who appears in classical literature most often in the pose of a father advising his son, Amphilochus, that he should adapt himself to whatever surroundings he encounters.[42] To locate a conversation where Pyrrho's own *diathesis* will be explicated next to a site resonant with similar adaptability is quite appropriate.[43]

From Diogenes (DL 9.67) we learn that in this work Timon 'makes clear Pyrrho's disposition' (διασαφεῖ τὴν διάθεσιν αὐτοῦ). Pyrrho is a figure who, like an oracular response, requires explication. When Sextus calls Timon the προφήτης of Pyrrho (*M.* 1.53) he further underlines Timon's interpretative rôle; a προφήτης is one who interprets oracles.[44] Timon is no disinterested reporter. Pyrrho presents only a disposition, a *diathesis* to the world, with little or no accompanying reasoning. Timon offers himself in the privileged position of Pyrrho's 'official' interpreter, as the person with whom the man himself spoke while travelling to Delphi, but in doing so he simultaneously underlines his position as an interpreter, and frames his interpretation as such.[45]

Further evidence for there being a distinctive Timonian presentation of Pyrrho can be gathered from the traces which remain of

[41] On the title of the *Indalmoi* and its subtle use of Homeric parallels in the service of Timon's philosophical programme: Brunschwig (1994b). Bett (1994a) 327 n. 63 is unconvinced, but a close examination of the *Silloi* has revealed Timon's detailed knowledge of Homeric poetry. On Timon and Homer: Ax (1991).

[42] Untersteiner (1971). Decleva Caizzi (1980a) 59 relates this image to Odysseus' own renowned cunning and the *topos* that the wise man should be an actor able to play many rôles: Ariston of Chios notably uses this image at DL 7.160 See above p. 76.

[43] Untersteiner (1971) 644.

[44] Pind. *N.* 1.60, Eur. *Ba.* 551, Aesch. *Eum.* 19, Hdt. 8.36–7. Ferrari (1981) 348; Decleva Caizzi (1981a) 207, (1981b) 111; Di Marco (1989) 12 n. 53 compares Plut. *Pyth.* 397C, where Plutarch attacks the Ἐπικούρου προφῆται who refuse to accept the validity of divination. Cp. Decleva Caizzi (1992a) 324 where she discusses the context of SE *M.* 1.53 (cf. 1.279) and decides that the term was used by opponents of Timon and Pyrrho as a counter to the Pyrrhonian charge that the grammatical arts are unnecessary and useless: Timon himself uses such arts. (Cf. Blank (1998a) 123.) This dialectical move does not rule out Timon's own use of the term, and indeed if Timon did use the term then the grammarians' move is more powerful.

[45] Cf. Decleva Caizzi (1981b) 111.

competing views. Within Timon's lifetime there was some discussion between the early Pyrrhonians of the nature of Pyrrho's thought. Various interpretations were available. That of Timon was perhaps the most widely known, the most sophisticated and the interpretation which eventually filtered into Aenesidemus' 'Pyrrhonism'. Nausiphanes was rather impressed by Pyrrho's *diathesis*, but constructed his own theories for its attainment. Similarly, we might look for suggestions of other early interpretations of Pyrrho in order to explain Timon's desire to present himself as the 'genuine, and authorised' προφήτης of Pyrrho. I am inclined to believe that the brief testimony of Numenius, one of the συνήθεις of Pyrrho (at DL 9.102), preserved by Diogenes is a trace of such an interpretation:

μόνος δὲ Νουμήνιος καὶ δογματίσαι φησὶν αὐτόν. (DL 9.68)

Only Numenius says that he also had sure doctrines.

There is another report about Timon which has in the past been interpreted as including a critique of Numenius. If we view Numenius and Timon as competing interpreters of Pyrrho then it should become more acceptable to read it in this way.

[Τίμων] συνεχές τε ἐπιλέγειν εἰώθει πρὸς τοὺς τὰς αἰσθήσεις μετ' ἐπιμαρτυροῦντος τοῦ νοῦ ἐγκρίνοντας, 'συνῆλθεν Ἀτταγᾶς τε καὶ Νουμήνιος'. (DL 9.114)

[Timon] used constantly to say in reply to those who endorsed sensations when accompanied by the evidence of reason, 'Attagas and Numenius agreed'.

However we interpret this quotation of a proverb, which refers to the names – Attagas and Numenius – either of two famous brigands or two species of birds,[46] we should remember that it is clearly in the context of a polemic against the epistemological view that it is possible to make judgements on the basis of sensory evidence when that evidence is confirmed by the mind. Timon likens this view to a combination of 'Attagas and Numenius', and his point is not difficult to see. That two sorts of birds – or indeed two bandits – agree

---

[46] Cf. Wachsmuth (1885) 16 n. 1, Brunschwig (1999a) 1143 n. 1.

on something is no reason to believe that what they agree upon is true.

Beyond this, however, we can ask a further question. Is this Numenius in the proverb also supposed to recall the Numenius of DL 9.68, the Numenius who proposed the (semi-)dogmatic Pyrrho? Can we read the proverb as an attack on Numenius the follower of Pyrrho rather than simply a way of saying that the senses and the rational mind are each as bad as the other when it comes to making judgements, and that the judgement of one is confirmed by another is no indication of the truth of that judgement (that two thieves agree is no indication that what they think is trustworthy)?[47] Wilamowitz originally proposed reading Numenius the Pyrrhonian as the object of Timon's attack, suggesting that Numenius himself held the 'corroboration' view of sure judgement.[48] There is no further evidence to support this second suggestion, although if Numenius styled himself as a follower of a not-so-sceptical Pyrrho (DL 9.68), he is likely to have held a more dogmatic epistemology than Timon. Numenius' assertion of Pyrrho's dogmatism would therefore help to ground his own position in the thought of his master,[49] and Timon's cleverly-aimed proverb forms part of an epistemological debate between two Pyrrhonians, both of whom were looking to their teacher to ground their own particular epistemological theories. It is clear from Timon frr. 49–50 Diels, which discuss Eurylochus and Philo, two more of Pyrrho's immediate followers, that Timon did discuss other Pyrrhonians in his work, and so a

---

[47] Barnes (1986a) 399 n. 24 claims that if Numenius were referred to by the proverb 'renderebbe di fatto oscuro lo scherzo'. The joke seems to me to be erudite and plausibly Timonian.

[48] Wilamowitz (1965) 32 n. 8; cf. von Fritz (1937), Brunschwig (1999b) 249. Hirzel (1883) 44 suggests that the list of associates of Pyrrho should be excised as a later gloss on Diogenes' οἱ συνήθεις, and that the inclusion of Numenius by the interpolator was motivated by the similarity of what follows in Diogenes' original text to the report of Numenius at DL 9.68. Barnes (1986a) 399 is tempted by this. Brunschwig (1999a) 1133 n. 4 notes that συνήθης suggests an immediate follower, or acquaintance. He argues that Aenesidemus was certainly not a contemporary of Pyrrho, so Numenius need not be. Cf. Görler (1994) 770. Frede (1982) 183 and Brunschwig (1999a) 1105 n. 5 retain the possibility that the Numenius of 9.102 is the homonymous Platonist. For this Numenius' view of Pyrrho as a sceptical predecessor of Arcesilaus, see him *apud* Eus. *PE* 14.5.13–14, 6.4–6.

[49] Cf. Hirzel (1883) 40–1.

swipe at Numenius is quite plausible.[50] It is essential to remember this competitive arena when assessing Timon's presentation of Pyrrho – there were other interpretations on offer.[51]

If this is the case, then Numenius lost this particular publicity battle. Timon's Pyrrho prevailed, and Numenius is sometimes written out of the history of the sceptical tradition altogether. While he is listed as one of 'the companions' of Pyrrho at DL 9.102, along with Timon, Aenesidemus, Nausiphanes and 'others', he is missing from the list of Pyrrho's pupils at DL 9.70, which includes Hecataeus of Abdera, Timon, and Nausiphanes.

As we shall see, Nausiphanes was later to draw a distinction between Pyrrho's *diathesis* (disposition) and his *logoi* (arguments) (DL 9.64). The picture of the *diathesis* remains fairly constant (at least until Aenesidemus felt it necessary to remove the more bizarre elements (DL 9.62)), but Pyrrho's lack of written philosophical output encouraged the various interpreters of Pyrrho to debate the *logoi* behind this *diathesis*. The range of options was such that Numenius was able to insist that Pyrrho was (in part) a dogmatist (DL 9.68), Nausiphanes could use Pyrrho's disposition in his particular brand of atomist ethics, and Timon could begin to construct an epistemological scepticism around the figure of his master.

Pyrrho the god

In Timon's *Python* there a sense of Pyrrho's oracular status. In the *Indalmoi* he is likened to the sun, or perhaps to the sun-god, Apollo.

τοῦτό μοι, ὦ Πύρρων, ἱμείρεται ἦτορ ἀκοῦσαι,
πῶς ποτ' ἀνὴρ διάγεις ῥῆιστα μεθ' ἡσυχίης
ἀεὶ ἀφροντίστως καὶ ἀκινήτως κατὰ ταὐτά,
μὴ προσέχων δίνοις ἡδυλόγου σοφίης.

---

[50] Cf. DL 9.68. Usener (1887) 407 identified this Eurylochus with the addressee of a letter in which Epicurus denies being a disciple of Nausiphanes (DL 10.13). Cf. Gigante (1981) 79–81, Pratesi (1988) 136–8.

[51] Emphasised by Ferrari (1968) 215–17. Tsouna (1998b) 262 notes that Theodosius' remark at DL 9.70 blocks the possibility of such debates over Pyrrho's disposition. Perhaps it was provoked by the disagreements of Pyrrho's immediate followers.

μοῦνος ἐν ἀνθρώποισι θεοῦ τρόπον ἡγεμονεύεις.
ὅς περὶ πᾶσαν ἐλῶν γαῖαν ἀναστρέφεται,
δεικνὺς εὐτόρνου σφαίρας πυρικαύτορα κύκλον.[52]
(fr. 67 Diels: 1–2, 5 *apud* DL 9.65; 3–5 *apud*
SE *M.* 11.1; 5–7 *apud* SE *M.* 1.305)

This, O Pyrrho, my heart longs to hear, how ever you, a man, act easily and with tranquillity, always without care and uniformly unmoved, never paying heed to the whirls of sweet-argued wisdom. You alone among men show the way of god who turns in his path across the whole world, showing the fiery circle of his well-turned sphere.

Lines 3 and 4, cited only by Sextus at *M.* 11.1, add a sense of stability to the remarkable state which Pyrrho displays, in clear contrast to the whirling and disruption which characterise 'wisdom'. Pyrrho is an antidote to the kind of physical and philosophical speculation practised by other thinkers. Another of Timon's works, the *Silloi*, similarly depicts Pyrrho's self-removal from the conflicts of the various other engaged and busy-body (πολυπράγμονες fr.1 Diels) sophists: he is elevated beyond their petty squabbles (fr. 8 Diels).[53]

Sextus refers to this passage from the *Indalmoi* at *M.* 1.305, where he is arguing against the existence of a *technē* of grammar capable of making pronouncements on what poets and prose-writers say independently of any knowledge of the subject of the work. This comparison of Pyrrho with the Sun causes Sextus some difficulty. Surely the Sun illuminates what is obscure? This, Sextus explains, would be the interpretation the grammarians would follow. But if so then it conflicts (μάχεται: 1.305) with Pyrrhonist suspension of judgement and avoidance of assertion. Sextus therefore explains how he interprets the piece in a manner consistent with his Pyrrhonism:

ἡλίου τρόπον ἐπέχειν φησὶ τὸν Πύρρωνα καθόσον ὡς ὁ θεὸς τὰς τῶν ἀκριβῶς εἰς αὐτὸν ἀτενιζόντων ὄψεις ἀμαυροῖ, οὕτω καὶ ὁ σκεπτικὸς λόγος τὸ τῆς διανοίας ὄμμα τῶν ἐπιμελέστερον αὐτῷ προσεχόντων συγχεῖ, ὥστε ἀκαταληπτεῖν περὶ ἑκάστου τῶν κατὰ δογματικὴν θρασύτητα τιθεμένων. (*M.* 1.306)

---

[52] For this text: Decleva Caizzi (1981a) 252–3. δίνοις Nauck for the MSS δειλοῖς (as 841 L-JP). Gigante (1981) 44 compares Lucr. *DRN* 3.1042–4. Also cf. Epicurus *Ep. Hdt.* 77 on the life of the gods.

[53] Cf. Cortassa (1978) 153. The line is based upon Hom. *Il.* 3.223, where no one disputes with Odysseus, because he is such a good orator. Timon fr. 50 Diels extols the same tendencies in Philo of Athens; Di Marco (1989) 224–5. For αὐτολαλητήν cf. DL 9.64.

He says that Pyrrho suspends judgement like the sun, in so far as, just as the god dims the eyes of those who intently turn their gaze upon him, so too the sceptical argument confounds the mind's eye of those who pay stricter attention to it. As a result they fail to grasp each thing posited through dogmatic rashness.

Sextus assumes that likening Pyrrho to the Sun conveys an epistemological point. However, that Sextus does not cite Timon as the authority for this interpretation, but must provide the interpretation himself, suggests to me that it was not originally present in the Timonian context.[54] There is no reason to prefer Sextus' interpretation other than the convenience of its avoiding a conflict between Sextan Pyrrhonism and Timon's Pyrrho. Sextus has to work hard to explain Timon's metaphor in a way which will allow it to cohere with his own position.[55]

We might now return to the anxiety felt by many modern commentators over the interpretation of Timon frr. 67 and 68 Diels and their apparent promise to give a dogmatic statement of the nature of the divine and the good. Nothing we have seen so far in the general image of Pyrrho's moral thought precludes him from holding and expounding such a conception. Although the claim that 'things are equally indifferent, unweighed and unjudged' was given as a response to the question 'how are things by nature?', we are perhaps not compelled to include 'the nature of the divine and the good' within the scope of these 'things'. Whether we choose to restrict the significance of 'things' to (other) ethical qualities or extend it in line with Timon's extended philosophical interest to a more general metaphysical thesis concerning 'what is', there is no requirement

---

54 Sextus probably had the whole of Timon's works, although he tends only to cite him either for his lampoons of other philosophers (*PH* 1.223–4, *M.* 7.8, 10; 9.57; 11.171–2) or for positive messages about the tranquillity of the sceptic (*M.* 11.1, 20, 141, 164) and, occasionally, for what might loosely be called his 'philosophical views' (*M.* 3.2, 6.66, 7.30, 10.197, 11.140). Sextus refers to Pyrrho surprisingly little (Sedley (1983a) 20–1). The reference to a work τὰ Πυρρώνεια at *M.* 1.282 might be to a lost work (Sedley (1983a) 27 n. 59) or merely to the *PH* (Decleva Caizzi (1981a) 176). Cf. Blank (1998a) 305–6.

55 Cf. Blank (1998a) 338–9. A similar problem is posed at *M.* 1.53 by Timon fr. 61 Diels which appears to contradict Sextus' version of the Pyrrhonist stance on γραμματική (a knowledge of reading and writing is certainly necessary, but γραμματική in the sense of a more learned enterprise is to be avoided). Sextus must himself offer to show what Timon really means (1.54: ἀλλὰ μᾶλλον τοιοῦτό φησι) and in doing so alters the participle διδασκομένῳ in Timon to διδαχθέντι in his paraphrase. On this passage see Di Marco (1989) 259, Decleva Caizzi (1992a) 325, Blank (1998a) 123–4.

to include within the scope of things undecidable the nature of the divine and the good, as there would be if the scepticism of Pyrrho and Timon were driven by the method found in Sextus.

Antigonan anecdotes, pitfalls and pigs

Anecdotes of the sort found in Diogenes Laërtius' *Lives* form a 'biodoxography',[56] which created the popular image of each of the competing philosophers, and played a crucial public relations rôle. The recognition of this rôle prompted the schools to manipulate and focus considerable debate around the image of their founder, so these anecdotes are excellent sources for the construction of philosophical positions within this competitive arena. We are expected to read the stories and be suitably impressed by Pyrrho's disposition (as were Nausiphanes and Epicurus: DL 9.64). Admittedly, it is not universally accepted that the biography offers any independent evidence about Pyrrho,[57] and it would indeed be surprising if the picture of Pyrrho in Timon were entirely incompatible with that extractable from Diogenes' *Life*. But this is insufficient to conclude that the biography adds nothing to our knowledge of Pyrrho.[58] Not until we have looked at the biography can we conclude that it has nothing to offer.

I focus on two passages: Pyrrho's failure to avoid falling down wells (DL 9.62) and his calm during a sea-voyage (DL 9.68). The first produces a speculative reconstruction of the layers of re-presentation of Pyrrho's image; the second offers a possible corroboration of Pyrrho's philosophical position proposed above.

Much of the anecdotal evidence comes from Antigonus, who dates from around 240 BC.[59] Many commentators when discussing early scepticism point to Aristotle's comments at *Met.* Γ

---

[56] A phrase coined by Gigante (1986) 16. See Decleva Caizzi (1993a).

[57] E.g. Long (1978) 69, Annas and Barnes (1985) 11.

[58] Long now appears to share this view: (1996) 42.

[59] The view of Wilamowitz (1965), that all of Diogenes' biographical material comes from this single source is now rightly rejected. Dal Pra (1989) 41; Long (1978) 69, and n.10; Dorandi (1995b) 62–8, 89, (1999) xlviii–liii. Bett (2000) 8 is inclined to be suspicious of the value of Antigonus' anecdotes, since Antigonus lived too late to have met Pyrrho himself, and – so Bett claims – was probably insensitive to philosophical theories.

1008b15ff., where he criticises those thinkers who deny – explicitly or implicitly – the Principle of Non-Contradiction (PNC), since some of the arguments he presents there as used by his opponents pre-empt later more detailed sceptical arguments. Furthermore, the passage from Aristocles' *On Philosophy* which I discussed in detail earlier (above p. 87) concludes with what looks like a denial of PNC by the Pyrrhonians. However, they do not relate Aristotle's criticisms to anecdotes found in the Diogenean biography. If the biography's sources were composed after the Aristotelian passage, it is perhaps not unthinkable that their content might display modifications designed to reflect or counter that critique. I shall argue that this is in fact the case.

Where a Pyrrhonian response to Aristotle has been identified, then, it has usually been interpreted as a bare rejection of the Aristotelian assertion of the undeniability of the Principle of Non-Contradiction on Pyrrho's part.[60] (Whether and, if so, how Pyrrho read the esoteric Aristotelian works is still open to debate.)[61] This is itself based on a reading of the Aristocles passage which assumes that the 'things' (πράγματα) should be understood in the widest possible application. The crucial phrase in Aristotle's discussion is the following:

οὔτε γὰρ οὕτως οὔτ' οὐχ οὕτως λέγει, ἀλλ' οὕτως τε καὶ οὐχ οὕτως· καὶ πάλιν γε ταῦτα ἀπόφησιν ἄμφω, ὅτι οὔθ' οὕτως οὔτε οὐχ οὕτως. (*Met.* 1008a31–3)

He does not say that it is thus or not thus, but that it both is and is not, and again even the negation of these both – that it neither is nor is not thus.

This is said to correspond to the following in the passage from Timon reported by Aristocles (Eus. *PE* 14.18.3):[62]

---

[60] Long (1981) 88–91 finds in *Met.* Γ and *APo.* material which looks very much like the modes of Agrippa and Aenesidemus later to be used in Pyrrhonism.

[61] Sandbach (1985) does not treat the *Metaphysics* specifically. I assume only that the *sort of* critique recorded at *Met.* 1008b15ff. was noticed by the writers of these anecdotes. Stopper (1983) 273 finds it hard to believe that Pyrrho 'burrowed away in the Lyceum library'. Görler (1985) 327 thinks it unlikely that Pyrrho would have no general knowledge of the leading philosopher of the time, and (1994) 753 wonders if he might have learned of Aristotle from Callisthenes during Alexander's expedition. Cf. Decleva Caizzi (1981a) 153–4, who also (172) notes that, in order to rebuke Alexander, Callisthenes quoted a line of Homer (*Il.* 21.107, Plut. *Alex.* 54) which, so Philo tells us, was a favourite of Pyrrho (DL 9.67).

[62] E.g. by Long (1981) 92, Berti (1981) 67, Reale (1981) 315, Stopper (1983) 273. Aristocles certainly refers to 'Aristotle's refutation of people long ago' who thought μηδὲν

περὶ ἑνὸς ἑκάστου λέγοντας ὅτι οὐ μᾶλλον ἔστιν ἢ οὐκ ἔστιν ἢ καὶ ἔστιν καὶ οὐκ
ἔστιν ἢ οὔτε ἔστιν οὔτε οὐκ ἔστιν.[63]

About every single thing, saying that it no more is than is not or both is and is not
or neither is nor is not.

Aristotle charges that his opponent says:[64]

A   1   neither 'X is F', nor 'X is not-F'
     but 2   'X is and is not-F'
     or 3   'X neither is F nor is it not-F'

The Aristocles passage, however, can be understood in two ways:

B   about each thing one should say
     either 1   'X is no more F than not-F'
     or 2   'X is both F and not-F'
     or 3   'X neither is F nor is it not-F'

On this understanding B2 contradicts Aristotle's denial of A2 and
B3 contradicts Aristotle's denial of A3. However, there is another
possible interpretation of the Aristoclean quotation:

C   about each thing one should say
     1   'that it no more is F . . .
     2   . . . than not F'
     or 3   . . . than both F and not-F'
     or 4   . . . than neither F nor not-F'

This interpretation yields much less of a correspondence with the
Aristotelian formulation and does not imply a denial of PNC.[65] If

---

πεφύκαμεν γνωρίζειν at 14.18.2, and *Met.* Γ. 4–5 seems a reasonable candidate for the
reference. One might compare, e.g., *PE* 14.18.9.4 and *Met.* Γ 1006a31ff., or 14.18.8–9
with *Met.* 1006a18 and Alex. Aphrod. *in Met.* 274.25–7.

[63] Compare Favorinus' report that Pyrrho said: οὐ μᾶλλον οὕτως ἔχει τόδε ἢ ἐκείνως ἢ
οὐδετέρως (*apud* Aulus Gellius 11.5.4).

[64] On ἔστι in these formulations, see Bett (1994b) 158 n. 61 and (2000) 30, 36.

[65] B2 does not deny PNC if X is both F and not-F, but not 'simultaneously and in the
same respect'. Version C is preferred to B by De Lacy (1958a) 64ff., Stopper (1983)
273, Bett (1994b) 161 and (2000) 33–7, and Brunschwig (1997) 300–3. Brunschwig
(1999b) 244–6 shows how one might rescue version B without making Pyrrho deny
PNC. Cf. Annas and Barnes (1985) 11 and Robin (1944) 14. See Flintoff (1980) for
possible roots in Indian thought. It might be thought that C requires the text to read οὐ
μᾶλλον ἔστιν ἢ οὐκ ἔστιν ἢ ἢ καὶ ἔστιν καὶ οὐκ ἔστιν ἢ ἢ οὔτε ἔστιν οὔτε οὐκ ἔστιν, the
double ἢ being needed for the meaning 'or than'. Perhaps the duplication was avoided as
unstylish; perhaps the duplication is not necessary: the first ἢ of the three means 'than',
and the next two mean 'or' – these latter introducing alternatives to the second of the

C is preferred, it therefore becomes less likely that we can assert a strict dialectical relationship between the two.

It seems to me more profitable to look elsewhere in *Met.* Γ for relationships between the two thinkers, and especially to the argument which Aristotle offers at 1008b12–20 that someone who holds the sort of position he is arguing against cannot consistently act in a recognisably human way. I shall also attempt to provide an interpretation of Pyrrho's relationship to the passage in question by referring to the image of Pyrrho found in the biographical sources; if this is an argument about the impossibility of action, and if Pyrrho reacts to it, this reaction will be manifested in his actions.[66]

At *Met.* 1008b12ff. Aristotle claims to show that no one can live thinking a particular thing is simultaneously and in the same respect both F and not-F, by showing that the kind of conduct which would follow from such a disposition is impossible. There are clear parallels with the anecdotal biography of Pyrrho. First, here is Aristotle's argument:

οὐδ' εὐθὺς ἕωθεν πορεύεται εἰς φρέαρ ἢ εἰς φάραγγα, ἐὰν τύχῃ, ἀλλὰ φαίνεται εὐλαβούμενος, ὡς οὐχ ὁμοίως οἰόμενος μὴ ἀγαθὸν εἶναι τὸ ἐμπεσεῖν καὶ ἀγαθόν. (*Met.* 1008b15–17)

He does not immediately as soon as day breaks walk into a well or ravine if he comes upon one, but seems to pay heed as if not thinking it equally not good and good to fall into a well.

Crucially, the reason why this kind of thinker might fall into a well is not that he doubts that 'there is a well there', but that he does not consider it a bad thing to fall down a well. He thinks it is both not-good and good. This much would also be suggested by Aristotle's indignant comment at 1008b24ff.

ἀλλ' ὅπερ ἐλέχθη, οὐθεὶς ὃς οὐ φαίνεται τὰ μὲν εὐλαβούμενος τὰ δὲ οὔ· ὥστε, ὡς ἔοικε, πάντες ὑπολαμβάνουσιν ἔχειν ἁπλῶς, εἰ μὴ περὶ ἅπαντα, ἀλλὰ περὶ τὸ ἄμεινον καὶ χεῖρον.[67]

---

comparanda in the οὐ μᾶλλον phrase. Even then one might expect οὐδέ rather than ἤ since the whole phrase is negative. On Pyrrho's use of οὐ μᾶλλον see DL 9.76 (again from Timon's *Python*) and on Aenesidemus' use see Woodruff (1988).

[66] Cf. Long (1981) 94–7, Vander Waerdt (1989) 244 and n. 51.

[67] τό γε μᾶλλον καὶ ἧττον ἔνεστιν ἐν τῇ φύσει τῶν ὄντων (1008b32).

But as was said, everyone seems to be wary of some things but not others. As a result, so it seems, everyone accepts that this is the case generally, if not about everything then at least about what is better and worse.

He argues that it simply is untrue that anyone could refrain from making decisions of choice and avoidance which are based on giving items in the world a determinate nature. Even if someone were to deny the Principle of Non-Contradiction for certain matters, Aristotle insists that there must be some determinate view of goodness and badness in order for one to function as a human.[68] For comparison, note that when Pyrrho was angry with himself for obeying a reflex impulse to avoid an on-rushing dog, his anger is not because he trusted his senses' information that 'a dog is rushing towards me', but either because he ran away (as told by Aristocles *apud* Eus. *PE* 14.18.26) or was terrified by it.[69] Pyrrho is supposed, however, not to be inclined to pursue or avoid anything, given his view that nothing is in nature good or bad.[70]

We might now posit a link between the Aristotelian critique and the Antigonan anecdote that Pyrrho would not take evasive measures from carts or precipices (DL 9.62).[71] This story has generally been read as a critical picture of Pyrrho, an application of the Aristotelian refutation in an absurd biographical anecdote.[72] However, although the philosopher's indifference to what is at his feet was a common *topos*, Pyrrho does not in this case fail to avoid wells because his mind is on higher things. Moreover, there is no need to assume that Antigonus' biography was at all critical of Pyrrho.

ἀκόλουθος δ' ἦν καὶ τῷ βίῳ, μηδὲν ἐκτρεπόμενος μηδὲ φυλαττόμενος, ἅπαντα ὑφιστάμενος, ἁμάξας, εἰ τύχοι, καὶ κρημνοὺς καὶ κύνας καὶ ὅλως μηδὲν ταῖς αἰσθήσεσιν ἐπιτρέπων. σώζεσθαι μέντοι, καθά φασιν οἱ περὶ τὸν Καρύστιον Ἀντίγονον, ὑπὸ τῶν γνωρίμων παρακολουθούντων. Αἰνεσίδημος δέ φησι φιλοσοφεῖν μὲν αὐτὸν κατὰ τὸν τῆς ἐποχῆς λόγον, μὴ μέντοι γ' ἀπροοράτως ἕκαστα πράττειν. ὁ δὲ πρὸς τὰ ἐνενήκοντα ἔτη κατεβίω. (DL 9.62)

He lived a life in accordance with his doctrine, neither turning aside for, nor taking precautions against anything, but standing up to everything – carts, if he

---

[68] Cf. Alex. *in Met.* 299.1ff.; Syr. *in Met.* 73.15ff.; Cassin and Narcy (1989) 229.
[69] DL 9.66, from Antigonus.   [70] Timon fr. 72 Diels: ἀφυγής καὶ ἀναίρετος ἔσται.
[71] Cf. Thales at Pl. *Theaet.* 174a4.
[72] Long (1981) 95–6, Frede (1982) 181, Bett (2000) 67–9.

should come across them, precipices and dogs – generally paying no heed to his senses. But he was saved – so Antigonus of Carystus says – by his acquaintances who followed close by him. But Aenesidemus says that Pyrrho conducted his philosophy in accordance with the argument of suspension of judgement, but in his everyday actions did not lack foresight. Pyrrho lived to be nearly ninety years old.

The Diogenes passage does show Pyrrho paying no attention to his senses (μηδὲν ταῖς αἰσθήσεσιν ἐπιτρέπων), but that sits badly with other anecdotal evidence which suggests that he did, at least for practical purposes, obey the information of the senses. That Pyrrho's indifference to falling down a well was thought at one time to show an epistemological position is once again revealing of later trends of sceptical thought. Lucretius, for example, against those who do not trust sense-perception, argues that they will be prone to falling off precipices (*DRN* 4.507). But there is no need to think that the anecdote was occasioned by an original epistemological doctrine of distrusting all the senses.

At some time before Antigonus wrote, I suspect, a charge of the sort made by Aristotle in the *Metaphysics* was brought against Pyrrho, who was known to have denied that anything (even falling down wells) was by nature good or bad.[73] Aristotle's original formulation, remember, depends only on the individual not being certain that 'it is a bad thing to fall down a well'. The ideal state, for Pyrrho at least, is neither to pursue nor avoid anything – so he may indeed be prone to Aristotle's accusation. Yet the anecdote does not articulate solely a criticism, but also a response. We must remember that Pyrrho did *not* fall down a well, but lived to be nearly ninety (DL 9.62). His failure to avoid physical dangers can therefore remain as a positive sign of his indifference, rather than a potentially fatal eccentricity. Perhaps the point of the anecdote is that someone living like Pyrrho need not fall down a well, because his charismatic equipoise will attract followers who will hold him back from the edges of precipices

---

[73] The relative chronology of Pyrrho and Aristotle is unclear, so I evade a question of direct reaction of Aristotle to Pyrrho's oral teaching. De Lacy (1958a) 64 n. 1 suggests its possibility. Reale (1981) 316 notes the chronological difficulties but for other reasons thinks that for Pyrrho to be unaware of Aristotle's work would be 'assurdo'. For another view: Berti (1981) 68.

(the γνωρίμων παρακολουθούντων, DL 9.62). Because Pyrrho follows his doctrine (is ἀκόλουθος 9.62), he attracts 'followers' (παρακολουθοῦντες) in both the literal and the metaphorical sense. They 'follow' his teachings, and so 'follow' him around and allow him to 'follow' strictly the precepts of his teaching. Admittedly, this makes the viability of such a life parasitic on there being others who do have set beliefs as to what is or is not good, but its advantage is that it also makes the very attraction of this same equipoise the main reason for its viability as a mode of life.[74]

Then, when Pyrrho's philosophy was given an epistemological spin, the reason for his indifference became no longer an indifference to judgements such as 'falling off cliffs is bad', but an indifference to all information provided by sense-perception. This adds the tag noted above (μηδὲν ταῖς αἰσθήσεσιν ἐπιτρέπων, DL 9.62). Immediately after the anecdote, Diogenes notes that it provoked a reaction from later self-proclaimed heirs to Pyrrho's philosophy. When Aenesidemus reappropriated Pyrrho's name for his new school, he looked to the surviving accounts of the life of his chosen founder and felt it necessary to make some attempt to square the public image of Pyrrho with that of the new Pyrrhonists.[75] To this end, he censored what he considered to be the more absurd of the surviving popular perceptions of the earlier sceptic, including the anecdote about him failing to avoid cliffs.

Aenesidemus' Pyrrho would not fail to look at the ground in front of him. He might not be convinced that what he sees is really there, but like the later Pyrrhonists would live in accordance with his impressions (SE *PH*. 1.19–20). Aenesidemus evidently felt that the extreme indifference conveyed by the Antigonan anecdotes was not an attractive image to offer, and so saw fit to re-write Pyrrho as someone who retained a sceptical outlook on the world, but would still behave in a normal manner.[76] Later sceptics continued to use Pyrrho and not Metrodorus, say, as their 'founding father' because of the moral basis of Pyrrho's image. Pyrrhonist scepticism – at least in Sextus Empiricus' presentation – is a means to the end

---

[74] Frede (1982) 182 suggests that the 'parasitic' nature of Pyrrho's life is part of Antigonus' critique; cf. Bett (2000) 67–8.

[75] Cf. Sedley (1983a) 19ff.   [76] Cf. Brochard (1923) 68 n. 2.

of dispelling worries generated by dogmatism (SE *PH* 1.12). In Pyrrho, Aenesidemus could find a model of an ethical and practical ideal of tranquillity perfect for his own philosophical motivation.

Another feature of many of the anecdotes which has been insufficiently remarked, and which corroborates the story above, is the remarkable number of times pigs appear in the stories: Pyrrho personally sells pigs in the market (9.66), is so indifferent that he washes a pig (9.66) and uses a pig as the example of the desired composure during a rough sea-journey (9.68). These are the only occasions on which these animals appear in Diogenes.[77] It is therefore not unreasonable to conclude that they have some peculiar relevance to Pyrrho.

εὐσεβῶς δὲ καὶ τῇ ἀδελφῇ συνεβίω μαίᾳ οὔσῃ, καθά φησιν Ἐρατοσθένης ἐν τῷ Περὶ πλούτου καὶ πενίας, ὅτε καὶ αὐτὸς φέρων εἰς τὴν ἀγορὰν ἐπίπρασκεν ὀρνίθια, εἰ τύχοι, καὶ χοιρίδια, καὶ τὰ ἐπὶ τῆς οἰκίας ἐκάθαιρεν ἀδιαφόρως. λέγεται δὲ καὶ δέλφακα[78] λούειν αὐτὸς ὑπ' ἀδιαφορίας... καὶ κυνός ποτ' ἐπενεχθέντος διασοβηθέντα εἰπεῖν πρὸς τὸν αἰτιασάμενον ὡς χαλεπὸν εἴη ὁλοσχερῶς ἐκδῦναι τὸν ἄνθρωπον.

He lived piously with his sister, who was a midwife – so Eratosthenes says in his *On wealth and poverty*. He himself would take birds to sell in the market, and – if they had them – piglets, and he would clean the house in indifference. It is also said that he himself washed a pig out of indifference. And when he was once startled by a dog which rushed at him, he said to someone who reproached him that it is difficult entirely to strip away the human.

The first two stories, of taking of a pig to market and the careful washing of a pig, come from an essay by Eratosthenes of Cyrene (*c.* 285–194 BC) in which, presumably, a moral point about wealth is being made.[79] Perhaps by taking care over such a lowly animal, Pyrrho is displaying that it is wrong to hold any judgement such

---

[77] Janáček (1992) s.v. δέλφαξ, χοιρίδιον. ὗς appears in one of the modes: DL 9.80.

[78] Schaps (1996) suggests that δέλφαξ refers to an adolescent pig. The pig on the ship at 9.68 is a χοιρίδιον.

[79] Cf. Ferrari (1968) 221, Ioppolo (1980a) 24. Eratosthenes was the pupil of Ariston, and the fragments of his περὶ ἀγαθῶν καὶ κακῶν and his περὶ πλούτου καὶ πενίας show Aristonian influence. Eratosthenes' interest in Pyrrho might help to corroborate the suggestion found in Ciceronian evidence that Pyrrho's ethical thought was very much like that of Ariston. Cf. Decleva Caizzi (1981b) 108. Nussbaum (1994) 313 claims that Pyrrho's behaviour shows an absence of 'class consciousness' (which is surely anachronistic), and also (more convincingly) that Pyrrho is unconcerned by conventions about the work appropriate to men and women.

as that wealth is good. At 9.68, the pig is an animal to be imitated:

τῶν γὰρ συμπλεόντων αὐτῷ ἐσκυθρωπακότων ὑπὸ χειμῶνος, αὐτὸς γαληνὸς ὢν ἀνέρρωσε τὴν ψυχήν, δείξας ἐν τῷ πλοίῳ χοιρίδιον ἐσθίον καὶ εἰπὼν ὡς χρὴ τὸν σοφὸν ἐν τοιαύτῃ καθεστάναι ἀταραξίᾳ.[80]

When his fellow travellers were bothered by a storm, he remained calm and was untroubled in his mind. Pointing to a pig eating on the deck, he told them that they should stay in such a state of tranquillity.

While the storm tosses the ship and disturbs the other travellers, Pyrrho remains tranquil (γαληνός)[81] and the pig continues to eat, maintaining its *ataraxia*.[82] Pigs and humans stand at opposite ends of the hierarchy of animals.[83] As such, pigs are particularly useful subjects if one wishes to generate relativist or sceptical conclusions.[84] They are no strangers to philosophical contexts. In Plato's *Theaetetus*, during his refutation of the Protagorean thesis that 'man is the measure of all things', Socrates draws our attention to the inclusion of 'man' (161c2ff.):

τὰ μὲν ἄλλα μοι πάνυ ἡδέως εἴρηκεν, ὡς τὸ δοκοῦν ἑκάστῳ τοῦτο καὶ ἔστιν· τὴν δ' ἀρχὴν τοῦ λόγου τεθαύμακα, ὅτι οὐκ εἶπεν ἀρχόμενος τῆς 'Αληθείας ὅτι 'Πάντων χρημάτων μέτρον ἐστὶν ὗς' ἢ 'κυνοκέφαλος' ἤ τι ἄλλο ἀτοπώτερον τῶν ἐχόντων αἴσθησιν.

The rest he said, I think, very well – how what appears to each person is also the case. But I was amazed at the beginning of his argument that he did not begin his *Truth* by saying 'A pig is the measure of all things' or 'baboon' or some other more peculiar perceiver.

If Protagoras were to apply his relativism consistently, there is no reason why 'man' rather than 'pig' should be the measure of all things, and therefore there is even less reason to allow Protagoras personally any authority to present *his* theory as 'Truth' rather than Socrates', Theaetetus', yours, mine, or that of the pig we are fattening up for the winter. This is a *reductio* to a piggish *absurdum*.

---

[80] The anecdote also appears in Plut. *Prof. in virt.* 82F, presumably also from a Posidonian source.

[81] Cf. Timon fr. 63 Diels (SE *M*.11.141).

[82] Cf. Nussbaum (1994) 305, McPherran (1989) 156.

[83] Hom. *Od.* 10.239ff.: Odysseus' men are transformed by Circe into pigs but retain their human minds. The discrepancy between the bodily needs of a pig and the ambitions and desires of the men is what makes the transformation horrific.

[84] Heraclitus B13, echoed by Sextus Empiricus (*PH* 1.56).

No one would make a pig's judgement the criterion of truth, but that is what a consistently Protagorean position demands.

'A pig is the measure of all things' is absurd partly because it recalls a proverbial phrase: 'A pig would not know as much', which was used when a matter depended on some degree of fine judgement. Something that 'every pig' would know is something which requires no intellectual effort.[85] Pigs are not only intellectually, but also morally, defective. Aelian notes their gluttony (*NA* 10.16). Pigs have no desires or impulses beyond sating hunger. The pig on Pyrrho's boat is happy because it can eat. Similarly, in Plato's *Republic*, Glaucon comments that Socrates' first ideal state is a 'city of pigs' (Pl. *Rep.* 372d4), insinuating that it caters only for the most basic needs. Elsewhere Aelian says that pigs are so concerned with filling their stomachs that they will even, on occasion, resort to cannibalism (7.19).[86] This is evidence that a pig is beyond the reach of moral rules, and unable to make mutually compelling agreements.[87]

Although dogs are often linked to pigs in their lowly status,[88] literary dogs are regularly allowed a sense of memory and loyalty never granted to pigs. Argus (SE *PH* 1.68) is allowed the virtue of bravery and intelligence. The Stoics even allowed the dog some degree of ability to perform what looks like (but, Chrysippus insists, is not) syllogistic reasoning: *SVF* 2.726, SE *M.* 8.270 (it σημειοῦται).[89]

By holding up a pig as the ideal human state, therefore, Pyrrho is making a striking claim.[90] More importantly, this claim has no epistemological tone. A pig is to be imitated not because it doubts

---

[85] Cf. Aristoph. *Pax* 928; Pl. *Laches* 196d9, *Leg.* 819d; Βοιωτίαν ὗν in Pin. *Ol.* 6.152. Di Marco (1983) 59–67 collects a large number of references.

[86] Cf. Clem *Strom.* 7.4.24.

[87] Cf. Epicurus *KD* 32: animals are not able to choose to form covenants for mutual benefit. *KD* 31, 37. Horses have a *mens* at DRN 2.265, but Hermarchus *apud* Porphyry *De abst.* 1.7–12 denies that animals have *logos*. Cf. Annas (1992) 134–7, Sorabji (1993) 28–9.

[88] SE *PH* 1.63: the dog is the most worthless animal. This is what 'dogmatists' think, in order not to have to take into account the dog's perceptions. The scholion to the Pl. *Laches* 196d9 cites the proverb as 'a pig or dog would not know as much'.

[89] Sextus goes on to give a number of reasons why one should not deprecate the dog or its perceptions/beliefs. See Decleva Caizzi (1993b). On Chrysippus' dog: Sorabji (1993) 26, Floridi (1997).

[90] See Chrysippus *apud* Porphyry *De abst.* 3.20.1. A pig has a soul in order to keep pork fresh for humans. Cf. Cic. *Fin.* 5.38 and Deschamps (1998).

its senses, but because it is does not worry about whether a storm is bad.[91]

Pyrrho's inhumanity . . .

A phrase used in the biographical sources which seems to describe an injunction to which Pyrrho subscribed, and which will secure an understanding of why pigs in particular are used in the anecdotes was: ἐκδῦναι τὸν ἄνθρωπον, 'strip off the human' (DL 9.66).[92] We would all be happier, implies Pyrrho, if we lived as contentedly as pigs and the best way to achieve that is to strive to rid oneself of all aspirations and conceptions of what is 'good' and 'bad' which can be frustrated, and lead to anxiety and stress.

But if this attempt to strip ourselves of the baggage of human moral convictions is the result of theoretical and philosophical argument, or even of being impressed by images of Pyrrho's indifference, a problem arises. Only by the employment of reason can we be convinced that we would be better off without these anxiety-producing convictions. Can the ideal state be one in which we remove totally those higher psychological capacities? Can we do so if reason is required to suggest that this is the right thing to do? Would we want to do it? Does a pig recognise that it is happy? Surely some awareness of achieving *eudaimonia* is required for anyone to want to be in such a state?

Pyrrho would prefer us to strip away the human, but recognises, when he himself is terrified by the rabid dog, that this is not an easy task. Nor does it seem an attractive thing to do, if it prevents us from rationally considering and valuing our happy state. The desired state, we might object, would be one which, while piglike, nevertheless retained the capacity which originally saw the desirability of being like the contented pig on a storm-tossed ship.

---

[91] See Dierauer (1977) 191 n. 13.

[92] Also Aristoc. *apud* Eus. *PE* 14.18.26. Cf. Bett (1998) 204–5, 211. I am extremely tempted to make a close link between the ἄνθρωπος which Pyrrho strives to remove and the ἄνθρωπος at which the Democritus of the Hippocratic *Pseudepigrapha* (Littré vol. 9 360) laughs. Cf. Timon fr. 11 Diels: ἄνθρωποι, κενεῆς οἰήσιος ἔμπλεοι ἀσκοί. Cf. Timon fr. 48 Diels: ὦ γέρον, ὦ Πύρρων, πῶς ἢ πόθεν ἔκδυσιν εὗρες | λατρείης δόξων κενοφροσύνης τε σοφιστῶν; Di Marco (1989) 220–1. Some MSS have ἔκλυσιν for ἔκδυσιν. Cf. Ferrari (1981) 353–5.

We would like to strip off human weakness and anxiety, perhaps, but not everything that makes us humans rather than animals.[93] Pyrrho's indifference is definitively *in*human: it requires the removal of all that makes us human, for that is where Pyrrho locates the source of all our anxiety. There is therefore something deeply paradoxical in calling this the truly desirable *human* end.

Moreover, this consideration of what we should be happy to call a human end is simultaneously effective against the god-like image of Pyrrho. In Timon fr. 67 Diels the divinity of Pyrrho is conveyed in particular by two striking adverbs: ἀφροντίστως and ἀκινήτως. To live 'without thought' and 'without change or movement' is not to live the life of most humans. They are engaged in movement and change, and cling to certain things, thinking they are valuable. To live ἀφροντίστως is to live 'thoughtlessly', without the usual structures of choice and avoidance which inform most human decision making. Parallels can be found where ἀφροντίστως is used to describe how an action is performed 'without care for' something which otherwise would normally figure in someone's calculations.[94] This might be quite a normal attitude for a certain matter at a certain time, but were this attitude to be extended more generally as in fr. 67, one might see a more radical challenge to normal structures of decision making. To live a life in such a way is not to care generally, to have no preferences on which to base one's actions. Such an outlook would form the basis of a life very different from that of most humans.[95]

To rid oneself of preferences and therefore the basis of practical reasoning as the result of Pyrrho's exhortation to 'strip away the human' (ἐκδῦναι τὸν ἄνθρωπον) is a radical and striking manoeuvre which calls into question just what is required by and surplus to a human (good) life. If Pyrrho locates the source of human anxieties in our tendency to maintain moral convictions then it is understandable, at least, that he should prescribe the removal of

---

93 Nussbaum (1994) 305 recognises the importance of animal examples in sceptical ethics. Also note her remarks at 291–2. Barnes (1990c) 18–19 suggests the life of an animal as a useful model for how a Sextan sceptic might live.

94 Pl. *Leg.* 885a3, cf. 917c6; Polyb. 3.79.2. Cf. Soph. *Aj.* 355. Epic. *Ep. Hdt.* 77: gods have no φροντίδες.

95 Hankinson (1995) 282 likens the attitude of a *Sextan* Pyrrhonist to a robot or passive receptor. Cf. Velleman (1993) 354–7.

such judgements. This removal makes us less human, either in the sense of it making us more god-like, or in the sense of it making us less than human: pig-like.

Pyrrho thus presents a radical challenge to some Platonic and Aristotelian (as well as Epicurean) conceptions of human *eudaimonia*. The Platonic passage which most captures the aversion to Pyrrho's reduction of a human to the level of an animal is from the *Philebus*. Protarchus is defending the thesis that pleasure is sufficient for the good life. Socrates asks whether practical reason, thought, and calculation are required also (21a14ff.). Protarchus thinks not (21b2). He is then led to reject the necessity of memory, knowledge, and opinion. Socrates concludes that without such capacities Protarchus will compromise his pleasure by limiting his ability for enjoyment to the present moment:

καὶ μὴν ὡσαύτως μνήμην μὴ κεκτημένον ἀνάγκη δήπου μηδ' ὅτι ποτὲ ἐχαίρεις μεμνῆσθαι, τῆς τ' ἐν τῷ παραχρῆμα ἡδονῆς προσπιπτούσης μηδ' ἡντινοῦν μνήμην ὑπομένειν· δόξαν δ' αὖ μὴ κεκτημένον ἀληθῆ μὴ δοξάζειν χαίρειν χαίροντα, λογισμοῦ δὲ στερόμενον μηδ' εἰς τὸν ἔπειτα χρόνον ὡς χαιρήσεις δυνατὸν εἶναι λογίζεσθαι, ζῆν δὲ οὐκ ἀνθρώπου βίον ἀλλά τινος πλεύμονος ἢ τῶν ὅσα θαλάττια μετ' ὀστρεΐνων ἔμψυχά ἐστι σωμάτων. (21c1–8)[96]

And possessing no memory it is necessary then that you never remember that you felt pleasure in the past – and when pleasure arises, no memory of it remains from one moment to the next. And not possessing true opinion you do not think that you are feeling pleasure when you are doing so. And, deprived of reason, it is not possible to reason how to find pleasure in the future. So you live not a human life at all, but that of a jellyfish or those shelled creatures in the sea.

The insistence that memory and anticipation are able to increase one's pleasure by extending the range of one's possible objects in a temporal sense was to become a central tenet of Epicurean hedonism. Socrates here rightly emphasises that that possibility requires rational capacities. A life without such rational capacities is inhuman; specifically it is the life of a jellyfish or some other such sea creature. We shall see that this insult is reused in Epicurus' abuse of Nausiphanes (below p. 191). It is perhaps significant that Epicurus both insists on the essential use of rational capacities in

[96] Cf. *Phlb.* 22b5 (with Lefebvre (1999) 70 n. 3) and Arist. *Met.* 1008b11 where he asks of the person who denies the PNC τί ἂν διαφερόντως ἔχοι τῶν φυτῶν; Sextus responds to a similar attack at *M.* 11.163–4.

maximising human pleasure (this claim recurs in Polystratus – see below pp. 137ff.), and attacks a follower of Pyrrho in the same terms as are used here by Socrates to abuse Protarchus' position.[97]

Pyrrho's own position can be likened to Protarchus' thesis. The *Philebus* enacts the examination of the thesis that only pleasure is essential to enjoyment, which via the rejection of all other capacities except the capacity to enjoy (τὸ χαίρειν) is found to be mistaken: some of those capacities which it rejected are in fact essential to the maximisation of enjoyment.[98] Pyrrho proceeds in a different direction, not originally motivated by the thesis that pleasure is the only good, but that a life without anxiety (ῥῆιστα μεθ' ἡσυχίης fr. 67.1) is to be pursued. He then diagnoses the sources of that anxiety and seeks to remove them. Nevertheless, the question posed by Socrates to Protarchus is just that which I posed in reaction to the assimilation of a human life to that of a pig: is such a life choiceworthy for a human? (ἄρ' οὖν αἱρετὸς ἡμῖν βίος ὁ τοιοῦτος; 21d3). As humans, a life which is choiceworthy for us should be a human life.[99] Pyrrho offers the paradoxical suggestion that the best human life is the life least characterised by specifically human capacities.[100] Given this Platonic objection, it is perhaps not coincidental that Pyrrho is not portrayed engaging in philosophical discussions and expositions. He cannot do so without employing those capacities he would rather have stripped away. His life is an image for us to contemplate much as the pig which he points to on the deck of the ship (DL 9.68) is an image for the passengers to contemplate.

Comparison of the Platonic and Aristotelian attitudes to the assimilation to divinity is also instructive. Platonic insistence on the immortality of soul, and the transcendent reality of Forms, can combine in a dialogue like the *Phaedo* to provide the ethical

---

[97] Compare Mill's (1861) ch. 2 discussion of the common misconception that Epicureanism *reduces* humans to pigs and his famous conclusion: 'It is better to be a human dissatisfied than a pig satisfied; better to be Socrates dissatisfied than a fool satisfied. And if the fool, or the pig, are of a different opinion, it is because they only know their own side of the question.'

[98] Cf. Aristotle *EE* 1215b30–7, discussed by Nussbaum (1995) 113ff.

[99] Stressed by Nussbaum (1995) 100. This question is also the subject of Lefebvre (1999), esp. 72–4, and McCabe (2000) 128–34.

[100] Cf. Burnyeat (1980b) 53. Aristocles asks: ποῖος γὰρ ἂν γένοιτο πολίτης ἢ δικαστὴς ἢ σύμβουλος ἢ φίλος ἢ ἁπλῶς εἰπεῖν ἄνθρωπος ὁ τοιοῦτος; *apud* Eus. *PE* 14.18.18.

conclusion that one should indeed strive to be as inhuman as possible: philosophy is a preparation for death.

Aristotle comments in the *Politics* that man is a 'political' animal, and that this essentially distinguishes humans from beasts and gods (1253a27–9). Similarly beasts and gods are inhuman in as much as they have no share of virtue or vice (*EN* 1145a25). This much has been well noted by Nussbaum, who is keen to see in Aristotle a thinker who insists on the specifically human nature of the human ethical end. However, in certain passages of the *Nicomachean Ethics* Aristotle too eventually identifies the highest human end with the most godlike life possible for a human (1177b33), and therefore substitutes his own version of 'becoming like god'.[101]

If Timon chose to emphasise Pyrrho's inhumanity by deifying his mentor in his poetry, that might be a choice informed by such deification being a more palatable alternative than the dehumanisation and reduction to an animal implied by the biographical tradition. If someone wishes to publicise and praise a view which encourages the removal of human anxiety and weakness, deification is clearly a more positive metaphor than the reduction of humans to swine. Two options then suggest themselves: that the biographical tradition is indeed reflecting a critical and polemical interpretation of Pyrrho's inhumanity by reducing the removal to an *absurdum*, or that the biographical tradition preserves an important corollary of Timon's literary deification: the process can work in two ways, towards the divine or the bestial but always essentially to the 'less human'. Either option emphasises the growing awareness that becoming like god, and becoming like a pig, are rather more alike than might first appear. This critical interpretation might fit with that of the 'pitfall' anecdote. However, I did not find that reading of the 'pitfall' story compelling and am therefore inclined to reject the critical interpretation of the 'pig' stories. This view is reinforced by the appearance of pig stories not just in Antigonus' biography, but in a number of sources, one of which is a work by Eratosthenes,

---

[101] See Nussbaum (1986) 373–7, cf. Nussbaum (1995); cp. Sedley (1997). There are suggestions of an Epicurean assimilation to divinity in *Ep. Men.* 135 and in the deification of Epicurus by Lucretius (*DRN* 5.8). On this see Warren (2000a).

whose moral stance was probably close to that of Ariston and there-fore of Pyrrho himself. This source, therefore, is unlikely to have been hostile to Pyrrho but nevertheless tells this same anecdote. This positive interpretation is further supported by the Epicureans' retention of the pig as a symbol of *ataraxia* (see below p. 133).

. . . and its limits. His sister and a dog

There appear, however, to be limits to the possibility of strip-ping away peculiarly human anxieties. The biographical tradition retains notice of two 'défaillances occasionnelles',[102] which en-act these limits: one an involuntary reaction to circumstance, the other an apparently voluntary exception to Pyrrho's indifference. The very phrase 'strip away the human', ἐκδῦναι τὸν ἄνθρωπον, is introduced in an anecdote in which Pyrrho fails to retain his char-acteristic equipoise when attacked by a dog. As Pyrrho himself is said to remark, the end would certainly be difficult to achieve entirely (DL 9.66), although the suggestion is clearly not that it is impossible, nor that it is necessarily difficult to achieve in part.

Also, it appears that Pyrrho was not always concerned to make a display of his preferred disposition of indifference.

χολήσας τι ὑπὲρ τῆς ἀδελφῆς, Φιλίστα δ' ἐκαλεῖτο, πρὸς τὸν λαβόμενον εἰπεῖν ὡς οὐκ ἐν γυναίῳ ἡ ἐπίδειξις τῆς ἀδιαφορίας. [103] (DL 9.66)

Angered on account of his sister, who was named Philista, he replied to the man who took him aside that it is not necessary to display indifference in the case of a woman.

Alone, this brief scene is quite bizarre. Why should Pyrrho make a distinction between those to whom he makes a display of his indif-ference? To do so calls into question Pyrrho's unstinting dedication and embodiment of his own professed ethical aim. Aristocles pre-serves a longer and more informative version of this anecdote, drawn from the same Antigonan source as used by Diogenes:[104]

---

[102] Brunschwig (1992b) 135.
[103] Brunschwig (1992b) 134 and Dorandi (1999) 5 retain the MSS λαβόμενον against Kühn's ἐπιλαβόμενον.
[104] Cf. Dorandi (1995b) 71–2. The Aristoclean version is also preferred by Brunschwig (1992b) 140.

Φιλίστας δὲ τῆς ἀδελφῆς αὐτοῦ θυούσης, ἔπειτα τῶν φίλων τινὸς ὑποσχομένου τὰ πρὸς τὴν θυσίαν καὶ μὴ παρασχομένου, τοῦ μέντοι Πύρρωνος πριαμένου καὶ ἀγανακτοῦντος, ἐπειδήπερ ὁ φίλος ἔλεγεν ὡς οὐ μὴν ποιῆσαι σύμφωνα τοῖς λόγοις οὐδ' ἄξια τῆς ἀπαθείας εἰπεῖν αὐτόν· ἐν γοῦν γυναικὶ <τί>[105] δεῖ τὴν ἀπόδειξιν αὐτῆς ποιεῖσθαι; καίτοι δικαίως ἂν εἰπεῖν ὁ φίλος ὅτι· ὦ μάταιε, καὶ ἐν γυναικὶ καὶ κυνὶ καὶ πᾶσιν, εἰ δὴ τί σοι τῶν λόγων τούτων ἐστὶν ὄφελος. (Aristocles *apud* Eus. *PE* 14.18.26)

Philista, his sister, was making a sacrifice. Then one of his friends who had promised to provide what was needed for the sacrifice did not bring it. Pyrrho bought it himself and grew angry, especially when the friend said that he was not acting in accordance with his theories, nor in a way worthy of freedom from passion. He said: '[Why] is it necessary to display a lack of emotions in the case of a woman?' But in that case, the friend might also rightly have said: 'In the case of a woman, and a dog, and everything, if there is any benefit to you in these arguments.'

It is clear why Aristocles is so keen on this particular anecdote, and that of the dog which preceded it. They threaten an inconsistency in Pyrrho's adherence to his own doctrines. The point of the friend reminding Pyrrho of his official doctrine is that it casts doubt on the universality of his lack of emotion (ἀπάθεια). On occasion, Pyrrho appears to forget or at least chooses not to follow his own philosophy. If Pyrrho can be shown to claim that it is not always necessary to demonstrate this (ἀπόδειξιν ποιεῖν), then the implication must be that when he does appear to lack emotion, this is solely for the purposes of display. Aristocles is therefore quick to construct the friend's retort to Pyrrho's question (the optative construction in the Greek makes it clear that this is Aristocles' own addition). However, Aristocles does retain a reason for Pyrrho's anger missing from Diogenes' brief report: a friend had failed to provide the promised materials for a sacrifice. Pyrrho bought the victim himself. So Pyrrho is not angry *because of* his sister. Rather he claimed that it is not necessary to make a show of indifference *in the presence of* or *in the case of* a woman.[106] But this claim is also difficult to understand, especially in the light of other anecdotal evidence which suggests that Pyrrho's 'home life'

---

[105] Dorandi (1999) 5 n. 27 retains this insertion by Wilamowitz.

[106] Brunschwig (1992b) 136 n. 3 rightly rejects Decleva Caizzi's (1981a) 166 suggestion that this shows a streak of 'misogyny'. On the possible meanings of the ambiguous ὑπέρ in DL 9.66: Brunschwig (1992b) 134, 138 n. 8.

was characterised by the same indifference as his cliff-top walks (DL 9.66).

Perhaps this anecdote might be better understood if we stress its religious and sacrificial context. Brunschwig suggests that Pyrrho's anger was caused by the inconvenience and expense he incurs.[107] Certainly, Pyrrho is angered at a friend's broken promise, but I am not so sure that the text necessarily implies that Pyrrho is angered because he had to buy the sacrificial victim himself. Elsewhere in Diogenes' *Life* we are told that Pyrrho and his sister lived together piously (εὐσεβῶς 9.66). Perhaps we should leave open the possibility that Pyrrho held some sort of religious beliefs. (We are told that he held some kind of priesthood: DL 9.64.) We might remember that Timon fr. 68 Diels promised to divulge not only the nature of the good but also of the divine. Perhaps two things were exempted from Pyrrho's indifference; he is not indifferent to the ethical end (of indifference),[108] nor is he indifferent in matters concerning the divine. Both of these were given a determinate nature.

These anecdotes are followed by another injunction:

διαγωνίζεσθαι δ' ὡς οἷόν τε πρῶτον μὲν τοῖς ἔργοις πρὸς τὰ πράγματα, εἰ δὲ μή, τῷ γε λόγῳ. (DL 9.66)

Strive as hard as possible first of all in deeds against things, and failing that, in argument.

Pyrrho describes two methods of moving towards that end: one preferred, the other less effective.[109] The contrast between deeds and words or arguments (λόγοι, *logoi*) corresponds in a sense to the distinction made between disposition and arguments or theories by the later interpreters of Pyrrho, and Pyrrho's own professed preference here for struggling in deeds rather than words corresponds well with the previous interpretation of the injunction to 'strip away the human'. Let me explain.

---

[107] Brunschwig (1992b) 138.

[108] Brunschwig suggests (1992b) 141 that Pyrrho must be thought to have responded to his friend that 'one need not make a display of indifference on account of a woman', and that this reply can be interpreted ironically: 'Il va jusqu' à être insensible à ses propres manquements à l'idéal d'insensibilité'.

[109] Cf. Decleva Caizzi (1981a) 167.

In the discussion of the section of Timon cited by Aristocles, it was decided that the πράγματα ('things') were originally things accorded some moral value, and connected closely with action, but were later extended in significance in line with a Timonian re-working and epistemological interpretation of Pyrrho's thought (above pp. 92ff.). A similar line can be taken here. Clearly this injunction wishes us to alter the way we act. We are engaged in a struggle in which we should (preferably) adapt our actions and deeds. On a restricted 'moral' reading of πράγματα, then, this would suggest that we should modify our actions in line with the realisation that 'nothing is good or bad by nature' and, presumably, would end by acting very much like the Pyrrho of the biographical anecdotes: failing to avoid precipices and the like. The wider epistemological (Timonian) reading of πράγματα corresponds to a different reason for failing to avoid the cliff, not because 'nothing is good or bad by nature', but because 'I do not believe that there is a cliff there.' This struggle against the πράγματα becomes a concerted struggle against believing the contents of sense-impressions.

On either interpretation, Pyrrho's injunction prefers action to thought, deeds to *logoi*. Here, therefore, we should insist on a strict division between the two terms in which the deeds and actions are, so to speak, argument-free. It is better not to have to go through a process of thought and argument in order to free oneself from the surrounding πράγματα since that not only presupposes that one has to oppose within one's own soul various conflicting arguments, that one must convince oneself that such action against the πράγματα is justified and justifiable, but also denotes a failure to rid oneself of the necessity to base everything on arguments or theories. If it is necessary to go through a process of argument to be convinced that, say 'this is not a bad thing by nature' then one's resulting action might be acceptable to Pyrrho, but the mere fact that it required such deliberation indicates the incomplete nature of one's removal of what is human. Had one removed what is human there would be no need for nor possibility of argument; one would simply (re)act without thought just like the pig on the storm-tossed ship. Thus the attainment of the correct disposition for Pyrrho might entail, at its limit, the removal of any need for arguments with which to argue for that very disposition.

An interesting distinction can now be made between the biographical traditions of Pyrrho and Timon which would correspond to the apparent philosophical differences between the two. Where Pyrrho retires from active life once he begins to philosophise, Timon is an engaged man. He writes poetry and philosophical works, enjoys fine wine (DL 9.110), and is shown in discussion with other famous men such as Aratus (9.113). If anything characterises Timon it is an approval of *logoi*. Still, he too maintains an allegiance to the Pyrrhonian *diathesis* of tranquillity, despite his active life. Here, then, we begin to see a distinction between him and his master:

[Τίμων] θορυβούμενός θ' ὑπὸ τῶν θεραπαινῶν καὶ κυνῶν ἐποίει μηδέν, σπουδάζων περὶ τὸ ἠρεμάζειν. (DL 9.113)

When disturbed by maids or dogs [Timon] did nothing, and tried hard to remain tranquil.

This brief anecdote shows a progression from Pyrrho's exceptions to the indifference rule; it is not coincidental that the two causes of disturbance noted here are barking dogs and maidservants, which correspond nicely to Pyrrho's two exceptions to indifference: his sister, Philista, and the dog of 9.66. Timon takes great pains (σπουδάζων) to retain his indifference to the very two situations in which Pyrrho failed to maintain his composure. Does it also suggest that there was some rule or theory guiding Timon's route to maintaining tranquillity which was not only missing but actively banished by Pyrrho? Timon seems not to have relegated the struggle against the πράγματα with *logoi* to the same level as did Pyrrho. *Logoi* are as essential, one suspects, not only to the dissemination but also to the attainment of Timon's view of the ethical end, as they are much later to Sextus Empiricus and his view of Pyrrhonism.

One-eyed Timon and blind Democritus

A further footnote can be made to this section. Timon is said to have had only one eye. Diogenes notes:

τοῦτον ἐγὼ καὶ ἑτερόφθαλμον ἤκουσα, ἐπεὶ καὶ αὐτὸς αὐτὸν Κύκλωπα ἐκάλει. (9.112; cf. 9.114)

I heard too that he also had only one eye, since he used to call himself 'Cyclops'.

It is of course possible that Timon did in fact only have one eye, but it is clear that Timon's loss of an eye is inferred by Diogenes (ἐπεί) from his calling himself a Cyclops. In that case, I prefer to read Timon's 'Cyclopean' nature as a comment by Timon on his own moral thinking.[110] The Cyclopes figure elsewhere in Greek moral thinking, and tend to represent a state of low social and political development. They also share some aspects of 'Golden Age' imagery. In Homer, for example, their island spontaneously generates crops (*Od.* 9.109–10). As such they are the object of some discussion: are they bestial, proto-human, or in some ways close to divinity? This can be seen not only in Euripides' satyr play, the *Cyclops*,[111] but also in the scholia to Homer *Odyssey* 9.105ff.

Particular attention is paid by the scholiasts to the description of the Cyclopes at 9.106 as 'without laws', ἀθέμιστοι, which they generally link to line 9.114–15:

θεμιστεύει δὲ ἕκαστος
παίδων ἠδ' ἀλόχων, οὐδ' ἀλλήλων ἀλέγουσι.[112]

Each lays down the law for his children and wives, and they do not have any regard for one another.

To be a Cyclops is to be one's own moral legislator. Here we should certainly feel echoes of Anaxarchus' picture of Alexander the Great legislating for the subjects under his sway. Without such power relationships all humans are in the moral world of the Cyclopes, each dictating norms to himself and his family.[113]

---

[110] Di Marco (1989) 5 is unconvincing: 'E prova di indifferenza, se dobbiamo credere a quanto ci viene riferito, egli diede anche in relazione ai propri difetti fisici: pur essendo orbo, infatti, trovava il modo di scherzarvi su, fino al punto di autodefinirsi "Ciclope".'

[111] Cf. Seaford (1984) 54–5.

[112] *ad.* 9.105: ἀθεμίστους δὲ τοὺς μὴ νόμῳ χρωμένους ἐγγράφως διὰ τὸ ἕκαστον ἴδιον ἄρχεσθαι. *ad.* 9.115: οὐ φροντίζουσιν ἀλλήλων ὅσον ἕνεκεν ὑποταγῆς. ἕκαστον γὰρ αὐτοκράτωρ ἐστὶ καὶ οὐχ ὑποτάσσεται τῷ ἑτέρῳ.

[113] Cf. Arist. *EN* 1180a24ff. Immediately after the introduction of the nickname at 9.112 Diogenes tells us that Antigonus characterised Timon as ἰδιοπράγμων.

Of course, the loss of sight, whether partial or total, cannot fail to have epistemological overtones as well as the moral tone of how one bears such a loss. It is instructive to compare the biographical tradition surrounding Democritus. Cicero (*Tusc.* 5.114) has this interpretation of Democritus' blindness:

luminibus amissis alba scilicet discernere et atra non poterat: at vero bona mala, aequa iniqua, honesta turpia, utilia inutilia, magna parva poterat, et sine varietate colorum licebat vivere beate, sine notione rerum non licebat. atque hic vir impediri etiam animi aciem aspectu oculorum arbitrabatur, et cum alii saepe quod ante pedes esset non viderent, ille in infinitatem omnem peregrinabatur, ut nulla in extremitate consisteret.[114]

When he lost his eyes, no doubt he could not tell apart white and black. But he *was* able to discern what was good and bad, virtuous and vicious, useful and useless, great and small. And he could live a happy life even without the variety of colours – but he couldn't do so without any conception of things. But this man thought that the power of his mind was even hindered by his eyesight, and while others often failed to see what was at their feet, he travelled across the whole infinite expanse, stopping at no boundary.

Democritus was free from the constraints of sense-perception and was able instead to range with his mind without the obstacles and impediments which hamper those who are sighted but who nevertheless do not 'see' what is at their feet. Note that Democritus' blindness is probably inspired by his metaphysical pronouncements concerning the status of secondary perceptible qualities: *alba et atra* belong to the class of things which are merely 'by convention' in Democritus' fragment B9.[115] The blind Democritus is free to peer into things 'in truth' – although here, unlike B9's reference to atoms and void as what exist 'in truth', Cicero also includes moral properties. Also, we should consider the last sentence in the general tradition of the *topos* of the distracted philosopher who cannot see what lies at his feet, and who risks falling into a well or off a cliff (e.g. Thales in Pl. *Theat.* 174a4). While Pyrrho could see but either did not believe what he saw, or did not care if he fell (above p. 110), Democritus is unable to see but for that reason

---

[114] In some stories Democritus deliberately blinded himself, e.g. Aul. Gell. 10.17. Plut. *De curios.* 521D claims that is untrue. Cicero *Fin.* 5.87 is unsure.
[115] Noted by Salem (1996) 155–7.

is able metaphorically to range unimpeded in thought through his atomic universe, leaving the sighted to stumble in his wake.[116]

If, besides the ethical connotations I have outlined, Timon's 'Cyclopic' nature may also have been supposed to recall his having only one eye, it too can be placed in an epistemological context. Perhaps to live 'with both eyes open' is to live with some acceptance of what our senses tell us. If Timon called himself 'one-eyed', or was later styled so, could this not be seen as a similar image, of someone who lives without full and uncritical acceptance of sense-impressions, but who nevertheless recognised the inevitable phenomena of experience? That at least seems to be Timon's position as revealed in this fragment of the *On Senses*, in which he agrees that honey appears sweet but does not conclude that it is so (DL 9.105, cited above, p. 99).

---

[116] Cf. Lucr. *DRN* 1.72ff.: Epicurus *extra/processit longe flammantia moenia mundi/atque omne immensum peragravit mente animoque . . .*

5

POLYSTRATUS AND EPICUREAN PIGS

In what has now become known as the 'cradle argument', Epicurus pointed to the behaviour of pre-rational human babies and animals in order to show that pleasure was that at which every living thing naturally aimed. He claimed that they naturally and without any opinions about questions of value seek pleasure. (A number of sources report this argument: Cic. *Fin.* 1.29–30, 2.31–3, 2.109; SE *M.* 11.96–7; DL 10.137.)[1] By taking such a line, however, Epicurus may set for himself a problem similar to that identified in the case of Pyrrho. The point Epicurus wishes to press home is that in the case of these infants and animals – two classes of beings which do not hold, or are not yet capable of holding, mistaken opinions about what to aim for – we can see that there is a natural drive towards pleasure, which can therefore be installed as the natural goal of life. Our task, therefore, is in some sense to approximate to this state once again, and rid ourselves of the mistaken opinions which cloud our general opinions about what should be valued. In general, we no longer aim as a baby or a pig 'naturally and without reasoning' (φυσικῶς χωρὶς λόγου, DL 10.137) for what is simply pleasant. Now, in just what sense is Epicurus extolling this uncorrupted state? Is he, like Pyrrho before him, intending us to strip away the human, and reduce ourselves to this level? If so, then he has indeed set himself a difficulty. If the uncorrupted natural state of a baby is the ideal, surely it is unattainable once we have got as far as to be able to listen to Epicurus' argument – since in order to do that we must be in a position to exercise our reason, and no longer be free of corrupting opinions. To avoid this difficulty, we must see in just what sense Epicurus does extol the natural state of an infant or animal – and by doing this we can begin to distinguish his view from that of Pyrrho.

---

[1] See on this argument: Brunschwig (1986); cf. Sedley (1996) 319–21.

Like Pyrrho, Epicurus maintains that not all of the desires which we feel in our everyday lives are natural or necessary (*Ep. Men.* 127). Nor must we satisfy them all in order to attain happiness:

τούτου γὰρ χάριν πάντα πράττομεν, ὅπως μήτε ἀλγῶμεν μήτε ταρβῶμεν· ὅταν δ' ἅπαξ τοῦτο περὶ ἡμᾶς γένηται λυέται πᾶς ὁ τῆς ψυχῆς χειμών, οὐκ ἔχοντος τοῦ ζῴου βαδίζειν ὡς πρὸς ἐνδέον τι καὶ ζητεῖν ἕτερον ᾧ τὸ τῆς ψυχῆς καὶ τοῦ σώματος ἀγαθὸν συμπληρωθήσεται. (*Ep. Men.* 128)

For it is for the sake of this that we do everything – so that we may feel neither pain nor anxiety. And as soon as we achieve this, the whole storm of the soul is calmed, since the animal cannot go off as if towards something it needs and in pursuit of something else with which the good of the body and soul will be fulfilled.

Here Epicurus returns to the image of *galēnē* seen both in Democritus' conception of the good life (DL 9.45) and in the Pyrrhonian anecdote of the sea-voyage (DL 9.68). An ataraxic Epicurean is *galēnos*, because his desires can always be satisfied. This does not entail, however, that an Epicurean's desires and psychological capacities are those of a pig. For example, Epicurus is adamant about the need for friendship in the good life (*KD* 27) – something of which animals are not capable (see *KD* 32). Also, *KD* 20 states unequivocally that *reason* is necessary to drive out empty desires. Epicurus therefore does not want us to return to the cradle or the sty, for then we would miss the pleasures of friendship and philosophy.[2]

It is made clear in the fifth book of Lucretius' *De rerum natura* that the bestial state of the early humans is not to be admired. Living *more ferarum* (5.932), they remain *miseri* (944), since they are still unable to consider the common good, or fashion laws and communities (958–9). Indeed, these miserable early humans are explicitly compared to swine:

saetigerisque pares subus silvestria membra
nuda dabant terrae nocturno tempore capti. (5.970–1)

Like hairy boars they would lay their naked bodies down to earth in the woods, overcome by night-time.

---

[2] Nussbaum (1994) 109–10 insists on a more primitivist version of Epicurus than I would accept.

This is no idyllic 'city of pigs', however, like Socrates' first Republic (at Pl. *Rep.* 372d4). These humans live a harsh and difficult life, since they have not yet learned to make maximal use of their rational capacities in the provision of the necessary goods and context for the attainment of *ataraxia*.[3] Indeed these piggish humans are attacked and driven off only a few lines later by a 'frothing boar' (*spumiger sus,* 985): they cannot organise themselves sufficiently to defend against their fellow swine. Pigs cannot make contracts of non-aggression against each other (*KD* 32), but humans must cooperate in producing the required conditions for the good life, basic security against wild beasts included.

Despite such clear indications that the Epicurean good life is a life which requires the use of reason and includes the pleasures of human friendship and community, by setting up a form of pleasure, of desire-satisfaction, as the highest state for human attainment, and declaring this to be true *eudaimonia* Epicurus laid himself open to attacks which ridicule his hedonism as reducing us to the level of the lower animals, concerned only with the bliss of a full stomach.[4]

On one of a pair of silver cups from Boscoreale (around 30 AD) skeletal figures represent the various contemporary philosophical schools. On the first cup, a pair of philosophers is depicted (see fig. 2). The identity of the figure on the left, gesticulating as if in heated debate, is a little unclear, but he is usually thought to be a Stoic since the figure is labelled 'ZENO' although the staff and wallet he carries are more usual in Cynic portraits. He is disagreeing with Epicurus on the right. This latter figure is not only intent on the meal in the pot at the centre of the picture (above which is written an Epicurean tag: 'pleasure is the *telos*'), but he is identified as a hedonist also by the presence of the pot-bellied pig jumping up to smell the cooking. By this time, in conjunction with the explanatory tag, it seems that the cooking pot and greedy pig are as common identifiers of Epicureanism as the staff, wallet, and dog are of a Cynic.[5] Piggish-ness becomes a philosophical insult.

---

[3] See Dierauer (1977) 28.   [4] See e.g. SE *M.* 11.97.

[5] Zanker (1995) 209–10 suggests that the cup pokes fun at intellectuals by claiming that no amount of philosophising can ward off death. Cf. Scatozza-Höricht (1986) 157, 164; Erler and Schofield (1999) 642.

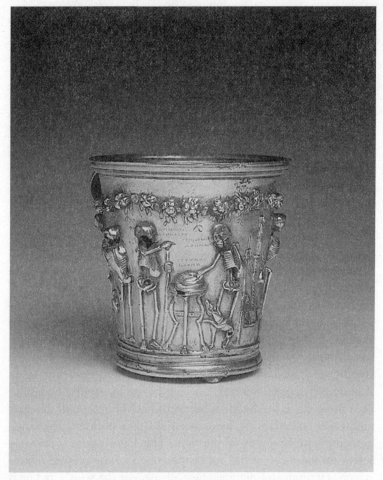

Fig. 2   A silver cup from Boscoreale depicting a pair of philosophers in debate, one of whom is Epicurus. AD 30.

A hedonist, who furthermore would make all pleasure physical in as much as it is based in motions of a corporeal soul, can be mistaken for someone who makes all pleasures physical in the sense of solely concerned with the fulfilment of bodily desires.[6]

---

[6] Mill (1861) ch. 2: 'The Epicureans have always answered that it is not they, but their accusers, who represent human nature in a degrading light; since the accusation supposes human beings to be capable of no pleasures except those of which swine are capable. If

Fig. 3   Statue of a pig from the Villa of the Papyri, Herculaneum.

Just as Pyrrho seems to have done, Epicurus and later Epicureans may have reappropriated the pig as a positive symbol of the *ataraxia* which they promoted. Although the pig on the Boscoreale cup seems to be indicative only of gluttony, a bronze pig with raised forelegs was discovered as part of the sculptural decoration of the Villa of the Papyri at Herculaneum (see fig. 3). This villa was the

this superstition were true, the charge could not be gainsaid, but would then be no longer an imputation; for if the sources of pleasure were precisely the same to human beings and to swine, the rule of life which is good enough for the one would be good enough for the other. The comparison of the Epicurean life to that of beasts is felt as degrading, precisely because a beast's pleasures do not satisfy a human being's conception of happiness. Human beings have faculties more elevated than the human appetites, and when once made conscious of them, do not regard anything as happiness which does not include their gratification. But there is no known Epicurean theory of life which does not assign to the pleasures of the intellect, of the feelings and imagination, and of the moral sentiments, a much higher value as pleasures than to those of mere sensation.' This position owes much to Mill's insistence on a qualitative distinction between 'higher' and 'lower' pleasures, not shared by Epicurus: Edwards (1979) esp. 30–48. Compare Russell (1957) 117.

focal point for a Campanian group of Epicureans, among them Philodemus. If the pig here is, as Gigante suggests, a 'well known Epicurean symbol',[7] then one would expect it to be a positive symbol of *ataraxia* rather than the mascot of a gluttonous hedonist.[8] The Epicurean pig, when used as a positive symbol, recalls only the tranquil state of that animal rather than its psychological incapacities. Epicurus insists that we become like pigs only in so far as we should strive for tranquillity. The Roman poet Horace is even able to claim defiantly that he is happy to be called 'a pig from Epicurus' sty' (*Ep.* 1.4.16).[9]

It might be possible to locate historically the origin of the 'pig' accusation against Epicurean hedonism. Much of the negative propaganda surrounding the school seems to derive from the disgruntled student Timocrates, the brother of Metrodorus, who left the Garden and dedicated some effort to spoiling Epicurus' reputation.[10] Diogenes Laërtius (10.4) notes that he wrote a work impugning Epicurus' Athenian citizenship, and Plutarch (*Non posse* 1098C–D) cites sections of a letter from Metrodorus to his brother Timocrates of which the latter seems to have made public certain carefully edited quotations. Diogenes cites a work of Timocrates where he claims that Epicurus vomited twice a day from over-indulgence (10.6), and the mention of two works by Epicurus and others by Metrodorus against Timocrates make it clear that a definite public-relations battle is being waged over just what kind of 'piggishness' Epicurus is extolling. This battle occurs within the first generation of the school.

With that we return to Pyrrho, or rather to 'Pyrrhonism' as interpreted by Timon. A fragment of his *Silloi* (fr. 7 Diels), which seems to use as its source, and even to echo the wording of, Timocrates' edited letter from Metrodorus (e.g. the term γαστρὶ χαρίζεσθαι found *apud* Plut. *Non posse* 1098C–D), attacks Epicurus, Timon's

[7] Gigante (1996) 10 and n. 43. But contrast the view of Gigante (1981) 46 on DL 9.68.

[8] Pandermalis (1983) suggests a special Epicurean relevance. Wojcik (1986) 124 disagrees. Sider (1997) 16 n.13 points to *POxy.* 3724 viii.7 (an anthology of first lines of Greek epigrams, many of which are Philodeman) where Rea restores ... τὸν θ' ὑικόν.

[9] The word for sty, *grex*, was often used as a term for a philosophical school, e.g. Cic. *Fin.* 1.65. The pun here in Horace is intentional.

[10] Sedley (1976a) 127ff.

elder contemporary, for 'pleasing the stomach – the most greedy thing of all' (γαστρὶ χαριζόμενος τῆς οὐ λαμυρώτερον οὐδέν).[11] Here we see evidence of the early divergence of Pyrrho's followers descending from Timon and those of Epicurus. This divergence would lead to both Aenesideman and Sextan Pyrrhonists and Epicureans espousing *ataraxia* as the ethical goal, but is attainable now by very different routes; one attacking the other's 'gluttony', the other claiming that scepticism was absurd and self-refuting.

One further fragment of Timon is often cited in support of the general conception of a strict division and polemical relationship between the Pyrrhonians and Epicureans:

ὕστατος αὖ φυσικῶν καὶ κύντατος ἐκ Σάμου ἐλθών
γραμμοδιδασκαλίδης[12] ἀναγωγότατος ζωόντων. (Timon fr. 51 Diels)

The most recent, most piggish, most doggish came from Samos – Son of School Teacher, the most uneducated of all creatures.

The first word is a pun. Epicurus is the last (most recent) and most 'piggish' of the philosophers. The possible ambiguity of the 'pig' accusation is reinforced by the related adjective, 'most doggish': κύντατος. Of course, there is plenty of evidence for the negative image of the stupid, gluttonous pig, and for a similarly negative image of the dog.[13] However, neither adjective is necessarily so univocally critical.[14] There are good reasons for rescuing a more ambivalent meaning. First there is the possible Cynic influence on Pyrrho. Second, recall the use of the phrase 'dogged strength'

---

[11] Athenaeus cites this at 279F and notes its anti-Epicurean nature. Compare *SV* 59, *KD* 20, and Us. 409: ἀρχὴ καὶ ῥίζα παντὸς ἀγαθοῦ ἡ τῆς γαστρὸς ἡδονή. On γαστήρ and its connotations: Gargiulo (1982). While λαμυρός comes to mean 'greedy', LSJ note that its primary sense is 'full of abysses' like the sea. The stomach therefore is the enemy of γαλήνη: Di Marco (1989) 127ff. Hipponax fr. 126 Degani mentions τὴν ποντοχάρυβδιν τὴν ἐγγαστριμάχαιαν ὅς ἐσθίει οὐ κατὰ κόσμον. At DL 6.51 Diogenes the Cynic τὴν γαστέρα Χάρυβδιν ἔλεγε τοῦ βίου.

[12] On γραμμοδιδασκαλίδης: Di Marco (1982).

[13] For a 'critical' reading, see Di Marco (1983) and (1989) ad loc. Similarly, De Martino (1986), who also remarks on the Samian's famed use of boar's-head rams on their ships (Plut. *Per.* 26.4; Choirilos of Samos 322 L-JP). Choirilos (little χοῖρος?) also puns on the word ὕστατοι in the proem of his *Persica* (317 L-JP). Cf. Pl. *Pol.* 266d8 and Shorey (1917).

[14] Noted by Lilja (1976) 126, cf. 34–6. Cf. Di Marco (1983) 67 n. 16.

(κυνέον μένος) in fr. 58's description of Anaxarchus, which does not give a wholehearted condemnation of Pyrrho's mentor (above p. 81). Similarly, given Pyrrho's own apparent use of a pig as a positive model, for Timon to call Epicurus this is perhaps not so unreservedly critical.

Like some other philosophers, Epicurus may, in Timon's eyes, have been not entirely without merit. After all, he did profess something like the same ethical end as Timon himself did, and Pyrrho had done. Timon's ambivalent attitude to Epicurus – reflected in these ambivalent epithets – is appropriate to the relationship between the two thinkers. Epicurus had (despite his protestations otherwise) been influenced by Nausiphanes, himself an admirer of Pyrrho, but whose interpretation of Pyrrho appears to have been opposed to that of Timon. Despite their vast differences on epistemological issues, Epicurus and Timon were perhaps not such bitter or irreconcilable enemies. Our reading of this fragment of the *Silloi* should in that case reflect their ambivalent relationship. What bitterness we find in their mutual polemics is driven by the combination of their similarities and differences.

In the examples of Epicurean pigs we see confirmed both stereotypical images of pigs identifiable from Plato and Pyrrho. The pig is an amoral, unintellectual glutton, and also a symbol of *ataraxia*. We have, perhaps, also seen an unexpected example of the influence which Pyrrho exerted over Epicurus. We can also provide further evidence of a common source in Pyrrho of the two strands of thought which were later to be articulated by Pyrrhonist (i.e. Aenesideman) ethico-epistemology, and Epicurean hedonism, both of which aim at the now apparently 'porcine' goal of *ataraxia*.

Epicurus admires the disposition or *diathesis* of the happy pig, but – unlike Pyrrho – recognises that it is not desirable to rid oneself, as a human, of all those rational psychological capacities which provide mental pleasures, allow one to use memory and future-directed planning, to reason and argue and so on.[15] Pyrrho advocates a life that is not recognisably 'human', at least in some of the more extreme anecdotal evidence. We should live entirely according to instinct and habit. Reason produces anxiety.

[15] Cf. Mitsis (1988) 42.

This distinction, at least the Epicurean side of it, can be supported with two Epicurean texts. The first of these is Polystratus' *On irrational contempt for common conceptions* (περὶ ἀλόγου καταφρονήσεως or *De contemptu irrationali*, found on *PHerc.* 336/1150). The relevant portion of Polystratus' text is the very opening of what has been preserved on the Herculaneum papyri, and is particularly poorly preserved. However, the overall argument seems to proceed as follows. Polystratus is attacking the position that, since animals have no conception of the gods, human conceptions of the gods have no ethical force. This position rests on the assumption that human and animal psychologies are relevantly similar and that therefore if animals do not develop a conception of the gods, then such a conception is neither necessary nor natural. Polystratus' defence of the Epicurean insistence on the natural and necessary construction of a conception and recognition of the gods' existence by humans therefore rests on distinguishing human from animal souls. The former can recognise and form preconceptions of the gods while the latter cannot. Polystratus can then conclude that what animals cannot do has no bearing on the status of Epicureans' insistence on the existence of the gods.[16] Polystratus goes on in the better preserved later sections of the work (e.g. cols. VI–VII) to continue his insistence on the important distinctions to be made between human and animal psychological abilities.

The opening of the extant text is in a poor state and much of the exact reconstruction of it must remain highly speculative. I therefore give Indelli's text, but have removed some of the longer editorial additions.

[... δυνατόν ἐστι καὶ τοῖς ζώιοις ὑπ|άρχ]ειν [ἕ]καστα τού|των, ἀλλ᾽ οὐ συνορᾶται | ὑπ᾽ [α]ὑτῶν· ἢ οὐδ᾽ ὑγιει|νὰ καὶ νοσ[ε]ρὰ καὶ ἄλλα | συμφέροντα καὶ ἀσύμ||[φορα- - -]| ...

... ὁ αὐ[[μασ]]||τὸς {ὁ} λόγ[ο]ς ἐφαρμόσει.| ἔστι γὰρ πάντα ταῦτα, φή|σει τις, κἀκείνοις, ἀλλ᾽ οὐ... [... οὔτε διὰ ση]||μείων εὑ[ρεῖν οὔ]τε δι᾽ ἄλ|λου τρόπου ἀπὸ τῆς αὑ|τῆς αἰτίας. ὅθεν οὐδ᾽ εὐ|λαβεῖσθαι πρὸ τοῦ παθεῖν | [ἐκεῖνα] δύνατα[ι, οὔ|τε τὰ παρελθ]όντα μνη||[μ]ονε[ύειν] ὥστε μὴ πά|λιν

---

[16] Cf. Polyst. v.26ff., vi.25ff.; for the reconstruction of the argument see Kleve (1963) 30–2, Indelli (1978) 145, Zacher (1982) 219, Annas (1993c) 68–9.

περιπ[εί]πτειν, οὔ|τε τὰ συμ[φ]ε|ροντα πο|ρίζεσθαι ἐφ' [ὅ]σα μήθ' αὐ|τῆι . . .
(I–IV Indelli (with omissions))

[. . . it is possible] that each of these [exists for animals also], but it is not reflected
upon by them, or things which are healthy or unhealthy and other beneficial or
harmful things . . .

. . . the self-same argument will apply in every case. For there are all the same
things for them too, someone might say, but not . . . nor [can they] make discoveries
[through] signs nor in any other way for the same reason. For this reason, neither
can they take precautions in anticipation of [these] sufferings nor recollect things
past to prevent them occurring once more, nor provide things of benefit in so far
as not . . .

Despite the textual difficulties, there is a relatively clear insistence on the psychic differences between humans and animals which are then led to produce implications for the relative
happiness of the two groups. Polystratus begins by conced-
ing that health and illness, and in general things of benefit or
harm might apply to animals but insists that these states are
not understood or dwelt upon (συνορᾶται) by them.[17] An animal might be healthy but will not reflect on this state. The
rest of the passage explores the consequence of this psychological handicap. The opponent might see this as a concession in his favour: animals suffer but are spared the occasion
of dwelling upon, or even dreading in advance their suffering.
Polystratus, however, contends that this psychological incapac-
ity counts *against* animal happiness. They are not able to be
aware and take care (εὐλαβεῖσθαι) in the face of suffering, nor
are they able to remember past events in order to avoid their
recurrence, nor actively provide things of benefit. Animals are
affected by health and illness just as humans are, but a pig
with renal calculus, say, would be entirely incapable of the kind
of recollection techniques which allowed Epicurus, when suffering from the same illness, to remain in a state of *ataraxia*
(DL 10.22).[18]

The second Epicurean text which deals with this issue is also preserved – in a rather better state – in the Herculaneum papyri, namely

---

[17] See Annas (1993c) 68 and n. 51; (1992) 135. Polystratus restates this claim using the
same vocabulary at col. VII. 4–5.
[18] Cf. Philippson (1909) 491.

the first book of Philodemus' *On the gods* (*PHerc.* 26). Col. XII imagines an objection by one of an unnamed group of people (ἰδιῶται, XII.2 Diels) who claims that animals are happier than humans because they are not disturbed by theological worries. This lack of worry is presumably linked to their inability to reason whether in fact there is a god and so on.[19] However, Philodemus is quick to resist this objection (XII.19–23 Diels). Rather than being assailed by less anxiety, Philodemus replies that animals suffer just the same sorts of worry and disturbance as humans,[20] but for animals this disturbance is deeper rooted (πολὺ σφοδροτέρ[αν] οὖσαν, XII.21), because they lack the capacity for correct reason which Epicureans regard as a necessary condition for the removal of anxiety. These two themes – that animals suffer no less disturbance than humans, and are less capable of soothing that disturbance – are then pursued through the subsequent text.[21]

Philodemus restates the claim that animals are happier than humans and makes his disagreement clearer at XV.16–33:

πολλῶν | ζῷα [μα]καριζ[όν]των ἐπὶ ταλαιπ[ω]ρισ|μῶι τοῦ παντὸς αὐτῶν βίου κατὰ τἆλ|λα καὶ κατὰ τὸ μηδὲ γεινώσκειν θεούς | ὑπὲρ ὧν ἡμ[εῖ]ς τ[οι]αύταις πεφύκαμεν | συνέχεσθαι φρείκαις, ὁ διαλογισμὸς οὗτος [ἀ]|φαιρ[εῖ] τε τὸ προσ[ε]πισωρευόμενον βά|ρος, ἐνφανίζων ὅτι ταῖς ἀναλόγοις κἀκε[ῖ]|να συζῇ καὶ προσέτ[ι διδ]άσκων ὅτι καὶ | μείζοσιν κατά τ[ι]να τρόπ[ο]ν, ἀλλὰ δὴ κα[ὶ] | τὸ μακάριον, ὅτι τοῖς [μ]ὲν ἀθεράπευτός | ἐστιν ἡ [τα]ραχή, [μ]έχρι<ς> ἂν τὴν τοιαύτην | φύσιν ἔ[χηι], τοῖς δ' ἀνθρώποις ὁ λογισμός, | ὥσπερ οἷος τ' ἦν ε[ἰ]ς ἄπειρο[ν ἐκβάλλειν] | καὶ τ[ὸ] δεινὸν καὶ τὸ [μά]λα φαῦλον, οὕτω δ[ύ]|ναται [τ]ά [τε] πάθη κα[ὶ τ]ὴν τῶν ὀλίων ὕ|παρξιν κατανοήσας τὸ[[ι]] μὲν εὐκατα|φρόνητον ἡγήσασθαι, τὸ δ' εὐποριστότ[α]τον.

Many people count animals as happy, because of the miserable nature of their own lives in other respects and because of their (the animals) not knowing the gods, on account of whom we humans naturally are embraced by such anxieties. But this reasoning removes the additional burden by making it evident that those animals too live with similar (anxieties), further informing us that in a certain way these anxieties are greater, and it removes the (animals') happiness too because their disturbance is incurable, so long as they have such a nature, whereas humans possess reason which, just as it is able to extend to infinity both what is terrible and exceedingly bad, so, having recognised the affects and the availability of the few aids of life,[22] can consider one easy to despise, the other most easy to procure.

[19] Cf. Plut. *Non posse* 1092B; Adam (1974) 37–8 and n. 81; Dierauer (1977) 197.
[20] Cf. Philod. *De piet.* 235–8 Obbink.   [21] Cf. esp. XIII.1–7, 16–22, 29–41.
[22] Cf. Diels (1916) 73.

The identity of those who are convinced of the happiness of animals is vague, but they are said to be numerous. This is not too surprising, since the *topos* of the 'happy beast' was not uncommon.[23] However Philodemus' opponent expands and explains this common conception with some argument. Animals are happier because they have no conception of the gods, on account of which we humans naturally tend to be disturbed. The objector's reasoning, while pointing out the supposed additional burden to human anxiety, namely the realisation that 'animals are happier than humans', proceeds on Philodemus' view to undermine and remove that very claim. Philodemus turns the reasons for the objector's claim against his thesis, by pointing out why animals' lack of particular psychological capacities counts against rather than for their chances of happiness.[24]

He first asserts that animals do suffer disturbances (ταραχαί). It is not necessary in order for an animal to suffer disturbance that it be rational, nor *a fortiori* that it must have disturbing thoughts about the gods. Furthermore, animals' anxieties are greater in one particular respect. Their lack of reason prevents them from doing any philosophy, from arguing away their fears (τοῖς [μ]ὲν ἀθεράπευτός | ἐστιν ἡ [τα]ραχή). For Philodemus, as for Polystratus, *logismos*, a specifically human trait, is a necessary tool for the attainment of happiness.[25] Irrational animals are, by definition, unable to reach that goal.

The Epicureans' statement of their views seems to have provoked a response, which can be seen in a work by Plutarch – himself a vociferous critic of Epicureanism in general. During his extended critique of Epicurean hedonism, Plutarch restates the position attacked by Philodemus, namely that animals are in no worse a position with regard to physical pleasures, and are indeed less susceptible to mental anxieties – specifically those related to the gods, and to death (*Non posse* 1091Cff., esp. 1092A–B).[26] This line of argument is also used by Plutarch in his witty dialogue,

---

[23] See the sources collected in Lovejoy and Boas (1965).
[24] For this interpretation of the argument see Diels (1916) 73.
[25] As noted by Dierauer (1977) 196ff.
[26] Cf. Adam (1974) 35–8; cp. Cic. *Fin.* 2.109–11.

Bruta ratione uti, also named *Gryllus* after its main speaker.[27] This short – and probably incomplete – dialogue has a Homeric setting. Odysseus has come to rescue his men from the spell of Circe. Before the witch releases her enchantment, however, she allows one of the man-pigs (Gryllus) to speak. There follows a brief discussion of whether humans or animals are the happiest or the most virtuous, and the dialogue is suffused with pointers to and parodies of Epicurean tenets.[28]

Surprisingly, Plutarch's dialogue has never before been discussed in relation to the Pyrrhonian suggestion that we should strive to 'strip away the human'. An influential article suggested that Plutarch's *Gryllus* was a response to Polystratus' *On irrational contempt*, further conjecturing that Polystratus' main opponents were Cynics, and that Plutarch drew his work from an earlier Cynic original.[29] The existence of a Cynic original of Plutarch's dialogue is a hypothesis based on the supposition that Polystratus' single opponent in *On irrational contempt* is a Cynic. However, the comparison of human and animal lives is not an exclusively Cynic practice, nor is the form of Plutarch's dialogue necessarily Cynic in origin.[30] Further, the Cynics are mentioned by name only at XXI.8, and in any case there is no reason to think that the opponents of Polystratus' text belong to a single school.[31] So there is no reason to suppose a Cynic prototype for Plutarch's work.

Once freed from the conviction that Polystratus is attacking – and Plutarch defending – only the Cynics, we are in a position to see a wider range of opponents in the Epicurean's sights. One of those opponents could be Pyrrho, who would indeed deny that anything is good or bad 'in nature', a thesis which Polystratus attacks

---

[27] For an introduction to this dialogue: Kidd (1992) 375–82. The most recent edition is by Indelli (1995).

[28] See Usener (1887) lxx–lxxi, Indelli (1995) 23–34.

[29] Philippson (1909), esp. 507–9. Philippson's insistence on this point was partly due to his acceptance of a reference to Bion in Polystratus' περὶ φιλοσοφίας (*PHerc.* 1520). Capasso now reads τῶι βίωι rather than τῶι βίωνι: (1976) 81, 84 and n. 26.

[30] *Contra* Dierauer (1977) 188.

[31] Cf. Indelli (1977), (1978) 53–4, (1996) 948–9. Cf. Gigante (1981) 102–6, (1990) 81, (1992) 81–2. Sedley (1983c) argues that Polystratus' opponents are Arcesilaan Academics; cf. Ioppolo (1986) 187–9.

at XXI.18–XXIX.1.[32] What admiration Epicurus did have for Pyrrho was certainly not unequivocal and there is little reason on these grounds to exempt Pyrrho from all of Polystratus' accusations. In support of this suggestion, I would also emphasise the choice of subject of Plutarch's *Gryllus*: a pig.[33] We know that Plutarch was aware of the Posidonian anecdote of Pyrrho and the storm-tossed pig, since Plutarch refers to it in one of his works, and can therefore be alluding to both Pyrrho's idealisation of the pig and also the Epicureans' arguments – preserved by Polystratus – against such idealisation of animals to the detriment of human powers of reason.[34] So by producing a dialogue in which he makes a pig discuss happiness with the man of reason *par excellence*, Odysseus, Plutarch can display the greatest possible division between humans and animals: the most rational and the least rational.[35] Thus it is a fitting and witty way in which to dramatise the philosophical discussion, and also a fitting and illuminating way for us to imagine the distinction between Epicurean 'rational' tranquillity and Pyrrhonian 'instinctive' tranquillity, both of which might turn to the happy pig as a model and an ideal, but with very different conceptions of the psychology underlying that desired tranquillity.

In the same work – *On irrational contempt* – Polystratus also produces a fine refutation of a view not unlike that we have found attributed to Pyrrho and Anaxarchus. Polystratus offers an argument against some unnamed opponents who argue that certain things, particularly moral properties, cannot be part of the fabric of the world. The terms in which this debate is originally played

---

[32] Wilke (1905) xiii–xvii suggests that οἱ ἀπαθεῖς (XXI.8) are Pyrrhonian sceptics. At XXI.17ff. Polystratus attacks those who deny that anything is good or bad φύσει. Cf. Indelli (1978) 57–66, Decleva Caizzi (1986) 157ff.

[33] Indelli (1996) 940 n. 6; Hesychius s.v. γρύλλος· χοῖρος, γρύλλη· ἡ ὑῶν φωνή. Philodemus uses the verb γρυλλογραφεῖν in the *Rhet.* (*PHerc.* 468 fr. 6 Sudhaus vol. II, 297), but *contra* Usener (s.v. *Glossarium Epicureum*) this does not mean '*porcos pingere*' but 'to draw a caricature': Plin. *NH* 35.114.

[34] Plut. *Prof. in virt.* 82F.

[35] Twice Plutarch refers to a proverb 'a sow might as well teach Athena' which conveys the same idea: *Praec. ger. reip.* 803D, *Dem.* 11.5. In the *Gryllus* a pig corrects Athena's favourite hero.

are those familiar from the *nomos / physis* contrast – between what is 'in nature', and what is 'merely conventional'. These opponents argue that certain putative existents are not independently in the nature of things, but are merely by convention.

ψευδής ἐστι ἡ δόξα τῶν οὔτε κα|λὸν οὔτε αἰσχρ]ὸν οὔτε [ἄλλο ἁπ]λῶ[ς τῶ]ν τοιού|[των] οὐθὲν [φ]ασκόντων | [εἶναι, ἐ]πεὶ[δ]ὴ οὐχ ὥσπε[ρ | λ]ίθ[ος κ]αὶ χ[ρ]υ[σ]ὸς καὶ τὰ | [ὅ]μο[ια] τούτοις, ὧν φα|μεν φύσει, οὐ νόμωι ἔ|[κ]αστον ὑπάρχειν, οὕτω | [κ]αὶ ταῦτα π[ᾶ]σιν τὰ αὐτὰ | ἐστιν, ἀλλ' ἄλλοις ἄλλα. [ο]ὐ|θὲν γὰρ τούτων εἶναι | κατ' ἀλήθειαν· δεῖν γάρ || εἴπερ ἦν, ὥσπ[ερ] ὁ κατ' ἀ|λήθ[ε]ιαν χαλκὸ[ς ἢ χ]ρυσὸς | πᾶσ[ι] καὶ παντα[χοῦ] ὁμοί|ως ἐ[σ]τίν, καὶ οὐ τ[ῶι]δε | μέν ἐστίν χαλκός, <τ>ῶιδε | δ' οὔ, οὐδ' ἐμ μὲν <τ>ούτωι | τῶι ἔθνει ἐστίν, [ἐ]ν δ[ὲ τοῖς] | λοιποῖς οὐκέτι, [ἀλλὰ παν]|ταχοῦ ὁμοίως, οὕ[τω κ]αὶ | τὰ καλὰ καὶ τὰ α[ἰσχρά, ε]ἴ|περ κατ' ἀλήθειαν ἦν], οὐ τῶ<ι>δε μὲν δι[ώ]κε[σθαι], | τῶι[δε δ'] οὐκέ[τι] ὠ[μολ]ο|[γῆσθαι] . . . (XXI.18–XXII.18)

[False is the opinion of those who say that neither the fine, nor the foul,] nor generally any of the other things of that sort exist because they are unlike stone and gold and similar things, each of which we say exists by nature and not by convention as these are the same to all and not different to different people. For none of these [sc. the fine etc.] exist in truth. For if they were to exist they would have to be like bronze or stone and the same to all and everywhere. Bronze is not bronze to one and not to another, nor to one tribe and not the others but is everywhere the same. Just so, if fine things and foul things existed truly they would not be such to one but not agreed upon by another . . .

The opponents have set a particular requirement on things if they are truly to exist. If something is to exist, then it must be the same to all people everywhere, and presumably, although this is not stated explicitly in the text, at all times. In this way bronze is bronze no matter who uses it, or where, or when.

This is contrasted with 'the fine' (*to kalon*). Different tribes of people, indeed even different individuals, will have a different notion of what is fine (again, this holds regardless of the particular word used to express the notion of '*kalon*'). So, these people claim, we cannot make a case for 'the fine' to be inscribed on the list of things which make up the world, since it fails the requirement of universal consistency.

It is worth noting at this stage that the debate centres on ethical properties such as *to kalon*, since it explains to some degree Polystratus' motivation in trying to rescue the existence of some of the things which fail the universal consistency requirement.[36] Polystratus, as an Epicurean, is committed to a dogmatic stance on what would provide for the good of a human. That is merely to say that as an Epicurean he has a particular ethical theory which he believes to be true, and which he believes can produce *eudaimonia* in all humans. But the very possibility of there being such a theory is undermined if the argument I have just outlined goes through, because it claims that there is no such thing in the world as *to kalon*.

First, Polystratus points out that in addition to the fine and the foul – which were mentioned explicitly by his opponents – a number of other things would swiftly pass from existence if their position were true, namely properties such as 'being bigger', or 'being smaller', 'being pleasant' and 'unpleasant', and importantly 'producing health', 'causing growth', and 'being destructive'.

Each of these fails the test of universal consistency. Person X may be taller than person Y, but he is not 'taller' *simpliciter*. We always need to specify 'than whom' (τινος), because Person X may not be taller than person Z. Similarly, a particular treatment will cure one person but not another; it is not 'healing' *simpliciter*. By the criterion set down by Polystratus' opponent these properties are not part of the fabric of the world.

Here Polystratus begins to turn the tables.

οὔτε γὰρ ὑγιεινὰ | ταὐτὰ πᾶσιν ὑπάρχει | οὔτε θρεπτικὰ ἢ φθα|ρτικὰ οὔτε τὰ τούτοις | ἐναντία, ἀλλὰ ταὐτὰ τοὺς | μὲν ὑγιάζει καὶ τρέ||φει, τοὺς δ' ἐκ τ[ῶν ἐ]ναν|τίων διατίθησιν. ὥσ|τε ἢ καὶ ταῦτα πάντα φατέ|ον [[λ]] ψευδῆ εἶναι, ἃ περι|φανῶς ἕκαστος θεωρεῖ ὃ | ἐργάζεται, ἤ, μὴ βουλό|μενον ἀναισχυντεῖν | καὶ μάχεσθαι τοῖς φανε|ροῖς, οὐδὲ τὰ καλὰ καὶ τὰ | αἰσχρὰ ἀρτέον ὡς ψευδῶς | νομιζόμενα, ὅτι οὐ πᾶ|σι ταὐτά ἐστιν ὥσπερ | λίθος ἢ χρυ[σὸ]ς ἢ [ἄλλ]ο | [τι τῶν τοιούων]. (XXIV.24–XXV.16)

For healthy things are not the same to all, nor nutritious or destructive things, nor the opposites of these. Rather, the same things make some healthy and nourish them but do the opposite to others. So one must say either that all these things whose results each of us can see manifestly do not truly exist or, not wanting to

---

[36] Striker (1983) 108ff. argues that this text is evidence that the debate may have begun as a result of a contrast between mass terms and value terms. She assigns the argument which Polystratus attacks to the Pyrrhonians on the basis of DL 9.61. Cf. Alberti (1995) 183. On the 'Universality Requirement' and its use in SE *M.* 11, see Bett (1997) xiv–xvi.

act shamelessly and conflict with the evidence, that the fine and the foul should not be eliminated as false products of convention just because they are not the same for everyone like stone or gold [or some other thing like them].

Polystratus takes his opponents' premise and demonstrates that it results in a vicious dilemma. First he takes the premise of the criterion of universal consistency and demonstrates that it rules out more than the fine and its opposite from true existence. Next he takes one of these newly discarded properties and shows that on pain of falling into absurdity the opponent cannot in fact rule it out of true existence. This is where the dilemma bites.

Imagine Polystratus and his opponent visiting a hospital and watching a doctor administering a particular drug to a patient. The patient recovers. So the drug is healthy for this patient. 'But', says Polystratus to his opponent, 'surely you must agree that no such things as health-producing drugs can exist. Since if the doctor gave the same drug to a different patient that patient would not necessarily recover. In that case it fails your criteria for true existence.' Here two options are available: the opponent can maintain his position or abandon it. Perhaps the opponent agrees and does therefore think that the drug is not truly health-producing. In that case Polystratus will accuse him of a blatant contradiction of what evidently happened. The patient did, after all, recover. Why did this happen unless the drug is truly health-producing, and therefore the property of producing health is part of the world? Polystratus can then convict the opponent of absurdity. Alternatively, the opponent would have to say that his criterion for existence does not apply – the quality of producing health does exist, even if it is not universal and consistent. So his starting thesis is false.

The particular example chosen is significant. Polystratus feels on safe ground here with the example of a curative drug because he can claim that everyone sees that these things have an effect, i.e. that things which are curative do indeed cure certain people. It is only then, once he has pointed to this indisputable empirical fact, that he can construct a dilemma, one of whose alternatives is the absurdity of fighting against what is evident.

Polystratus' opponents are not denying that some people clearly think that certain things are good, just that the disagreement over the subject shows that these things are not unequivocally and therefore not by nature good. The very difference of opinion over what is and is not *kalon* is presumably what first motivated a position of the kind they are taking. The problem is, of course, that it is not possible for Polystratus to point to any uncontroversial instance of something actually being *kalon*, even for a particular person at a particular time, since he can be accused of begging the question. His opponent can claim that in fact this is not an instance of something *kalon* since nothing is truly *kalon* – that is precisely what his argument sought to show. But Polystratus cleverly moves the discussion away from the *kalon* to one of the other properties which he has shown to be subject to the same fate according to his opponents' criterion. And this property is not as controversial, in the sense that Polystratus can and does point to concrete examples of people recovering after the administration of a particular drug. Whether something cures a particular patient is not merely a matter of opinion.[37] It is not therefore possible in this case for his opponent to deny that this example is actually an instance of effective medical treatment on pain of clear disagreement with the *phainomena*.

Notice that at this stage the opponent can now make the claim that his criterion still stands, but in a restricted way. He can claim that in fact the quality of producing health passes the universal consistency requirement in the sense that this particular drug will always cure this particular kind of patient. But then the criterion is rescued at the cost of admitting many more properties into the class of things which are *physei*: the quality of 'producing health in this sort of case' can be listed as part of the world – just what the original argument sought to deny. Or the opponent must give a relational analysis of the evident property of the drug (the drug is healing in relation R), and try to insist that this still does not pass the consistency requirement (since it is not healing in relation R*), and therefore the property does not exist 'in nature'.[38] Either way, Polystratus can claim that he has won. In the first case the

---

[37] A point noted by Alberti (1996) 532.

[38] Bett (1994c) 144ff. tries to rescue the opponents' position by claiming that the opponent could accept that the drug has a particular property but nevertheless maintain that it does not have that property 'by nature' precisely because it is not a universal property of that drug. He goes on to argue that Polystratus is relying on a dogmatic stance on there being an underlying *physis* to the drug which is not directly perceptible but can be inferred

opponent has simply accepted that these relations are 'in nature'. In the second, the opponent may claim a victory since it looks as if his consistency requirement is intact, but the relational analysis of the properties he has conceded is all that Polystratus needs. The debate has become a simple disagreement over classification. The opponent calls only consistent and universal properties *physei*, but importantly has now been forced by Polystratus to recognise in some sense the existence of other relational properties – which will include such things as the fine.[39]

Polystratus goes on to explain how his opponents made their mistake.

[ὅτι τ]ὰ πρό[ς τ]ι κατηγ[ορού]||μενα οὐ τ[ὴ]ν αὐτὴν χ[ώ]||ραν ἔχει τοῖς κατὰ τ[ὴ]ν | ἰδίαν φύσιν λεγομένοις | [κ]αὶ μὴ πρό[ς] τι, οὐδὲ τὰ | μὲν ἀληθῶς ὑπάρχει,|τὰ δ' ου. (xxv.18–24)[40]

... because relative predicates do not occupy the same space as things said in virtue of a particular nature and not relatively. Nor do the latter exist truly and the former not.

They have mistakenly applied criteria relevant for one sort of existent to another, and as a result have been misled into denying the reality of these relative properties – which Polystratus calls τὰ πρός τι κατηγορούμενα – because they do not display the sort of consistency to be found in the case of an entirely different class of existents – which Polystratus calls 'things said in accordance with their own particular nature' (τὰ κατὰ τὴν ἰδίαν φύσιν λεγόμενα) and which we might roughly call 'substances' – such as gold and

from its various different relational properties – and this stance is not something which Sextus can accept since he is only prepared to talk about phenomenal properties and aspects of the object.

[39] So Sextus, while arguing along these lines that good and bad are not *physei*, nevertheless states that an object may be good or bad in a relative sense (*M.* 11.114; cf. *M.* 11.78, 118). But this is a perfectly good moral realist stance, since moral realists need not be moral absolutists (Annas (1986) 9). Even Bett (1997) 143 agrees that for Sextus in *M.* 11, ' "X is good for A at t" is not a claim about A's impressions, or even about how X appears to A, but a suitably relativised claim about how X is *in its real nature*' (original emphasis).

[40] Striker (1983) 110. Cf. Annas and Barnes (1985) 138. The terminology here is interesting. Indelli (1978) 179–80 is happy to think that Polystratus has borrowed this from the Academy. Cf. Isnardi Parente (1971). Krämer (1971) 84 also argues that Polystratus is borrowing Academic, specifically Xenocratean, classifications (cf. ibid. 92–6). For a further example of the striking metaphorical use of χώρα here, see xviii.25.

bronze. In essence, then, his opponents have made a category mistake in the sense that they have attempted to view everything as if it were a substance.

Polystratus does not explicitly raise the question of the position of these properties within the Epicureans' own scheme, and he need not do so.[41] His argument is a purely dialectical one against an opposing thesis. In the process of the refutation of this argument it nevertheless follows that Polystratus establishes a negative thesis, namely that the relativity of certain properties is not itself sufficient grounds for concluding that those qualities are not real. But metaphysics is not his primary concern in this work. Rather, the moral significance of Polystratus' overall project is confirmed towards the end of the text, where the protreptic call to Epicureanism is combined with a further attack on the opposing schools whose doctrines have been scrutinised in the work. Polystratus concludes that not only are the opinions of these schools false, but they are a positive hindrance to the attainment of happiness. One of the principal shortcomings highlighted is their . . .

. . . τὸ μὴ δύνασθαι | διαγνῶναι, τί ἡ φύσις ἡ|μῶν αὐτὴ ζητεῖ τέλος | καὶ ἐκ τίνων τοῦτο συμ|πληροῦσθαι πέφυκεν. ἡ | γὰρ τούτων ἀβλεψία πάν|των [ἀ]ρχηγὸ[ς] κακῶ[ν]. (xxxii.8–14)

. . . inability to distinguish what goal our very nature requires and with what it is by nature satisfied. For the non-recognition of these is the architect of all evils.

Especially worth noting here is the emphatic and repeated reference to human nature, and to the natural end for humans – which only Epicureanism, or so it is claimed, can identify. Clearly, Polystratus is content that he has done enough to rescue the possibility of such claims to moral naturalism (there is a natural and objective good for humans) against the attacks of the moral eliminativists.

It is not novel to claim that in this brief argument of Polystratus we find a refreshing and clear-headed resistance to the common inference from inconstancy and relativity to unreality. But previous discussions have not, I think, always appreciated the connection between this argument and Epicurean ethical theory – not only in terms of the conclusion which it seeks to provide, but also in

---

[41] Alberti (1995) 183 n. 36. Cf. Goldschmidt (1977) 184, Adorno (1980) 158.

terms of the method (and the particular examples) by which it reaches that conclusion. In particular, the example of the varying curative powers of a single drug not only offers to Polystratus' opponents an undeniable example of a real and effective property which nevertheless fails their criterion of universal consistency, but it adds further support to the ultimate goal for which Polystratus is producing his argument, namely the reinstatement of moral properties into the class of things which are by nature. That this need to justify moral realism, and the Epicurean version of it in particular, is what underlies Polystratus' argument is made clear by the common Epicurean use of healing drugs as a metaphor for the workings of their ethical theories. If Polystratus' opponents are forced to agree that medicinal drugs do in fact have real if inconstant properties, then they are a step closer to agreeing with the Epicureans that dogmatic moral theories can have real effects and produce objective human happiness.

6

HECATAEUS OF ABDERA'S
INSTRUCTIVE ETHNOGRAPHY

The next philosopher in my successional list is Hecataeus, whom both the *Suda* and Hesychius list as 'an Abderite philosopher' ('Αβδηρίτης φιλόσοφος). This is generally taken to mean that he was indeed from Abdera, but it has also been suggested that Hecataeus was not originally from Abdera, but from its metropolis Teos (Strabo 14.644, Pseudo-Scymnus 869), in which case he was probably known as the 'Abderite' because of some other connection to this colony, perhaps by association with the atomist tradition founded there. This name would therefore be another case of the use of 'Abderite' to denote a follower of Democritus (above p. 23).[1] That Hecataeus was linked with the Democritean tradition is confirmed by his appearance in Clement's doxographical list at *Strom.* 2.130, where his chosen *telos* is listed as 'self-sufficiency', *autarkeia* (above, pp. 20–1).[2] Also, Diogenes lists Hecataeus along with Timon as one of those who were 'pupils' of Pyrrho at DL 9.69.[3] So like Nausiphanes, Hecataeus appears to bridge the gap between early Pyrrhonism and Democriteanism.

This is as much as can be ascertained from Clement and Diogenes. However, we do have evidence from elsewhere for Hecataeus' major preoccupations. Above all, he was an ethnographer. The two major works known to us are *On the Hyperboreans* and *On the Egyptians' philosophy*.[4]

---

[1] Jacoby (1943) 31.   [2] Cf. Jacoby (1943) 33.

[3] Müller (1848) 384n. suggested that at DL 9.61 the 'Ασκάνιος ὁ 'Αβδηρίτης should be 'emended' to Ἑκαταῖος. Cf. Jacoby (1912) 2751, who later rejected the emendation as unnecessary: (1943) 33, and Decleva Caizzi (1981a) 135. Bar-Kochva (1996) 8 n. 5 thinks that Hecataeus' appearance at DL 9.69–70 shows later attempts to legitimise Pyrrhonism by linking it with as many well-known others as possible.

[4] Hecataeus also wrote an excursus on the Jews, now retained in Photius' epitome of Diodorus book 40 (*FGrH* 264 F6). The work Περὶ τῶν 'Ιουδαίων, attributed to Hecataeus and used by Josephus (*FGrH* 264 F21–4), is probably spurious. Cf. Jacoby (1943) 61–75, Bar-Kochva (1996) 18ff.

The curious position of the Hyperboreans

The subject of the first of these works shows that Hecataeus' ethnography is heavily tainted with moral concerns. The Hyperboreans were generally conceived as living 'beyond the North wind' in an ideal climate and state. They are close to the gods – especially Apollo – and associated with Delos and Delphi.[5] This general conception is mirrored in what we can discover of Hecataeus' presentation. Aelian (*VH* 11.1) includes Hecataeus as one of those who celebrate (ὑμνοῦσι) the Hyperboreans, and both the scholiast on Apollonius (see DK 73 A4) and Diodorus (2.47.7) mention their connection with Apollo in contexts where they are clearly taking their information from, among others, Hecataeus. Diodorus further includes what looks like a Hecataean description of the Hyperboreans' country as a remote land where the Golden Age still prevails:

Ἑκαταῖος καί τινες ἕτεροί φασιν... νῆσον οὐκ ἐλάττω τῆς Σικελίας. ταύτην ὑπάρχειν μὲν κατὰ τὰς ἄρκτους, κατοικεῖσθαι δὲ ὑπὸ τῶν ὀνομαζομένων Ὑπερβορέων ἀπὸ τοῦ πορρωτέρω κεῖσθαι τῆς βορείου πνοῆς· οὖσαν δ'αὐτὴν εὔγειον τε καὶ πάμφορον, ἔτι δ' εὐκρασίαι διαφέρουσιν, διττοὺς κατ' ἔτος ἐκφέρειν καρπούς. (2.47.1)

Hecataeus and some others say that... there is an island no smaller than Sicily which is in the North. It is inhabited by people called the Hyperboreans, since it lies beyond the furthest breath of the North Wind. The island is fertile and fecund, and the climate is extraordinarily good – it produces two crops every year.

Certainly some utopianism is at work here, and Jacoby is probably correct in identifying an ideal of self-sufficiency in the Hyperboreans' divinely blessed island,[6] but his suggestion that they function as a sort of protreptic to correct religious practice is very speculative, and not easy to fit into either the Democritean or the Pyrrhonian background. Previously, the generally perplexing nature of the work *On the Hyperboreans* has been resolved by commentators by retaining from it only its utopianism, and viewing it

---

[5] Pind. *Pyth.* 10.34–44, *Ol.* 3.17–45, Hdt. 4.32–5, Philod. ΠΡΑΓΜΑΤΕΙΑΙ (*PHerc.* 1418) xxx.4. On Greek conceptions of this people: Jacoby (1943) 52–9, Romm (1989) and esp. (1992) 6off., Dillery (1998) 26off., Militello (1997) 281–2.

[6] Jacoby (1912) 2757.

in close connection with the second of Hecataeus' works: *On the Egyptians' philosophy*. Where commentators have found in the latter work similar idealising or utopian elements, these have been viewed as a version of those same elements in the mythical Hyperborean island.[7] *On the Hyperboreans* becomes protreptic to Hecataeus' more influential work which itself contains some similarly idealising features but in a less mythical setting. I cannot help but think that this interpretation is driven in part by the nature of the surviving sources. There is more to say about Hecataeus on the Egyptians because of its more extensive use by later writers.

On the Egyptians: date, content, sources

Diogenes Laërtius consulted Hecataeus' work *On the Egyptians* in the composition of the preface to his *Lives*,[8] and it has been thought that Hecataeus is the major source for most of Diodorus Siculus' description of Egypt (from 1.10). This wholesale attribution of Diodorus' first book has now been discredited, but there are still those who confidently attribute greater or lesser parts of it to Hecataeus.[9] Diodorus names Hecataeus only once in the book (1.46.8),[10] on which basis we can attribute some of the subsequent description of Ozymandyas' tomb to him, but any other ascriptions are speculative.[11] One might assume that Hecataeus' work was a full and comprehensive study of the country, including geographical, historical, and ethnographic sections, but it is impossible to be sure where Diodorus has retained Hecataean material, let alone

---

[7] So Schwartz (1885) 250, Jacoby (1912) 2757–8. Dillery (1998) 26off. claims to find the influence of Hecataeus' work on Egypt on his utopia of the Hyperboreans.

[8] Hecataeus' work ran to more than one book in length: DL 1.10.

[9] Suggested by Schwartz (1885), supported by Jacoby, and retained but modified and refined by Cole (1967) 159, n. 35, and Murray (1970) 145, (1971) 332ff. Burton (1972) 3ff., building on Spoerri (1959), takes a more sceptical view, concluding that only 1.47–9, 70.11, 80.6 can securely be attributed to Hecataeus. Murray (1975), Wallbank (1984) 77 and n. 46, Burnstein (1992) 45 n. 1, and Dillery (1998) 256 n. 4, reject Burton's scepticism. Hornblower (1981) 20–1 recognises Burton's challenge to her reading of Diodorus' books 18–20 as deriving heavily from Hieronymus. Her case studies using parallel texts (27ff.) generally suggest that Diodorus used a single main source per subject. Hornblower (21) recognises that Burton might be correct about the first book.

[10] The Hecataeus at 1.37.3 is probably Hecataeus of Miletus.

[11] Even in the section at 1.47.1–49.5, Diodorus only inserts ['E.] φησίν once (1.47.1), and at the end uses a plural: φασίν, 1.49.6: Burton (1972) 6 n. 2.

Hecataeus' own wording and order of composition. It has also been suggested that Hecataeus is the source for the cosmogonical section in Diodorus (1.7–9), mainly on the assumption that it tells a recognisable Democritean story, but this too seems to me unlikely.[12] There is no reference to atomism in that passage – the primary elements are earth, air, fire, and water – and the only 'philosopher' named is Euripides, 'the pupil of Anaxagoras' (1.7.7).

We can nevertheless try to date Hecataeus' most famous work. Theophrastus in *De Lapidibus* (dated by reference to Athenian archons to 315/314 or slightly later) twice mentions a work on the kings of Egypt (*De Lap.* 24, 55) which might be that of Hecataeus; we know of no other plausible candidate. Hecataeus thus predates 315/314.[13] There are also parallels between Theophrastus *apud* Porph. *De abst.* 2.5 and Diodoran material on Egypt.[14] It is also generally thought that Hecataeus was writing under the patronage of Ptolemy I, the son of Lagus (*c.* 367/6–283 or 282 BC). His *Suda* entry states that he lived at the time of Alexander's successors, and Diodorus mentions him as one of the many Greeks who went to Thebes under Ptolemy I (1.46.8).

On kingship

Even without the ascription of large chunks of Diodorus to Hecataeus, we can more soberly comment on the political context of this lost work. Hecataeus' ethnography certainly discussed the Pharaonic traditions and might therefore be placed within a long tradition of writing *On kingship* (περὶ βασιλείας). As such,

---

[12] Suggested by Reinhardt (1912) and supported with modifications by Vlastos (1946), and Cole (1967). Salem (1996) 265ff. summarises Cole's conclusions. Cf. Murray (1970) 169–70, (1971) 532–5. Reinhardt's thesis was attacked by Spoerri (1959) who thinks that 1.7–8 derives from late Hellenistic ideas into which Stoicism and Platonism are also interwoven. Cf. Burton (1972) 15–16, 44–51; Bertelli (1980); Sacks (1990) 56–7. This is thought 'uncharacteristic' of Diodorus by Fraser (1972) vol. II, 721, n. 19. Gigon (1961) suggests Posidonius as the most probable direct source. DK print Diodorus 1.7–8 as a Democritean fragment (B5), as does Luria (§558). In any case, the usefulness of this section as a source for Democritus is limited: Vlastos (1946) 58.

[13] Cf. Fraser (1972) vol. II, 719 n. 7. See the debate over dating between Stern and Murray (1973).

[14] Cole (1967) 156 n. 35: 'The *Aegyptiaca* of Hecataeus was the most up-to-date source of information on Egypt in Theophrastus' day and it would have been natural for him to use it.' For the success and popularity of Hecataeus' work: Murray (1971) 383ff.

Hecataeus is engaging in one of the most pressing debates of his age. While it is true that theoretical and protreptic discourses on kingship were being written before the Hellenistic period (Plato's political philosophy in particular, but also Xenophon's *Cyropaedia*, and the oratory of Isocrates), the political change brought about by the conquests of Alexander the Great and the emergence of the Hellenistic kingdoms provided the major impetus for such works.[15] The new political climate demanded a rethinking of the rôle of the philosopher at the court of one of these new monarchs.[16] It required the delicate negotiation of the demand for the opportunity for frank and open advice and criticism and of the necessities of living under the autocracy of one's pupil.[17] The presentation of Egyptian monarchy might have offered to Hecataeus an indirect means of commenting on the new monarchy of Ptolemy, perhaps even offering a positive model for him to emulate. Ptolemy himself held a delicate position as the new Greek ruler of a country with its own traditions of kingship. It is tempting, therefore, also to see Hecataeus' work of ethnography functioning within this negotiation of a new order in Egypt.

Hecataeus can also be placed within the narrower context of the Democritean tradition. Democritus himself had little to say about kingship, but – as we have seen – Anaxarchus most certainly did. Furthermore, it is likely that Hecataeus was aware of Anaxarchus' discussion of kingship, especially if that work was written in the light and context of Alexander's absolute monarchy and Hecataeus was writing under the derivative but analogous rule of Ptolemy in Egypt.[18] Further evidence for Hecataeus' view might come from

---

[15] See Wallbank (1984) 76–9, Gruen (1993) 3, Delia (1993) 200, Schofield (1999) 742–4. The most comprehensive work on this genre is by Murray (1971). Diogenes Laërtius lists nine works *On Kingship*: by Ecphantos (2.110), Aristotle (5.22: Ross collects meagre 'fragments'), Theophrastus (two works: 5.42, 5.49), Strato (5.59), Persaeus (7.36), Kleanthes (7.175), Sphairus (7.178), Epicurus (10.28). There are works *On the philosopher king*: by Dionysius the Renegade (7.167), and Strato (5.59). On dating Ecphantos (Stob. 4.7.61–3) to the Hellenistic period, along with Diotogenes (Stob. 4.7.64–6): Thesleff (1961), cf. Goodenough (1928) 64ff., Murray (1971) 245.

[16] On the complex and varied nature of Hellenistic kingship: Gruen (1996).

[17] See, e.g. Plut. *Reg. et imp. apoph.* 189D (= Stob. 4.7.27).

[18] Cole (1967) 120 constructs a 'Democritean' theory of good kingship, based on suggestions of εὐεργασία in B157, 255, 258, 263. None these fragments have any particular relevance to monarchy.

Plutarch, who quotes an anecdote in the *Life of Lycurgus* (repeated in *Apoph. Lac.* 218B):

Ἀρχιδαμίδας δὲ μεμφομένων τινῶν Ἑκαταῖον τὸν σοφιστήν, ὅτι παραληφθεὶς εἰς τὸ συσσίτιον οὐδὲν ἔλεγεν, 'ὁ εἰδώς, ἔφη, 'λόγον καὶ καιρὸν οἶδεν.' (Plut. *Lyc.* 20.3)[19]

When some were criticising the sophist Hecataeus, because when he was brought into the mess hall he said nothing, Archidamidas said, 'The wise man knows what to say and also knows when to say it.'

Diels (*ad* DK 73 A6) wonders whether this should be attributed to Anaxarchus, presumably on the basis of the reference to 'the opportune' (καιρός, Anaxarchus B1 – see above, p. 83). Jacoby notes that it is quite possible that Hecataeus was used on embassies to Sparta, and rejects Diels' proposed reattribution on chronological grounds. An embassy by Anaxarchus to Sparta is unlikely.[20] Further, it is unlikely that Plutarch has confused Hecataeus with Anaxarchus; he is quite well informed about Anaxarchus' life (Plut. *Alex.* 28, 52; *Tranq.* 466D). Hecataeus is indeed the philosopher intended by Plutarch, and if the reference to καιρός is a resonance of Anaxarchan thought, it implies at least that Plutarch thought Hecataeus was influenced by Anaxarchus, and perhaps that Hecataeus was indeed influenced by the former's discussion of kingship.[21]

Hecataeus stands to Ptolemy I in a relationship analogous to that of Anaxarchus and Alexander: the Abderite philosophical adviser and the new monarch. There are, however, important disanalogies. In the wake of Alexander's extraordinary exploits which might well have occasioned Anaxarchus' view of a king as global moral legislator, the Diadochi required a less radical philosophical justification for their monarchy, one which would perhaps be acceptable to the native population of their respective areas. If Diodorus' discussion of Egyptian kingship is even a pale reflection of Hecataeus'

---

[19] This Archidamidas is otherwise unknown. Jacoby (1912) 2752 suggests that we should understand a reference to Archidamus IV (*c.* 305–275). The name Archidamidas occurs in both of Plutarch's versions of the anecdote, so if there was a mistake, then it occurred in Plutarch's source or earlier.

[20] Jacoby (1943) 34.

[21] However, the idea that one should know the appropriate λόγος for the appropriate occasion is not uncommon: Hdt. 9.87; Soph. *El.* 1292; Pl. *Phaedr.* 272a1–7, *Leg.* 727e5–6; Isoc. *Evag.* 34, *Panath.* 86.

work, Hecataeus' presentation was perhaps appropriate to such a desire.

The philosophical successors of the Democriteans had similarly cordial relationships with Hellenistic monarchs, the Ptolemies included. Colotes dedicated his work *That it is impossible even to live according to the opinions of other philosophers* to Ptolemy II Philadelphus.[22] Near its conclusion, that work also contains some views on the nature of good kingship:

τὸν βίον οἱ νόμους διατάξαντες καὶ νόμιμα καὶ τὸ βασιλεύεσθαι τὰς πόλεις καὶ ἄρχεσθαι καταστήσαντες εἰς πολλὴν ἀσφάλειαν καὶ ἡσυχίαν ἔθεντο καὶ θορύβων ἀπήλλαξαν· εἰ δέ τις ταῦτα ἀναιρήσει, θηρίων βίον βιωσόμεθα καὶ ὁ προστυχὼν τὸν ἐντυχόντα μονονοὺ κατέδεται. (Plut. *Adv. Col.* 1124D)

Those who set up laws and customs and established the governance and rule of cities delivered human life into great security and tranquillity and freed it from turmoils. If anyone removes these, we will live the life of beasts, and whoever chances upon anyone else will all but devour him.

Unfortunately we have no evidence for the views of Epicurus on the desired conduct of the king.[23] Most of his thoughts on kingship are driven by the consideration of how as a form of government it might allow for the *ataraxia* of those who live under it.[24] We might begin to form a picture of his personal view, however, from what we know of his own life. Epicurus himself seems to have been on good terms at various times with Antigonus Monophthalmos and Demetrius Poliorcetes,[25] and a number of other Epicureans are linked to prominent Hellenistic rulers.[26] The later history of the Epicurean school, particularly that of the Campanian Epicureans in the first century BC, shows evidence of a revival of sustained meditation on the nature of kingship, specifically tied

---

[22] Plut. *Adv. Col.* 1107E. Colotes refers to the views of Arcesilaus, who became head of the Academy in 268–264. Ptolemy II ruled from 282 until 246.

[23] Long (1986) 291: 'Colotes stated a position we have every reason to think would have been endorsed by any member of the school.'

[24] Grimal (1986) 260ff. Gigante and Dorandi (1980) 484–6 construct a positive Epicurean attitude towards monarchy. For a sustained criticism of their view: Fowler (1989) 130–3. Gigante (1992) 35 remains unconvinced. Cf. Dorandi (1982a) 24–7.

[25] Cf. Momigliano (1935).

[26] Philonides was the instructor of the young Demetrius (later Soter), and an adherent of Antiochus IV Epiphanes. Cinesias, the tutor of Pyrrhus, is shown offering Epicurean advice to his charge at Plut. *Pyrrh.* 14, and esp. 20. Cf. Murray (1971) 200–10, Grimal (1986) 262–3, Gigante (1995) 66.

to these Hellenistic rulers, numerous busts of whom were found in the Villa of the Papyri at Herculaneum.[27] Philodemus' work *On the good king according to Homer (PHerc.* 1507), addressed to L. Calpurnius Piso,[28] might well be recalling such Hellenistic works *On Kingship* at a time when the Roman Republic was threatening to collapse into monarchy.[29] It too contains references to Hellenistic kings as they are compared and contrasted with their Homeric predecessors.[30]

Hecataean kings and Anaxarchan kingship

The most pressing question for my concerns is whether we can indeed attribute to Hecataeus the section of Diodorus which discusses the institutions of Pharaonic kingship (1.70ff.). Hecataeus did mention the Egyptian customs according to which the kings' consumption of wine was regulated by law (Plut. *De Is.* 353A–B), but this is insufficient support for those commentators who have accepted all of the Diodoran material as deriving from Hecataeus, and have begun on that basis to speculate on the relationship of the picture of kingship portrayed there to Ptolemy's position in Egypt, and to Anaxarchan models of kingship.

This is how Diodorus' section begins:

πρῶτον μὲν τοίνυν οἱ βασιλεῖς αὐτῶν βίον εἶχον οὐχ ὅμοιον τοῖς ἐν
μοναρχικαῖς ἐξουσίαις οὖσι καὶ πάντα πράττουσι κατὰ τὴν ἑαυτῶν

---

[27] Pandermalis (1983) 23–31, Wojcik (1986) 267–71, Gigante (1995) 65, Tepedino Guerra (1991) 131. Long (1986) 295 finds Lucr. *DRN* 6.1ff. 'a highly positive account of the external amenities of Hellenistic Athens'.

[28] As is Philodemus epigram 27 Sider.

[29] Murray (1965) 181 suggests dating the work to Piso's consulship in 59 BC, at which point he would be counted as one of the *principes*, a position, Murray suggests, analogous to one of the Homeric kings. Grimal (1986) 266 prefers 45 BC and places it firmly within a discussion of the impending civil war.

[30] Demetrius Poliorcetes: XXXVII; Niomedes (III Euergetes: Dorandi (1982a) 160–1): XXII.35; Cambyses: XXIV.18. In the surviving portions of the text these particular rulers are generally offered as negative *exempla*, of vanity (Demetrius), profligacy (Nicomedes), and a lack of concern for one's family (Cambyses). On the 'Epicureanism' of the text opinions are divided: Murray (1965) 174 finds it 'popular and exoteric' and (1984) 158–9, a meditation on the patron–client relationship of Philodemus and Piso; Asmis (1991) 24 can see 'no technical philosophical analysis, nor even any outright assertion of distinctively Epicurean doctrine'. The importance of παρρησία for the Epicureans is clear. Philodemus wrote a treatise on the subject (*PHerc.* 1471), on which see Glad (1995) chs. 2–3, and (1996); Konstan et al. (1998).

προαίρεσιν ἀνυπευθύνως,³¹ ἀλλ᾽ ἦν ἅπαντα τεταγμένα νόμων ἐπιταγαῖς, οὐ μόνον τὰ περὶ τοὺς χρηματισμούς, ἀλλὰ καὶ τὰ περὶ τὴν καθ᾽ ἡμέραν διαγωγὴν καὶ δίαιταν. (1.70.1)

First of all their kings led a life quite different to those who live among the licences of monarchy and who do everything according to their own choice without the need to account for it. Rather everything was established by the laws' commandments, not only when it came to matters of possessions, but also concerning day-to-day behaviour and diet.

The account begins by declaring that this is unlike the familiar brand of monarchy. Unlike the monarchs familiar to Diodorus' audience, these early Egyptian monarchs are all obliged to follow pre-existing laws and customs (νόμοι) not only in their administration of the country, but also for their everyday lives – for example, what they eat and how they bathe. This picture might even have been unfamiliar to early Hellenistic Egyptians.³² It certainly conflicts with Anaxarchan views of the king as moral legislator.³³ One might be tempted to reach for Hecataeus' Pyrrhonian connections, perhaps suggesting that they instilled in him a notion of the importance of following laws which tempered the Anaxarchan thesis.³⁴

But this is highly speculative. I prefer not to base any interpretation of the relationship between Hecataeus and Anaxarchus on such slim evidence. Even if some portion of Diodorus could be attributed to Hecataeus, I doubt that significant headway could be made towards an outline of Hecataean 'philosophy' based on such

---

31 Without being subject to εὔθυναι; cf. ps.-Arist. *AP* 48. ἀνυπεύθυνος power is the mark of an autocrat: Pl. *Leg.* 875b3, Arist. *Pol.* 1295a20, Murray (1971) 300, 369.

32 See Fraser (1972) vol. I, 501. Murray (1970) 166 suggests that Hecataeus' views on the workings of Egyptian kingship derive from the opinions of the Egyptian priests (cf. 1.44.4, 1.46.7, 1.69.7). Compare Murray (1971) 351–4, Burton (1972) 29–30, Sacks (1990) 206. For more general discussion of Ptolemaic kingship: Koenen (1993), Samuel (1993).

33 Murray (1970) 165 n. 1: 'If [Anaxarchus'] doctrine was in any way unorthodox, it was probably in the direction of an emphasis on the absolute power and autonomy of the king . . . This attitude is specifically rejected by Hecataeus – for [Anaxarchus] the king is above the law.'

34 Murray (1971) 378: 'From Pyrrho, Hecataeus perhaps inherited a respect for foreign political philosophy, Hyperborean, Indian, Jewish or Egyptian. Scepticism in politics, when not coupled with total abstention, might lead to a relativism which saw that no one ideal state was inferior to another . . . But this is pure speculation; a certain distaste for luxury (τρυφή) in kings and an emphasis on ethical and political self-sufficiency, and the moderation of desires, are the closest links between Hecataeus and his philosophical tendencies.'

second-hand and probably paraphrased material. Still, Hecataeus' significance remains twofold. As a member of both Clement's 'Abderites' and Diogenes' 'Pyrrhonians' he highlights the close links between these two groups, and as a court ethnographer he belongs firmly in a tradition of writing for and about Hellenistic monarchies, a tradition to which the Epicureans later contributed.

NAUSIPHANES' COMPELLING RHETORIC

When Nausiphanes met Pyrrho . . .

Nausiphanes of Teos plays a crucial rôle in any history of the Democritean and sceptical schools, since not only is he the famously reviled teacher of Epicurus, but there are also hints that he received some kind of instruction from Pyrrho. However, Nausiphanes is given no *Life* of his own by Diogenes (although he plays a part in the *Lives* of the philosophers which surround him doctrinally and chronologically), and no clear *verbatim* citations of his thought survive. We are reliant on the few references to him in other philosophers' *Lives*, a brief appearance in one of Seneca's letters, and the hostile Epicurean sources, notably Philodemus' *Rhetoric*.

We should first consider whether and when Nausiphanes was exposed to Pyrrhonian influences. The major evidence for such an exposure is from Diogenes' life of Pyrrho:

[Πύρρων] ἔν τε ταῖς ζητήσεσιν ὑπ' οὐδενὸς κατεφρονεῖτο διὰ τὸ ἐξοδικῶς λέγειν καὶ πρὸς ἐρώτησιν· ὅθεν καὶ Ναυσιφάνην ἤδη νεανίσκον ὄντα θηραθῆναι. ἔφασκε γοῦν γίνεσθαι δεῖν τῆς μὲν διαθέσεως τῆς Πυρρωνείου, τῶν δὲ λόγων τῶν ἑαυτοῦ. ἔλεγέ τε πολλάκις καὶ 'Επίκουρον θαυμάζοντα τὴν Πύρρωνος ἀναστροφὴν συνεχὲς αὐτοῦ πυνθάνεσθαι περὶ αὐτοῦ. (DL 9.64)

In his inquiries Pyrrho was looked down upon by no one because he would speak continuously even when replying to a question. For this reason Nausiphanes, a youth at the time, was captivated by him. At any rate, he used to say that one ought to cultivate Pyrrho's disposition, but his own arguments. He also often said that Epicurus was amazed at Pyrrho's behaviour and constantly pestered him about it.

This passage has created the chronological problem of trying to engineer the opportunity for Nausiphanes to have heard Pyrrho lecturing when Nausiphanes was still only around twenty years old: ἤδη νεανίσκον ὄντα. If Epicurus studied with Nausiphanes in Teos before his *ephebate* in Athens (before 323), this threatens to push the time of Nausiphanes' supposed exposure to Pyrrho back before Pyrrho accompanied Alexander on his expedition (327–325 BC). Yet Pyrrho's disposition which so impressed Nausiphanes (DL 9.64) was at least in part inspired by the experiences on that expedition (DL 9.61, 63). There have been numerous attempts to reconstruct the whereabouts of Pyrrho, Nausiphanes, and Epicurus in the latter part of the fourth century BC, and more recent commentators tend to place Epicurus' contact with Nausiphanes after the former's *ephebate*.[1] This allows time after Pyrrho's return from India in about 325 for Nausiphanes to be impressed by his *diathesis* and then relate this information to Epicurus some time after 323.

It has also been suggested that the reference to Nausiphanes' age should be ignored as an error of transmission,[2] but I would read it in a manner which will reveal its importance for the way in which we are led by Diogenes to conceive of the power of Pyrrho's *diathesis* and its relevance for Nausiphanes' thought, but which lessens its status as a piece of evidence for any chronological reconstruction.

My proposed interpretation focuses on the use of 'young man', νεανίσκον, when combined with the verb 'to capture', θηρᾶν. When referring to young men this verb often carries erotic overtones. A parallel passage from the *Life* of Polemo will clarify my point.[3] Polemo has already been introduced as a profligate young debauchee. On one particular drunken spree, this happens:

καὶ ποτε συνθέμενος τοῖς νέοις μεθύων καὶ ἐστεφανωμένος εἰς τὴν Ξενοκράτους ᾖξε σχολήν· ὁ δὲ οὐδὲν διατραπεὶς εἷρε τὸν λόγον ὁμοίως· ἦν δὲ περὶ σωφροσύνης. ἀκούων δὴ τὸ μειράκιον κατ' ὀλίγον ἐθηράθη καὶ οὕτως ἐγένετο φιλόπονος... (DL 4.16)

[1] Susemihl (1901) 190 n. 28 suggests that Nausiphanes taught Epicurus in Teos before 323, but followed Epicurus to Athens and then went to Elis to hear Pyrrho (after the expedition of 325). Nausiphanes then returned to Athens to tell Epicurus about Pyrrho. He accepts that the sequence given in Strabo 14.1.18 describes consecutive stages in Epicurus' training: καὶ δὴ καὶ τραφῆναί φασιν ἐνθάδε [sc. ἐν Σάμῳ] καὶ ἐν Τέῳ καὶ ἐφηβεῦσαι Ἀθήνησι, and therefore must reject DL's suggestion (9.64) that Nausiphanes was young when he heard (about) Pyrrho: 189 n. 26. Von Fritz (1935) 2021ff. raises a number of objections, suggesting (p. 2022) that Nausiphanes accompanied Pyrrho in 325 and then taught Epicurus before 323. Cf. Blank (1998a) 76. Sedley (1976a) 121 and 149 n. 2, argues that Strabo's report need not show a strict chronological sequence, and suggests that Epicurus studied with Nausiphanes *after* the age of 18. This is accepted by Vander Waerdt (1989) 235. Cf. Dorandi (1991b) 45–7.

[2] Von Fritz (1935) 2022; cf. Gigon (1946) 19–20.

[3] On Antigonus of Carystus' *Life of Polemo* and our sources for its reconstruction: Dorandi (1995b) 85–7, (1999) liii–lvii.

Once, in the company of some youths, drunk and garlanded, he came into Xenocrates' lecture room. Xenocrates paid no attention and gave his lecture – which was about temperance – as if nothing happened. As he listened the young man was gradually captivated and thus became industrious ...

A latter-day drunken Alcibiades bursts into a *Symposium Platonicum* at the Academy and is 'captivated' by the beauty of the speech on temperance.[4] Immediately he is converted and eventually rises to the heights of scholarch.

There is another peculiar irony in Polemo's story, since in the following chapter Diogenes finds a story in Antigonus of Carystus' biography that Polemo had been a defendant in a lawsuit brought by his wife on the charge that he spent time with young boys (μειρακίοις, DL 4.17). So for Polemo the usual progression from *erōmenos* to *erastēs* is reversed: the 'captivator' of little boys 'grows up' when 'captivated' by the words of the philosopher.[5] The version which survives in Philodemus' *Historia Academicorum* (*PHerc.* 1021 and 164), again from Antigonus, makes the connection more explicit, passing immediately from a description of Polemo's profligacy and unrestrained desires (in which context his wife's lawsuit is mentioned) to his conversion by Xenocrates.

φυγεῖν | δίκην αἰσχρὰν κακώ{σ}|σεως ὑπὸ τῆς γυναικός·[6] εἶναι | γὰρ φιλόπαιδα καὶ φιλομειράκιον· ὅς γε περιέφερε νό|μισμα παντοδαπόν, ἵνα τῷ | συναντή[σ]αντ[ι χρῆσ]θαι προ|χείρως ἔχη· θηραθεὶς δ' ὑ|πὸ Ξενοκράτου[ς] καὶ συστα|[θε]ὶς αὐτῷ τοσοῦτο μετήλ|[λ]αξε κατὰ τὸν βί[ο]ν, ὥστε... (XIII.3–13 Dorandi)

He was defending himself against a shameful charge of misconduct levelled by his wife, for he was a lover of youths and young men. He used to carry all sorts of coins with him, so he would have some to hand should he meet someone. Captivated by Xenocrates and reformed by him, he so changed his lifestyle that...

---

4 Dumont (1987) 87 rejects the pederastic overtones. Cf. Chantraine (1956) 70–2, Wolff (1997) 45–6, Clay (1998) 115–16. Dumont claims that Polemo is captivated by 'le divin appel du Souverain Bien', although no such thing is mentioned in the anecdote. At Plut. *Adv. Col.* 1124B a philosophical doctrine selected for its popularity is a θήρα μειρακίων; cf. *Comm. not.* 1073B and Schofield (1991) 28ff.

5 Polemo himself goes on to captivate Crantor at 4.17 (again from an Antigonan source), and 4.24. Also see DL 4.29–30: Crantor loves Arcesilaus and seduces him away from Theophrastus' school. Cf. DL 2.114, 125; 6.94; 9.112.

6 On this text cf. Dorandi (1999) 8 n. 40.

The emphatic positioning of θηραθείς not only enacts the sudden radical conversion to philosophy, it must surely recall the preceding description of Polemo as φιλόπαις καὶ φιλομειράκιος.[7]

Such parallel texts reveal that the story of the enraptured young Nausiphanes is neither a necessary historical fact to be fitted into a chronology, nor an epitomiser's error, but a *topos* of philosophical biography, and particularly of Antigonus of Carystus' biographies. The story of Polemo and Xenocrates in both Diogenes and Philodemus derives from Antigonus, as (probably) does Diogenes' story of Nausiphanes and Pyrrho.[8] It therefore offers little help in constructing a chronology, or (modern) biography of Nausiphanes or Pyrrho, but instead suggests ways in which the reader of Diogenes is asked to construct images of the various philosophers through their interrelation. It is an enactment of the perceived relationship between the two thinkers' philosophical stances. Indeed, there is support for such a reading from the text itself. After the description of Nausiphanes' 'captivation', Diogenes comments:

ἔφασκε γοῦν γίνεσθαι δεῖν τῆς μὲν διαθέσεως τῆς Πυρρωνείου, τῶν δὲ λόγων τῶν ἑαυτοῦ.

At any rate, he used to say that one ought to cultivate Pyrrho's disposition, but his own arguments.

The particle γοῦν is important. Nausiphanes' supposed endorsement of Pyrrho's general attitude is included by Diogenes as evidence for the supposition of his being captivated as a young man in a manner which is a common *topos* in philosophical biography. This is quite different from the thought which gave rise originally to the impulse to locate the historical event of Nausiphanes' conversion. On that interpretation, the assumption is that the inference was in the opposite direction – that Diogenes has notice of an accurate biographical account of a meeting between the two philosophers, and has surmised that this was the occasion at which Nausiphanes'

---

[7] *Contra* Dorandi (1991a) 234: 'θηρᾶν è qui usato, come spesso in Diogene Laerzio (2.125; 4.16, 17, 24 e 9.64) senza nessun valenza erotica.' Gaiser (1988) 506 insists that there is no direct connection between Polemo's profligacy and later conversion.

[8] Antigonus is named twice in 62, and invoked with a φησί in 63. It is probable that the story of Nausiphanes in 64 is Antigonan also. Cf. Wilamowitz (1965) 55–6, Dorandi (1995b) 72.

opinion was formed. Instead, we see here that Diogenes knew of Nausiphanes' approval of Pyrrho's disposition and uses this to justify his inclusion of a story about how the two met. Nevertheless, one might insist that the anecdotal biography should provide at least a *plausible* chronology for the thinkers in question, and such a chronology is perfectly possible. If we do not require Nausiphanes to be a young man when he meets Pyrrho – since that particular piece of the story owes more to the commonplaces of philosophical biography than historical fact – then we might locate that meeting after the expedition of 325 (see above, p. 161 n. 1). The Diogenes passage gives us no independent evidence for *when* that meeting took place.

We can now pass to more pressing concerns. Why did Nausiphanes approve of Pyrrho's outlook *alone*, while commending his own theoretical basis for this outlook?[9] Why did biographers illustrate Nausiphanes' approval for Pyrrho's *diathesis* by his being captivated in this way?[10] To answer these questions we will need to look more closely into what can be gathered about Nausiphanes' own philosophy.

Towards a reconstruction of Nausiphanes' thought

Nausiphanes' telos

Diogenes' biographies give us no indication of Nausiphanes' theories. The most promising source for any attempt is Philodemus' *Rhetoric*, which contains an extended attack on Nausiphanes' rhetorical theory.

We can learn little from sources outside Philodemus' *Rhetoric*. Nausiphanes is said by Clement to have described the *telos* of life as *akataplēxia* (see above, pp. 20–1). If Nausiphanes did use this term, we might ask whether it resembles Democritus'*athambia* (as Clement says Nausiphanes claimed) or Epicurus'*ataraxia* or neither?[11]

---

[9] Cf. Purinton (1993) 300 n. 31.

[10] Decleva Caizzi (1981a) 182: perhaps 'Antigono ricavasse le notizie sul metodo di Pirrone da uno scritto di Nausifane, lo stesso forse di cui Filodemo ci ha conservato qualche notizia.'

[11] Von Fritz (1935) 2024: Nausiphanes' ἀκαταπληξία 'scheint im wesentlichen nur eine Anpassung des demokriteischen Ausdrucks an den Sprachgebrauch der Zeit des N. zu sein'. Cf. Decleva Caizzi (1981a) 184.

Although *akataplēxia* is introduced as Nausiphanes' *telos* it does not correspond to any of the terms Clement uses to describe that of Democritus. Instead, Nausiphanes' *telos* is said to correspond to something else in Democritus' system: *athambia*.[12] But as Cicero warns us, Democritus' own words were anything but clear on this matter (*Fin.* 5.87–8, see above pp. 43–4). Democritus felt no need to maintain a consistent terminology for a *telos*, instead discussing a number of interrelated ideas: *euthymia*, *athambia* and the like. It is therefore clear that these doxographic reports on their own offer little help in the search for the content or meaning of Nausiphanes' *telos*.

So we might look elsewhere at other uses of the word. *Akataplēxia* is not a common term, but where it occurs, it appears to carry the meaning of 'unshakeability' or 'steadfastness'.[13] This would confirm Clement's report that it was linked to Democritus' *athambia*, glossed by Cicero as *animum terrore liberum* (*Fin.* 5.87).[14] Interestingly, it is rather common in Epicurean texts. At *De morte* XXXIX.23 Philodemus describes someone dying with the correct Epicurean attitude as passing away ἀκαταπλήκτως. Similarly:

τὸ δ' ἰδίωμα τοῦτο π[ερι]φερόμενο[ν] | ἀκαταπληξίαν ἔχει πρ(ὸς) τὰ [δ]εινὰ τὴ[ν τε]|λειοτάτην... (*On the Gods* 3 fr. 81.2–4 Arrighetti)[15]

This renowned peculiarity comprises perfect imperturbability towards what causes fear...

We might conclude, therefore, that for the Epicureans *akataplēxia* designates a correct attitude to things which normally cause fear or astonishment.[16] A true Epicurean, having internalised the ideas distilled in *KD* 1 and 2 attains *akataplēxia*. He is unafraid of the gods and of death because he has the correct opinion about divinity and annihilation. Epicurus, in the first book of his *On*

---

[12] Noted by Alfieri (1979) 161 n. 2.

[13] Diog. Hal. 1.57.3, 1.81.2; Appian *BC* 1.110, 2.142; Julian *Const.* 36.22.

[14] Procopé (1971) 116 n. 3. Where ἀθαμβία appears in Democritus' fragments it could carry the meaning of 'fearlessness': B215, 216.

[15] See Arrighetti (1955) 347–8.

[16] An analysis of the much more common positive cognate terms confirms this. καταπλήσσειν generally means 'to terrify' or 'to astonish': e.g. Hom. *Il.* 3.31; Thuc. 1.81.6, 2.65.9, 4.10.2, 7.42.2; Xen. *Cyr.* 3.1.25, ps.-Arist. *AP* 38, Epict. *Diss.* 2.19.8. Clement himself uses the word regularly: *Prot.* 2.27.5; *Paed.* 2.3.35, 2.5.48, 3.11.61; *Quis dives salvetur* 20.3, but this is no reason to suspect his report in the doxography above.

NAUSIPHANES' COMPELLING RHETORIC

Metrodorus described his pupil as 'unafraid in the face of disturbances and death' (ἀκατάπληκτος πρός τε τὰς ὀχλήσεις καὶ τὸν θάνατον, DL 10.23).[17]

Although this makes *akataplēxia* a necessary part of *ataraxia* it does not necessarily make the two states identical; *akataplēxia* is not simply a synonym for *ataraxia*, and the Philodeman texts above actively dissociate the two terms. In Epicurean terminology – as far as I can see – *akataplēxia* is restricted to one's attitude toward certain things which might normally be expected to induce fear, and while this contributes to and is a necessary condition of *ataraxia*, it is not a sufficient condition.[18] I might fear neither the gods nor death, but nevertheless be ambitious, or otherwise be infected by unnecessary or unnatural desires. Of course, the Epicureans will have a story to tell about *how* the presence of unnecessary desires and empty opinion more generally play a part in the generation of the common fears of death and divinity in particular, but even this appears to me to be evidence for the superimposition of a wealth of theorising onto whatever basis the Epicureans may have inherited from Nausiphanes.[19]

Philodemus' *Rhetoric*: texts and contexts

So at last we turn to the most promising source of information about Nausiphanes. Two papyri found at Herculaneum contain portions of Philodemus' *Rhetoric* and include an attack on Nausiphanes', and then Aristotle's, views on rhetoric (*PHerc.* 1015 and 832). Sudhaus numbered columns of the former in Roman numerals, of

---

[17] Some MSS have ἀκατάληπτος for ἀκατάπληκτος. Cf. Laks (1976) 94.
[18] The removal of θάμβος in *Ep. Hdt.* 78–9 is only part of the attainment of ἀταραξία. Cf. Gale (1994) 194 on Lucr. *DRN* 3.29.
[19] The Stoics also took something like *akataplēxia* into their ethical vocabulary: Epictetus *Diss.* 2.8.23, DL 7.97, Julian *Const.* 36. In a fragment of the *De Stoicis* (*PHerc.* 339, fr. 7 x.4; see Dorandi (1982b)), Philodemus describes how Antipater was καταπλη[τ | τ]όμενος at the ἀπάθεια of Zeno and Diogenes the Cynic as revealed in their *Republics*. It would be nice to see this as a Philodeman jibe: Antipater is astounded (a vice in Stoic terms) by the founder's impassivity, the very virtue which he has failed to attain. In Aristotelian moral psychology, ὁ καταπλήξ suffers from the vice of a surfeit of the characteristic whose mean is αἰδώς: *EN* 1108a34, *EE* 1233b27, *MM* 1.29.1. The relationship between the Stoics and Aristotelian theory remains controversial. Cf. Long (1968) and Sandbach (1985) 24.

the latter in Arabic; I retain that method.[20] Previous interpretations have relied on the extracts in Diels–Kranz, which print von Arnim's supplements to Sudhaus' text of the *Rhetoric*, which were made without independent examination of the papyri.[21] There col. XVI appears to give a Nausiphanean account of the 'natural *telos*', but Blank's new edition shows this to be unsupported by the text.[22]

Better evidence for Nausiphanes' *telos* comes in col. XVII, but again the state of the text and the fragmentary context do not provide unequivocal support. Philodemus ridicules the idea that Nausiphanes' orator-philosopher will have any particularly esoteric or specialised knowledge on which to base his advice:

ἀλλ' εἰ πυνθά|νοιτό τις ἄν[τι]κρυς αὐτῶν· |'ἢ βούλ[ε]σθ' ἢ[δ]εσθαι καὶ μη|θὲν μήτε ἀλγεῖν μήτε λυ|[πε]ῖσθαὶ;' τίνες οὐ φήσουσιν; | [ὥ]στε πως οὐ χαλεπόν, ἃ πε|[ρὶ] τῶν ὑποκ[ει]μένων ἔ|[κα]στοι [β]ούλ[ο]ντα[ι, γι]νώσ|κειν, ὅτε οὐδὲ περὶ τοῦ συμ|φ[ύ]του τ[έλ]ους ο[..]ντες μὲν ... (XVII.11–20 Blank)

But if one of them was to ask explicitly, 'Do you wish to feel pleasure and not to feel pain, nor to be distressed?', who would say no? So in a way it is not difficult to know what each of these people wants regarding these matters in hand, when not about the natural goal ...

Clearly, this is a *reductio*, but it is unclear whether the choice of ethical truism is Nausiphanean rather than Epicurean. Philodemus' criticism would appear to have more force if the self-evident information in the parody ('people want to feel pleasure and not

---

[20] They were identified as two pieces of a single text by Sudhaus (1893) 321 and in the preface to his second edition and cited as book six of the *Rhetoric*. Longo Auricchio (1985) lists fragments of these papyri as from *liber incertus*. Dorandi (1990) 73 suggests that they come from the fifth book, on the hypothesis that they form a continuous exposition with *PHerc.* 1015 against, in chronological order, Nausiphanes, Aristotle, and (in 1004, listed as the sixth book) Diogenes of Babylonia. He is followed by the bibliography in Obbink (1995) 277. Longo Auricchio (1996) 171 (or (1997)) claims to read H in the *subscriptio* of 1015 and 832, which makes it part of the eighth book, and I in the *subscriptio* of *PHerc.* 1669, which would then be the tenth book. On the history of the papyri and their apographs: Longo Auricchio (1994) 389, Blank (1998b). New texts are currently being prepared by David Blank and Francesca Longo Auricchio.

[21] Von Arnim (1898) 51, 46. On Sudhaus the papyrologist: Schmid (1979) 37–8 and n.13; Gigante (1996). On methodological causes of error in these early editions, with reference to and examples from Sudhaus' *Rhetorica*: Turner (1971). Cf. Longo Auricchio (1978) 32.

[22] The Nausiphanean origin of the text found in DK is accepted without much question by Indelli and Tsouna-McKirahan (1995) 171 in their edition of *PHerc.* 1215, where they refer to von Arnim (1898) 51, and also by Obbink (1997) 276.

pain') is indeed a piece of understanding which Nausiphanes attributed to his wise man, but it is equally possible that Philodemus is attempting to deny that Nausiphanes' wise man has any special knowledge by claiming that what he asks his audience is *like* asking them whether they want to feel pleasure and not pain. On this reading the question, 'Do you wish to feel pleasure and not to feel pain, nor to be distressed?', in col. XVII does not refer to the actual content of the orator's insight, but rather to a ridiculous counterpart of that content, whose truistic nature is clear. We can say only that whatever Nausiphanes did claim his orator could teach, Philodemus thought it was so ridiculously obvious that it was like asking one's audience if they wanted to be happy. There is no need to claim that Nauisphanes' *telos* was ever described in such a way, and therefore no grounds for reading ἥ[δ]εσθαι καὶ μη|θὲν μήτε ἀλγεῖν back into what Diels–Kranz print as a description of Nausiphanes' view of the natural *telos* in col. XVI.

The following section of Philodemus offers another tantalising clue. It suggests that the content of the knowledge of Nausiphanes' natural philosopher – *physiologos* or *physikos* – is indeed 'what one naturally desires':

..χαί[ρο]υσι μ[έ]ν, ἄχθο[ν]|ται δ[ὲ] τὸ τ[ὸ]ν φυσικὸν | μόνο[ν] τοῦτο τεθεωρηκό|τα τῷ γινώ[σκ]ειν ὃ βού|[λεθ' ἡ] φύσις καὶ [..]λέγειν [[λέ]] | καὶ λέγοντα τὸ πρὸς τὴν | βούλησιν ἀεὶ [...(.)]στα δυ|νήσεσθαι πολλά· καὶ πῶς| οὐ γελοῖ[ο]ν τοῦτο καὶ με |[μ]ε[ι]γμέ[νο]ν τῇ κατὰ[.]ω...(8.2ff Blank)

'...they rejoice, but also are grieved at the statement that only the *physikos* has seen this by coming to know what nature desires...and, when saying what is related to desire...always will be capable of many [things]'. And how is this not ridiculous and mixed with...?

This assigns to the *physikos* the knowledge of 'what nature wants' (ὃ βούλεται ἡ φύσις). It is more certain in this case that the section I have put into inverted commas (ἄχθονται to δυνήσεσθαι) is at least a paraphrase of a Nausiphanean argument cited in order to be refuted by Philodemus in the following section. We can therefore be reasonably confident that Nausiphanes said that only the *physikos* knows what the *physis* desires, and it is plausible to interpret *physis* here as 'the nature of men' (ἡ τῶν ἀνθρώπων φύσις), which appears in XV.11.

Physiologia, rhetoric, and the grounds of ethical advice

We should also attempt to understand Philodemus' engagement with Nausiphanean theory by approaching the *Rhetoric* more generally. The second book of Philodemus' *Rhetoric* centres around a disagreement between – on one side – Philodemus and his teacher Zeno of Sidon, perhaps the current scholarch of the Garden, and – on the other – a group of unnamed Epicureans apparently based in Rhodes. The question is this: is rhetoric an art (*technē*)? If so, is all rhetoric a *technē* or only some branches, or only one branch?[23] The closest we come to a definition of a *technē* in the *Rhetoric* is in the second book (*PHerc.* 1674, XXXVIII.5–18, p. 123 Longo).[24] Two qualities are made essential for a *technē*. First, it must be able systematically to describe its subject matter in such a way that one who has learned the particular skill may produce the desired effect in each particular instance without failure or guesswork. Second, the same results cannot regularly be produced in the absence of this *technē*.[25]

The precise positions taken by the various sides in that debate do not concern us now, but it is worth noting that Philodemus excludes *political* oratory from being a *technē*. Both sides of the Epicurean debate agree on one point, which seems to have been made clear in Epicurus' own work *On Rhetoric*. Political oratory is a knack acquired by experience (ἐμπειρία ἀπό τινος τριβῆς καὶ τῶν ἐν ταῖς πόλεσι ἱστορίας *Rhet.* 2, *PHerc.* 1672, XXI.25–XXII.3, p. 217 Longo) rather than a systematised body of knowledge which

---

[23] Text in Longo Auricchio (1977). Comment in Isnardi Parente (1966) 367–92, Longo Auricchio and Tepedino Guerra (1981) 25–32, Ferrario (1981), Asmis (1983) 38–40, Longo Auricchio (1984 and 1985), Barnes (1986b widens the debate to Sextus, Quintilian, and Cicero), Sedley (1989) 107–17, Kleve and Longo Auricchio (1992), Blank (1995), Karadimas (1996) 169ff. The ancient debate rages around what the four *kathēgemones* thought, each side offering texts from Epicurus, Metrodorus, Hermarchus, or Polyaenus in support of their cause. At *Rhet.* 1 (*PHerc.* 1427) VII.4ff. (Longo Auricchio (1977) 21), Philodemus accuses those who 'disagree' with the founders of the school of parricide. Kleve and Longo Auricchio (1992) 223–4 suggest that Philodemus' interpretation of Epicurus' remarks was motivated by the Herculaneum *contubernium*'s use of media such as Lucretius' poetry to disseminate the Epicurean message.

[24] A new edition of this text is currently being prepared by David Blank.

[25] Barnes (1986b) 6 compares SE *M.* 2.10. Philodemus, in contrast, does not require the τέχνη to have a good or useful end, and adds that the τέχνη must attain its goal firmly and reliably.

can be taught.[26] Philodemus' attack on Nausiphanes must be read against the background of this attack on the technicity of political oratory.

Nausiphanes is the object of the polemic in *PHerc.* 1015/832 from the beginning of the surviving papyrus rolls until XLVIII.15, at which point Philodemus signals that he has considered Nausiphanes' views and has shown that the true philosopher should not encourage the study of rhetoric.[27] He then passes on to Aristotle. Nausiphanes is referred to by name at 4.10 and XXIX.16 and is invoked in one further reference to Ναυ[σι]φάνης at XXIV.17 (the text here is in a poor state).[28]

There is also a reference to Nausiphanes' suggestion within the text of the second book of the *Rhetoric* in which Philodemus sets up his distinction between political oratory and *technē*. Here, Philodemus is citing Metrodorus in support of his view that the skill of political rhetoric is not a *technē*, but something picked up through practice.

πότερον οὖν τὴν ῥη|τορικὴν δύναμιν λέγει[[ν]] | τις βλέπων ἐπὶ τὴν διάγνω|σιν τού ἃ πρακτέον ἐστὶν τῷ μέλ|λοντι εὐδαίμον[[ε]]ι εἶναι τε | κ[α]ὶ ἔσεσθαι καὶ [οὐ πρ]ακτέον, | καὶ ταύτην φησὶν ἀπὸ φυσ[ι]ο|λογίας παραγείνεσθαι, ἢ[τ]οὶ | τὴν πολειτικὴν ἐμπειρίαν, | καθ᾽ ἣν ἐκ τριβῆς καὶ ἱστορί|ας τῶν πόλεως πραγμάτω[ν] | συνορ[[ο]]ώιη<ι> ἂν τις οὐ κακῶς | τὰ πλήθ[[η]]ει συμφέροντα; (*PHerc.* 1672 XXII.7–19 Blank)

Is it then that someone speaks of rhetorical ability looking to the discernment of what should be done by whoever is about to be and will continue to be happy, and what should not, and does he also say that this is acquired by natural philosophy, or [does he say that] political experience also [is so acquired], on account of which, through practice and inquiry into the affairs of the city, someone might see well what is advantageous to the many?

The φησίν – 'he says' – in line 13 is within the quotation from Metrodorus, so Metrodorus himself is not the subject,[29] and we

---

[26] Cf. Pl. *Gorg.* 462c4ff., 465a2ff.

[27] David Blank informs me that this line is preceded by a *coronis* in the papyrus, marking the end of a portion of text. See Capasso (1991) 216 and figs. LXVII–LXXII.

[28] He is also named in the third book, *PHerc.* 506 XL.33: Hammerstaedt (1992) 17.

[29] Philodemus introduces this quotation with: ἀρκέσει τὰ πα|ρὰ Μητροδώρωι σαφῶς διδά|σκοντα·, and marks the end of the quotation which I have given above with: καὶ μικρὸν προβάς. He then offers another quotation. That Metrodorus is the subject of this φησίν appears to be assumed by Longo Auricchio (1984) 467. Sudhaus (1896) x recognises this as a reference to Nausiphanes. Cf. Blank (1995) 187.

know that Philodemus used Metrodorus' work *Against those who say that good orators are the product of natural philosophy* (πρὸς τοὺς ἀπὸ φυσιολογίας λέγοντας ἀγαθοὺς εἶναι ῥήτορας) in which Metrodorus appears to have criticised Nausiphanes.³⁰ It is likely, therefore, that this citation also comes from that work, and we can expect that the indefinite τις characterised above might turn out to be offering claims meant to be recognisably Nausiphanean. Metrodorus wishes to know if the ability to give ethical advice comes about through natural philosophy – *physiologia* – (a claim with which he could agree to some extent, although for Epicureans natural philosophy does not of itself guarantee persuasiveness in one's ethical advice), or whether political skill also comes from this source. The proposal that *physiologia* might offer a means of teaching the skill of political persuasion is also prominent in Philodemus' explicit polemic against Nausiphanes.

It is important to note that the task of the rhetorical skill in question here is not merely persuasion, but ethically motivated persuasion. The orator can show how one should act in order to live a good life and be *eudaimōn*.³¹ This suggests not only that Nausiphanes was claiming to provide some oratorical training, but that this training was undergone with the further end in view of the provision of ethical advice.

Philodemus' position is restated in *PHerc.* 1015/832 in terms similar to those which informed the debate within the Epicurean school in the second book (cf. XXI.31–XXII.3 p. 215 Longo): political rhetoric is not a *technē*. Here Philodemus produces a possible opposition to that position: someone who claims that the persuasive skill of a fine orator *can* be taught as a *technē*:

εἰ ῥήτορα τ[ὸν] φυ[σι]κὸν ἄριστον | οἴεταί τις εἶναι, καθόσον ἀπὸ | φυσιολογίας
ἔστ[ι] τὴν πολι | τικὴν ἐμπειρία[ν] καὶ [[τὴν]] δει| νότητ[α] παραγίνεσθαι,
πότε | ρον [..(.)]ι³² προσλάβοι, λέγει, τὴν | τῶν [π]ολιτικῶν πραγμάτων|
ἐμπει[ρί]αν καὶ τοῦ πλήθους | κατα[μά]θοι τοὺ[ςἐ]θισμοὺς|καὶ [τὴν]
φυσ[ιολογ]ίαν ὁ φυσ[ικός]... ; (XXV.11–20 Blank)

If someone thinks that the natural philosopher is the best orator insofar as it is possible that political experience and skill can be acquired by natural philosophy,

³⁰ Us. 10, fr. 25 Körte; Longo Auricchio (1985) 35–6. Longo Auricchio and Tepedino Guerra (1980) 472.
³¹ Compare VII–VIII and X.10.   ³² εἰ suppl. Sedley.

does he mean [this provided] that the natural philosopher were similarly to receive in addition the experience of political matters, and also to learn the habits of the masses and natural philosophy too . . . ?

This opponent suggests that the student will learn to be a good orator by learning natural philosophy. Philodemus then asks whether he is also assuming that this orator has some experience of politics. He proceeds to offer his opponent alternative methods of grounding the claim that political experience is added to the knowledge of natural philosophy. These alternatives form col. 16ff.:

. . .]λ[.]τοιλ[. . . .]‖αθεναι ἢ μάλιστ' ἂν ἐπ[ιδέ]‖ξαιτο τὴν τῶν π[ολιτικ]ῶν |
λόγων δύναμιν μ[. . . .]μέ|νη τὰς ἐμπειρίας [συλλ]αμ|βάνειν, δι' ὧν
συλλογισθήσε|ται τὸ πλήθει συμφέρον, ἢ| καὶ ἕξιν αὐτὴν νομίζου|σιν εὐθὺς
ἐνεργά[ζ]εσθαι| τῆ[ς] δ[υνά]μεως ταύτης, | ὥστε μηδὲν ἔτι μελέτης | ἄλλης
προσδεῖσθαι τὸν φυ|σικὸν [μη]δ' ἱστορίας πλείο|νο[ς] . . . (16.1–14 Blank)

. . . or would it in particular receive the power of political arguments . . . to comprise experience from which it might deduce what is advantageous to the many, or do they think that the very state of this capacity is immediately worked up so that the natural philosopher requires in addition no other practice nor more research . . . ?

Either the *technē* of the ideal orator receives in addition the experience – ἐμπειρία – which will allow him to make deductions about what is advantageous to the many (16.1–7) or it creates directly the state of mind – ἕξις – of this persuasive ability. Col. XXVI.1–9 refutes the former alternative by pointing out that in this case the persuasive ability over the masses possessed by the orator comes in fact not from his *physiologia* but from the additional political experience (ἐμπειρία). By allowing this to act as a necessary condition of demagogic success Philodemus' opponent has allowed his position to collapse at least partially into that advocated by Philodemus himself: political skill is acquired by experience and practice, not – at least not only – through theoretical study. The second alternative is given longer discussion, and the state of the text through the next few columns becomes steadily worse, although XXIX.16 does mention the name Ναυσιφάνης (according to Sudhaus entirely preserved), which signals that the object of Philodemus' attack has not altered. That Philodemus did mount a refutation of the latter alternative, which he at least found powerfully persuasive, is shown by the following:

δῆλον το[ί]|νυν ἤδη καί, διότι μω[ρί]α | πολλή τίς ἐστιν τὸ φάσκειν | εὐθὺς ἕξιν [τ]ιν' ἐνγίνεσ|θαι πολιτικ[ῶν] λόγων | ἀπὸ φυσιολο[γίας . . . (XXXVIII.12–17 Blank)

. . . so it is now clear also why it is such lunacy to say that some state of [competence in] political speeches arises directly out of natural philosophy . . .

Note again the word [ε]ὐθύς.[33] It appeared also at 16.9, and picks up the suggestion of direct access to beneficial persuasive power through the theoretical study of *physiologia*. Not only does Philodemus reject *a priori* the notion that political rhetoric is a *technē*; he also rejects Nausiphanes' claim that he was able to teach (political) rhetoric by teaching natural philosophy. This would amount to making rhetoric indirectly teachable in the manner of a systematic *technē*, and threatens to make political success the goal of learning *physiologia*. Natural philosophy is certainly teachable, and if Nausiphanes can claim an immediate (εὐθύς) link between mastering that, and mastering political speech-making, then he might claim to be able to teach the *technē* of rhetoric. That would explain his appearance in this particular work. It also begins to allow us to speculate more generally on Nausiphanes' ethical theories.

The criticisms levelled against Nausiphanes and recorded by Philodemus do not attack the *telos* which the earlier philosopher might have expounded, but rather this insistence not only that a knowledge of the mechanics of the world is sufficient training in oratory but also that someone thus trained would make a good orator and would take up political oratory as a means of improving the lives of his fellow citizens by offering reasoned ethical advice. Nausiphanes' orator wins influence through his ability to advise his audience in matters of choice and avoidance. He is persuasive because of what he knows and what advice he can give. In order to be relevant to ethical choice-making, Nausiphanean natural understanding must encompass human nature, specifically the nature of the speaker's audience (XV.9).

---

[33] Highlighted also by Isnardi Parente (1966) 369.

Philodemus objects that it is absurd to suppose that a knowledge of *physis* is enough to provide useful and incontrovertible advice in questions of choice and avoidance. Moreover, he complains that Nausiphanes himself did not specify how *physiologia* might supply the requisite understanding.[34] Philodemus demands clarification of the exact link between natural philosophy and rhetoric early in the text: IX.11, X.11–20.

Philodemus himself offers a possible link:

τίν[....]ικαιτ[.]|σιν ἔχων ὁ φυσι[κὸς τῆς τῶν] | ἀνθρώπων φύσ[εως ..]υσο[.]|
ταύτης δύναιτο πείθειν | αὐτούς; ἆρά γε τὴν ἐκ τ[ί]|νων ἢ ποίων στοιχείων |
συνεστήκασι; (XV.9–15 Blank)

Having what [knowledge] of the nature of men might the natural philosopher
. . . be able to persuade them? Is it a knowledge of from what or what sort of
elements they are composed?[35]

In all likelihood, Philodemus has conjured up his own possible account of a link one might make between *physiologia* and rhetorical skill, and offers this ridiculous position to Nausiphanes.[36] This therefore tells us nothing directly about Nausiphanes' own position. Still, it might not be utterly unlike what vague specifications Nausiphanes did provide. If rhetorical skill is to be acquired through natural philosophy, and this rhetorical skill allows one to provide one's audience with genuine moral advice, then this natural philosophy presumably includes a knowledge of human nature, perhaps in physical terms. Philodemus' question here is intended to show just how ridiculous this position is. Does Nausiphanes think rhetorical skill is gained through knowing about the elements out of which people are composed? If this question is at least partly based in Nausiphanes' own view, we can therefore hypothesise that Nausiphanes was prepared to allow that the *telos* could be explained in physical – if not elemental – terms, and that there is a certain physical state of the individual which is the desired goal of all actions and which presumably can be obtained as a result of performing the correct actions.

---

[34] Cf. κα[τά τι]να τρ[όπον] X.19.

[35] Cf. VIII.10–12, XI.3–4; Isnardi Parente (1966) 370.

[36] As Alfieri (1936) 375 n. 28; von Arnim (1898) 51 assumes the elements are atoms.

Further speculation on the specific content of Nausiphanean *physiologia* depends upon one's preferred view of Nausiphanes' philosophical inheritance. Nausiphanes can be linked both to Democritean atomism and to the followers of Pyrrho. There is no need to discard either one of these possibilities; Nausiphanes' links to Pyrrho do not disqualify him from proposing a Democritean *physiologia*. In the report of Nausiphanes' view of Pyrrho at DL 9.64 (ἔφασκε γοῦν γίνεσθαι δεῖν τῆς μὲν διαθέσεως Πυρρωνείου, τῶν δὲ λόγων τῶν ἑαυτοῦ), Pyrrho's theory is not endorsed, only the resulting disposition. So it is quite plausible that Nausiphanes was a Democritean and an atomist, who nevertheless approved of Pyrrho's outlook. After all, Epicurus too is supposed to have asked Nausiphanes for information on Pyrrho's behaviour and comportment (DL 9.64). One might further suspect that if Nausiphanes had proposed that an atomist view of the world would be sufficient to provide accurate information for choice and avoidance, then there would be even greater cause for Epicurus' hostile denunciation of his tutor, and a greater motivation for the moves to distance Epicureanism from Nausiphanean ethical theory. I shall return to this suggestion below.

Cicero, in the guise of Cotta, offers this claim about Nausiphanes' philosophical heritage:

[Epicurus] ita metuit, ne quid umquam didicisse videatur. in Nausiphane Democriteo tenetur, quem cum a se non neget auditum, vexat tamen omnibus contumeliis. atqui si haec Democritea non audisset, quid audierat? quid est in physicis Epicuri non a Democrito? (Cic. *ND* 1.73)

[Epicurus] feared that he should appear to have learned something at some time. He is caught out in the case of Nausiphanes the Democritean, whom – although he does not deny he learned from him – nevertheless he pelts with all sorts of abuse. But if he had not heard these Democritean theories there, what had he listened to? What is there in Epicurus' physics which does not derive from Democritus?

Nausiphanes is offered as the source for Epicurus' knowledge of Democritus. This does not entail that Nausiphanes was a Democritean, but Cotta at least thinks it plausible to call him such (*Democriteo*).[37] Any direct contact between Democritus and

---

[37] I have surveyed the polemical use of the tag 'Democritean' against Epicurus in my Introduction (above p. 24). Cf. Huby (1978) 85 n.14. Huby's Pyrrhonian interpretation of

Nausiphanes would of course be chronologically impossible,[38] so Nausiphanes must have heard or read about Democritean theory, perhaps even reading Democritus' own works in some form. If we still wish to insist that Nausiphanes met Pyrrho in person at some time, then Pyrrho would make an excellent source for this information, given his own enthusiasm for Democritus (DL 9.67). In any case, it is quite acceptable to insist that Nausiphanes' philosophy displayed a dependence on both philosophers, as is implied at DL 9.64: on Pyrrho for his disposition and on Democritus for the basis of Nausiphanes' theories. Cicero, as Cotta, chooses to emphasise the Democritean part of Nausiphanes' heritage as part of his general attack on Epicurus – using a tactic I have discussed above (pp. 24–6).

Let us accept as a hypothesis that the theory constructed by Philodemus in col. xv approximates to Nausiphanes' own general position. It is an understandable development of Democritean ethical and physical theories to insist on a close link between a certain physical state and a desired psychological or emotional state (what I called E/Ph, above p. 59). Indeed, as I have noted, it has often been suggested that Democritus himself already held such a position. If he did not, then perhaps Nausiphanes was first proponent of such a close relationship, offering his proposal as a development and interpretation of the theories of Democritus himself and the hints at E/Ph found there. If he did, then Nausiphanes was the thinker who emphasised how such a systematic knowledge of men's nature might allow one to be a great orator, emphasising the medium of transmission now made possible by the infallible and universally applicable nature of the knowledge. The specific Epicurean

Nausiphanes is motivated by her insistence that Epicurus was not hostile to Democritus. She infers that since Epicurus was hostile to Nausiphanes, Nausiphanes cannot have been a Democritean. There is also a letter *To the philosophers on Mytilene* (Arr. 104, *PHerc.* 1005 fr. 116 Angeli, cf. SE *M.* 1.1–4; on the history of this text: Angeli (1988) 241ff.) in which Epicurus describes himself listening to lectures on Teos. Certainly the lectures are on Anaxagoras and Empedocles *as well as* the atomists (cf. Sedley (1976a) 136), but this does not exclude Nausiphanes from being a Democritean himself. The fragment refers to ὁ τοὺς 'Ερμοκο|πίδας ἐν Τέῳ συ[σ]τήσας | [κατὰ Δ]ημοκρίτον καὶ [Λεύκιπ]πον πραγματευ|[ομένους. On this characterisation of Nausiphanes' unruly pupils: Blank (1998a) 79. The reference to Leucippus might confirm Laks' reading of DL 10.13: Laks (1976) 70; cf. Luria (1936), Rohde (1901), Diels (1880).

38 Democritus was almost certainly dead before the mid-fourth century BC. Nausiphanes was probably not born until around 360.

hostility to Nausiphanes on this point might indeed be evidence against Democritus himself making a clear and systematic link between ethics and physics. Democritus is attacked generally for metaphysical eliminativism – a topic to which I will turn in my Conclusion – but Nausiphanes in particular is the target of Epicurean criticism of an attempt to reduce ethics to physics.[39]

Philodemus is intensely critical of Nausiphanes' implied insensitivity to the beliefs of his audience, since his orator would rely on a theoretical knowledge of the *physis* of a person. In contrast, the Epicurean therapeutic enterprise attacks the beliefs of its audience and requires a reassessment of what desires are truly necessary and natural (e.g. *SV* 59). Nausiphanes, on Philodemus' account, appears utterly unconcerned with changing the *doxai* of his audience, insisting instead that the words of the skilled *physiologos* will command universal assent always, based on his intimate knowledge of 'what nature desires'. The Epicureans maintain that it is no proof of sound reasoning that one's oratory is approved by the masses, since there is no guarantee that their *doxai* are sound.

οὐ τοιο|ῦ|[το δ' ἐστιν] τὸ ἐπάγγελμα, | ἀλλ' ὡς ἁπλῶς περὶ οὗ πο|[τ' ἂν] ἐθέλωσιν αὐτοί, πεί|σειν ἔφη τ]ῇ τέχνη[ι] τῆς πει|[στι]κῆς δυνάμεως, [ο]ὔτε δὴ γινώσκειν δυνατόν, οἷς | χ[αί]ρουσιν οἱ πολλοὶ κατὰ τὰς δόξας καὶ μὴ τὸ συ[γ]|γενικὸν τέλος, οὔτ' εἰ τό[ῦτό]|τις ὑποτεθείη γινώσ|κειν, κἂν πείθειν δύναιτ[ο.]. (XXIII.6–17 Blank)

This is not [his] promise, but he said generally that he will persuade them about whatever they want through this *technē* of the persuasive power. But it is not possible to know what the many enjoy in virtue of their opinions and not the natural end. Nor even if someone were hypothesised to know this would he also be able to persuade them.

Even if someone knows the natural goal and even if one is able to persuade the audience to do as one wishes, their compliance will always be according to their opinions, which may or may not coincide with the knowledge of the speaker. Philodemus has already

---

[39] Theodoret *Graec. Aff. Cur.* 4.1–2 (not in DK) comments: Δημόκριτον τὸν Δαμασίππου τὸν Ἀβδηρίτην φασὶ παραπλησίαν εἶναι τῇ φύσει λέγειν τὴν ἀρίστην διδασκαλίαν· μεταμορφοῦν γὰρ δὴ ταύτην καὶ μεταρυθμίζειν πρὸς τὸ βέλτιον τὴν ψυχὴν καὶ τοὺ παλαιοὺς ἀνανεοῦσθαι χαρακτῆρας, οὓς ἐξ ἀρχῆς ἡ φύσις ἐνέθηκεν. Theodoret is here paraphrasing Democritus B33, which he probably found in Clem. *Strom.* 4.151. On these remarks as evidence for E/Ph, see p. 71, n. 126.

undermined the technicity of rhetoric so that, even if it were possible to know for sure what the mob wants, it would not be possible on the basis of a *technē* to persuade them successfully. Now he offers another objection. The audience approves what it hears on the basis of its opinions and not solely with regard to the natural *telos*. These opinions are variable and possibly entirely misguided (XXIII.18–19). Therefore audience compliance is no sign of the speaker's knowledge or authority.[40]

The Epicureans offer an alternative means of education: the 'removal of false beliefs' (XLIV.18ff.),[41] which accepts that most people's decisions are made on the basis of their opinions and appetites, but that in the majority of cases those opinions are mistaken. In this case it is nonsense to claim that a knowledge of the underlying natural state of a person allows one to persuade a mass audience of the correct choice of action; people simply will not do as you wish against their own opinions, whether mistaken or not.

This same criticism can be extracted from one of the *Vatican Sayings*:

SV 29: παρρησία γὰρ ἔγωγε χρώμενος φυσιολογῶν χρησμῳδεῖν τὰ συμφέροντα πᾶσιν ἀνθρώποις μᾶλλον ἂν βουλοίμην, κἂν μηδεὶς μέλλῃ συνήσειν, ἢ συγκατατιθέμενος ταῖς δόξαις καρποῦσθαι τὸν πυκνὸν παραπίπτοντα παρὰ τῶν πολλῶν ἔπαινον.[42]

I would rather use my frank speech and in my natural philosophy give out oracles about what is of benefit to all humans – even if no one would understand it – than give in to others' opinions and live off the constant praise which falls from the lips of the many.

Epicurus would much prefer to use his knowledge of *physiologia* in telling all men what is to their advantage by speaking like an oracle (χρησμῳδεῖν), than be forced to tailor his advice to the opinions of a mass audience.[43] Nausiphanes' claim that *physiologia* has

---

[40] Cf. Us. 187: οὐδέποτε ὠρέχθην τοῖς πολλοῖς ἀρέσκειν· ἃ μὲν γὰρ ἐκείνοις ἤρεσκεν οὐκ ἔμαθον· ἃ δ᾽ ᾔδειν ἐγὼ μακρὰν ἦν τῆς ἐκείνων αἰσθήσεως. Cf. Sen. *Ep. Mor.* 29.10 and *PHerc.* 1232 fr.8 I.12–15 (see Clay (1986) 13).

[41] Which Epicurean's view is being cited here is uncertain. Metrodorus is named shortly afterwards (32.1). Longo Auricchio and Tepedino Guerra (1980) ad loc. suggest that the ἀνήρ cited in XLIV.15ff. is Metrodorus or Epicurus.

[42] Text as in Arrighetti. The MS has φυσιολογῶ χρησμῶ δεῖ τά. Crönert (1906b) 420 reads φυσιολόγῳ (as does von der Mühll).

[43] Cf. Diog. Oin. 112 Smith for the troubles oratory causes.

a universal appeal and commands unavoidable assent is false. If someone does stand up in public and tell the truth about what is good for people then they are unlikely to listen; if he wants a large and approving popular audience, he must fit his speech to their pre-existing opinions. If he wishes to persuade someone else of what is correct according to his philosophy of the natural goal of human action, then he must first align the opinions of his audience to that natural goal. The bare knowledge of the natural good is insufficient for this task. There is no direct (εὐθύς) shortcut from the philosopher's knowledge of the good to public acceptance of his informed advice.

Nausiphanes' insistence on the applicability of *physiologia* to ethics and politics offers a counter-charge to the often-voiced opinion that philosophy has no relevance to the life of the citizen or the *polis*. What good to us is speculation about the tiny building blocks of the universe? On Nausiphanes' view there is every reason to think about the physical basis of the world, since this will also provide knowledge of the physics of human nature which can be harnessed in political thinking and persuasion. Perhaps dissatisfaction was voiced about Democritus' own theory where an elaborate account of the nature of the universe might well have been felt (as it is still often felt now) to offer no basis for the *moralia*. Nausiphanes' insistence on the applicability of *physiologia* to ethics is in that case a response to such criticisms.

It is important to be clear about how the Epicureans differ from Nausiphanes, since one might argue that an understanding of the physics and underlying structure of the world is essential for a number of central Epicurean theories. More importantly, atomism plays a crucial rôle in a number of the central ethical claims which are intended to produce and ensure *ataraxia*. For example, in Epicureanism, atomic theory plays a large part in arguing for the conclusions 'that all perceptions are true', that 'death is nothing to us', and that 'god did not create the world'. However, the rôle given to physical concerns in these arguments is carefully delimited.[44] *KD* 11 and 12 recognise that some amount of *physiologia* is necessary given that we are affected by worries about celestial

---

[44] Generally on this topic see Manolidis (1987).

phenomena, death, and the like. A knowledge of 'the nature of the whole' (*KD* 12) is instrumental in banishing those kinds of fears.[45] However, the Epicureans are very clear in the insistence there is more to attaining *ataraxia* than mere *physiologia*; learning the nature of the mechanics of the universe is only a step on the road to the required adjustment of one's opinions – and this is where they part company with Nausiphanes. I shall return to the Epicurean use of *physiologia* when I come to describe more generally its reaction to Democritean natural philosophy in my Conclusion. More specifically anti-Nausiphanean is this *Vatican Saying*:

SV 45 οὐ κομπούς οὐδὲ φωνῆς ἐργαστικούς οὐδὲ τὴν περιμάχητον παρὰ τοῖς πολλοῖς παιδείαν ἐνδεικνυμένους φυσιολογία παρασκεύαζει ἀλλὰ ἀσοβάρους καὶ αὐτάρκεις καὶ ἐπὶ τοῖς ἰδίοις ἀγαθοῖς οὐκ ἐπὶ τοῖς τῶν πραγμάτων μέγα φρονοῦντας. (Metrodorus fr. 48 Körte)

Natural philosophy does not make people clever or good at speaking nor does it provide that education which is fought over by the masses – rather it makes people humble and self sufficient, taking pride in their own goods, not in the goods of external things.

This summarises the main criticisms of Nausiphanean theory found in Philodemus.[46] It recalls the Epicurean denial that political rhetoric can be a *technē*, and therefore that someone can learn to be a good speaker as a result of theoretical study. It claims that *physiologia* alone cannot make someone a great and clever speaker, nor is it sufficient to form an education (παιδεία) in all that one needs to know (at least in the eyes of the general public). Indeed *physiologia* seems to Epicurus to be quite irrelevant to the public sphere. Instead its use is in instilling the correct attitude to private goods (ἰδίοις ἀγαθοῖς). It is of no use to men of high ambition.

Often the main bone of contention between Nausiphanes and Epicurus has been thought to be the former's advocacy of a public and active philosophical life, as opposed to the injunction to 'live unknown' on which Epicurus insists.[47] They certainly disagree on this point, but that disagreement is grounded ultimately

---

[45] *Ep. Hdt.* 37, 83 φυσιολογία helps to produce γαλήνη. At *Ep. Hdt* 78–9 it removes θάμβος. (Cf. *Ep. Pyth.* 87: ἀθορυβῶς.)

[46] Isnardi Parente (1966) 383 cites *SV* 45 in her discussion of the Epicurean attitude to rhetoric.

[47] E.g. Longo (1969) 14; Longo Auricchio and Tepedino Guerra (1980) 470–1.

on a more theoretical disagreement. For a reductive atomist the natural philosopher is the possessor of the knowledge to which every choice and decision must be referred. For a non-reductive atomist, who, furthermore, is engaged in a therapeutic enterprise of soothing anxieties, the starting point must be the examination of the *doxai* of the audience, indeed of the individual pupils. Epicureanism is not a philosophy which can be preached from the *bēma*, but entails intense personal introspection on the part of the pupil.[48]

Compelling rhetoric

Before leaving this general topic, and moving to other aspects of Nausiphanes' thought, let us place his theory of the power of rhetoric in a wider context. The ability of oratory to 'move the soul', to compel assent in an audience, and the power which this placed in the hands of the skilled rhetorician were much debated in the fifth and fourth centuries. One particular term is commonly associated with this theme: *psychagōgia* (ψυχαγωγία). Originally a term used in discussions of the dead being 'led away' to Hades, it was later transferred as a metaphor to denote the 'bewitching' power of rhetoric.[49] The credit for the first use in this semi-technical sense is often given to Gorgias, who employs metaphors of enchantment in his *Encomium of Helen* (10).[50] This ascription is often made via Plato's use of the term, especially in the *Phaedrus* (e.g. 261a7). Socrates' attitude to rhetoric in this dialogue is particularly interesting. In an apparent retraction of his attitude to rhetoric expressed in the *Gorgias* (465a2), he suggests that rhetoric is indeed a *technē*. However, from the discussion which follows it becomes clear that he has a very particular image of the kind of *technē* it might be. It is certainly not a skill one can pick up simply by reading the rhetorical manuals which Phaedrus has seen for sale in the agora (266d5–6). Instead, the ideal rhetorician must have a thorough

---

[48] Sudhaus (1893) 341, cf. Isnardi Parente (1966) 368ff., Manolidis (1987) 34.

[49] Wigodsky (1995) 65–8 discusses the meaning of the term in the texts of Philodemus. Cf. Schächter (1927), Mangoni (1993) 319–20, Janko (2000).

[50] Cf. Wardy (1996) 41. For the ascription of this use of ψυχαγωγία to Gorgias, see e.g. Wehrli (1946) 13ff., Untersteiner (1954) 130 (and n. 83 where he traces the ascription back to Pohlenz in 1913; Wigodsky (1995) 66 n. 45 traces it back to Süss in 1910).

knowledge of psychology (271a4–8), and a knowledge of the relation between particular speeches and particular psychic reactions
(271b1–5). He will also have some practical experience of audience reaction (269d2–6). This is in fact no retraction of Socrates'
harsh appraisal of the so-called *technē* of rhetoric professed by
the followers of Gorgias. Instead this is a new, Socratic, *technē* of
'philosophical rhetoric'.[51]

Socrates' vision in the *Phaedrus* of a *technē* of philosophical
rhetoric based on psychology has been offered as the most likely
source for Nausiphanes' own theory.[52] But it is unclear what sort
of psychology Socrates has in mind, and in any case Socrates'
psychology is unlikely to be similar to Nausiphanes'. Moreover,
it has already been pointed out that Socrates is clear in the need
for his ideal orator to supplement his natural ability not only with
knowledge but also with practice (269d5). If part of the Epicurean
objection to Nausiphanes' rhetorical theory is that it did not give
sufficient (if any) importance to practical experience, then
Nausiphanes in this regard differs significantly from the ideal of
the *Phaedrus*. Further, although in both the *Phaedrus* and my reconstruction of Nausiphanean theory we have seen a close alliance
between successful rhetoric and a knowledge of psychology, I see
no reason on this basis to suggest a dependence of Nausiphanes
on Plato. The very term *psychagōgia* itself implies a link between
oratory and psychology which may have provoked a number of
thinkers independently to produce an explicit expression and the-
orisation of such a link.[53]

More interesting is a use of *psychagōgia* as the term for one of
the Democritean *telē* in Clement's list at *Strom.* 2.130.4:

Δημόκριτος μὲν ἐν τῷ περὶ τέλους τὴν εὐθυμίαν, ἣν καὶ εὐεστὼ προσηγόρευσεν... Ἑκαταῖος δὲ αὐτάρκειαν καὶ δὴ Ἀπολλόδοτος ὁ Κυζικηνὸς τὴν
ψυχαγωγίαν.

---

[51] Cf. Asmis (1986), Ferrari (1987) 75ff.

[52] Cole (1967) 168. In support, Cole cites Susemihl (1901) 190 who claims that Diotimus
of Tyre has also read the *Phaedrus*, and quotes SE *M.* 7.140.

[53] I do not claim that the discussions of the *Phaedrus* and *Gorgias* have no connection to
the discussion of the nature of rhetoric found in Philodemus. They are all markers of a
general preoccupation. Philodemus refers to the views of the Gorgias of Plato's *Gorgias*
at *PHerc.* 1007 XLIV.5ff.

Democritus in his *On the goal* calls it *euthymia*, which he also termed *euestō*...Hecataeus calls it *autarkeia*, Apollodotos of Cyzicus *psychagōgia*

Little is known about this Apollodotos. Natorp proposed relat-
ing the term *psychagōgia* to Democritus' *terpsis*, and I have already noted that an Apollodorus might have linked Democritus to
Pythagoras (DL 8.12 and 9.38).[54] In the light of the previous discussion, it is intriguing that the term – which surely must have retained
its link to rhetorical discussions – is included as the *telos* of this
Democritean immediately prior to the appearance of Nausiphanes,
for whose slightly better known philosophy the term has undeniable resonance.

Nausiphanes' epistemology: tripods, oracles, Epicurus

Nausiphanes also made some contributions to epistemology.
Diogenes records a tradition which made Epicurus' *Canon* directly dependent on a work by Nausiphanes entitled the *Tripod*
(DL 10.14).[55] From what we know of Epicurus' *Canon*, he set
down three criteria of truth and might well have outlined his empiricist methods of arguing for the 'non evident' from the 'evident'
(summarised by SE *M.* 7.203–26).

Nausiphanes' title is part of a long tradition associated with differing conceptions of wisdom, but is perhaps also relevant to the
specific epistemology reflected in Epicureanism. It is not unthinkable that the title *Tripod* would refer to ancestors of the three criteria
of truth which are used in Epicureanism: *prolēpseis*, perceptions,
and *pathē*.[56] On these three criteria all other knowledge is founded,

[54] Natorp (1893) 123.
[55] Diels–Kranz reprint their chosen portions of Philodemus' *Rhetoric* under the heading
ΝΑΥΣΙΦΑΝΟΥΣ ΤΡΙΠΟΥΣ. We have no titles of other works by Nausiphanes but not
all of the Nausiphanean material which can be extracted from Philodemus would fall
naturally into a work whose title suggests it was an epistemological treatise.
[56] The De Lacys (1978) 174 suggest that the *Tripod* refers to 'the basic principles of
empirical methodology: observation, *historia*, and inference from similar to similar'.
Cp. Asmis (1984) 338 n.14. Hirzel (1883) vol. I, 132 and n.I suggests a Democritean
source for Nausiphanes' *Tripod*. There is some evidence to link this with Democritus'
Τριτογένεια (DL 9.46) with his conception of practical reasoning. Eustath. *ad.* Hom. *Il.*
8.39 (p. 696); Τριτογένεια δὲ ἀλληγορικῶς ἡ φρόνησις, ἐπεὶ κατὰ Δημόκριτον τρία

just as a tripod balances its load on three legs. In the portions of Philodemus' *Rhetoric* which discuss Nausiphanes' theory we can see methods of argument from the evident to the non-evident, much as we would expect in Epicureanism: XL.8–13, 27.1ff. Tripods also have a long history of association with wisdom. Diogenes relates the fable of a tripod intended for 'the first in wisdom' which is passed around the Seven Sages and eventually dedicated to Apollo (DL 1.28ff). Diogenes also refers to a work by Andron on this subject, entitled *Tripod* (DL 1.30).[57] The tripod is also closely associated with insight in connection with the Oracle of Apollo. The Pythia would sit on a tripod, and its triplicity is associated by the *Suda* (s.v.) with knowledge of the trinity of past, present, and future.[58]

There are also references to tripods and Pythian oracles in sources concerned with Epicureanism. I noted above (p. 178) that *SV* 29 might be a rebuttal of Nausiphanean rhetorical theory. Here I draw attention to the verb χρησμῳδεῖν, which immediately connotes an oracular utterance such as might be provided by the Pythia sitting on her tripod. Other Epicurean texts use similar language, notably Lucretius *DRN* 1.738–9, repeated at 5.110–13:[59]

> qua prius aggrediar quam de re fundere fata
> sanctius et multo certa ratione magis quam
> Pythia quae tripode a Phoebi lauroque profatur,
> multa tibi expediam doctis solacia dictis.

Before I shall proceed to pour out the fates on the matter, more divinely and with much more certain thought than the Pythia who proclaims from Phoebus' tripod and laurel, I shall explain to you many comforts in learned words.

In book one this appears during Lucretius' criticism of earlier natural philosophers, where he notes that although they described the world 'with much more certain thought than the Pythia who proclaims from Phoebus' tripod and laurel', nevertheless they made terrible and grave errors (1.738–41). Of course, these Epicurean

γίνεται ταῦτα ἐξ αὐτῆς, τὸ εὖ λογίζεσθαι, τὸ λέγειν καλῶς τὸ νοηθέν, καὶ τὸ ὀρθῶς πράττειν αὐτό. Cf. *Suda* s.v. τριτογένεια (which seems to conflate it with the previous work in Thrasyllus' catalogue: περὶ τῶν ἐν Ἅιδου); Zeller and Mondolfo (1969) 258 n. 121, Taylor (1999) 67 n. 51.

[57] For Andron of Ephesus: *RE* s.v. (15), *Suda* s.v. Σαμίων ὁ δῆμος.

[58] Cf. Plut. *E apud Delphos* 387b–c.   [59] Cf. Gale (1994) 205.

texts do not endorse oracular authority, but rather say that even it would be preferable to the obscurities and errors of some other philosophers.[60] *SV* 29, for example, suggests that Epicurus would *rather* speak in oracular riddles than his advice be conditioned by mass opinion (above p. 178). Lucretius, *DRN* 1.740–1, suggests that Empedocles, for example, was an improvement on oracular authority, but nevertheless made some grave errors. *DRN* 5.110–13 states clearly that Lucretius will do *better* than a riddling oracular utterance. Nevertheless Epicurus seems to want his philosophy to stand in some way as a Pythian pronouncement.

μέμνησο ὅτι θνητὸς ὢν τῇ φύσει καὶ λαβὼν χρόνον ὡρισμένον ἀνέβης τοῖς περὶ φύσεως διαλογισμοῖς ἐπὶ τὴν ἀπειρίαν καὶ τὸν αἰῶνα καὶ κατεῖδες 'τά τ' ἐόντα τά τ' ἐσσόμενα πρό τ' ἐόντα'. (*SV* 10 (Metrodorus fr. 37 Körte), citing Hom. *Il.* 1.70)

Remember that as a mortal by nature and receiving a finite time you have ascended through natural philosophy to the infinite and have looked down upon 'what is, will be, and was before'.

Again we see the trinity/tripod of past, present, and future, and again the Delphic atmosphere of the *sententia* is pronounced; it begins with an injunction to '*remember* thyself'.[61] Epicureanism thought it was able to claim this Pythian knowledge because its natural philosophy offered a method of comprehensive knowledge, of the infinity of atoms and void, of the infinite variety of combinations. Any Epicurean knows all of what was, is, and will be, just like the Homeric seer Calchas (cf. *DRN* 1.72–7).

Some sources assimilate philosophical theories, and Epicurean theories in particular, to oracular utterances more closely. Cicero's criticism of Epicureanism brands the *Kyriai Doxai* as the book 'in which he is said to have expounded almost oracles of wisdom, briefly in a compilation of most portentous phrases' (*in quo breviter comprehensis gravissimis sententiis quasi oracula edidisse sapientiae dicitur, Fin.* 2.20), and returns to this motif elsewhere (*Fin.* 2.102, *ND* 1.66). While Epicurus appropriated the language of divination, the incongruity of such a characterisation with the doctrines of a school which rejected divine interventionism and divination was not lost on Cicero, nor, presumably, on the Epicurean

[60] Cf. Sedley (1998b) 13–14 esp. n. 59.   [61] On *SV* 10 also see Warren (2000a) 251–2.

targets of this attack. This *topos* of describing a philosophical doctrine as an *oraculum* is not unusual, but it is particularly significant
when applied by hostile sources to Epicureanism, not only because
of Epicurus' doctrinal opposition to *oracula*[62] but also, I suggest,
because of Epicurus' desire to distance himself from Nausiphanes.

The tradition which held that Epicurus' *Canon* was directly dependent on Nausiphanes' *Tripod* can be related to the Epicurean
rejection of oracles.

Ἀρίστων δέ φησιν ἐν τῷ Ἐπικούρου βίῳ τὸν Κανόνα γράψαι αὐτὸν ἐκ τοῦ
Ναυσιφάνους Τρίποδος, οὗ καὶ ἀκοῦσαί φησιν αὐτόν. (DL 10.14)[63]

Ariston says in his *Life of Epicurus* that Epicurus wrote his *Canon* on the basis
of Nausiphanes' *Tripod*. He also says that he was Nausiphanes' pupil.

The insistence that Epicurus did indeed study with Nausiphanes is
significant. To say that Epicurus' epistemological theory derived
from Nausiphanes' *Tripod* is to reject Epicurus' claim to have
been self-taught (again, see above p. 25). Further, since the title
of Nausiphanes' work is redolent of oracular connotations, this
polemical claim might also suggest that Epicurus' own version of
the 'route to knowledge' (his epistemological theory) was copied
from Nausiphanes' pronouncements as a scribe might copy the
Pythia's oracles pronounced 'from the Tripod' (ἐκ τοῦ Τρίποδος),
assimilating Epicurus' denied intellectual debt to the process of
divination which he also strained to reject. Further, another question then poses itself: if Epicurus did not learn his epistemological
theory from Nausiphanes' *Tripod*, where *did* he?

Diogenes (DL 10.12) preserves a brief epigram by Athenaios:

> ἄνθρωποι, μοχθεῖτε τὰ χείρονα, καὶ διὰ κέρδος
> ἄπληστοι νεικέων ἄρχετε καὶ πολέμων·
> τᾶς φύσιος δ' ὁ πλοῦτος ὅρον τινὰ βαιὸν ἐπίσχει,
> αἱ δὲ κεναὶ κρίσιες τὰν ἀπέραντον ὁδόν.
> τοῦτο Νεοκλῆος πινυτὸν τέκος ἢ παρὰ Μουσέων
> ἔκλυεν ἢ Πυθοῦς ἐξ ἱερῶν τριπόδων.

---

[62] Obbink (1996) 568–9 for references. Sedley (1998b) 13 n. 59 notes that Epicurean
theories are branded *oracula* only in hostile sources. There is an exception: Philodemus
De piet. 2043ff. Obbink says that he and other Epicureans ἐχρησμω[ι]|δήσαμεν their
theological theories. Obbink ad loc.: 'it is fair to say that there is at least some irony
imported by both Epicurus' statement and Philodemus' here'.

[63] See Laks (1976) 75–6 for textual discussion.

O you mortals who suffer the worse and, insatiable for gain, provoke quarrels and wars, the wealth of nature sets down a slender boundary, whereas empty choices set an endless path. This the wise son of Neokles heard either from the Muses or from the sacred tripods of Apollo.

The alternative possible sources for Epicurus' philosophy are the Muses or the Pythian oracle, neither of which Epicurus would have accepted. The author of this epigram, Athenaios, is unknown other than from two epigrams cited by Diogenes – of which this is one.[64] At 6.14 his other epigram is introduced in illustration of Antisthenes' belief that virtue is the only good and its relation to Stoicism. This is repeated at 7.30. The penultimate line raises doubts about the Antisthenic thesis by noting that other men (presumably Epicureans) hold pleasure to be the *telos* (σαρκὸς δ᾽ ἡδυπάθημα, φίλον τέλος ἀνδράσιν ἄλλοις). These two poems therefore oppose Stoicism and Epicureanism.[65] This is confirmed by the reference to the Muses as a source of inspiration at DL 10.12, and the final lines of the other epigram, where Epicureanism is said to be Muse-inspired (at DL 6.14, 7.30). Athenaios therefore offers to the Epicureans an answer to the dilemma of their theories' inspiration outlined at the end of 10.12. They should claim one of the Muses as the authority for their ideas.

Why this alternative? Athenaios is possibly aware of the Epicureans' reluctance to accept a Pythian oracle as their intellectual inspiration, not only because it would contravene their theology (as indeed would the second alternative, Muse-inspiration),[66] but also because of the Nausiphanean connotations of the Pythian tripod.

We have one other piece of information describing Nausiphanes' epistemology.

Nausiphanes ait ex his quae videntur esse nihil magis esse quam non esse. (Seneca *Ep. Mor.* 88.46)

---

[64] *RE* s.v. (16).   [65] Goulet–Cazé (1999c) 693 n. 6.

[66] The first line spoken by the Muses in Hesiod's *Theogony* (26: ποιμένες ἄγραυλοι, κάκ᾽ ἐλέγχεα, γαστέρες οἶον) is used by Timon in his *Silloi* (fr. 10 Diels, cf. fr. 11). The reduction of humans to the appetites of their stomach is often used in anti-Epicurean polemics: Di Marco (1983).

Nausiphanes said that of those things which appear none is any more than it is not.

Seneca is telling Lucilius how philosophy often descends into nit-picking and unnecessarily sophisticated discussions. A number of offenders are listed, starting with Protagoras, and passing via Nausiphanes to the Eleatics Parmenides and Zeno, and then on to Pyrrhonists and Academics. The examples of philosophical over-subtlety which Seneca presents are linked not by a sceptical leaning *per se* but by their paradoxical and self-defeating conclusions.[67]

Seneca attributes to Nausiphanes a thesis concerning appearances, *quae videntur*, which are relegated to a less than full degree of existence. This recalls not only Democritus B9 (see above, pp. 7–9) but also echoes the 'no more' (οὐ μᾶλλον) formula of which Democritus was also fond.[68] As we saw in the position maintained by Polystratus' opponents (above pp. 142–9), one reaction to the problem of perceptual or moral conflict is to declare that no object is any more F than not-F, and therefore F-ness (one of the *quae videntur*) is not 'in the nature of things'.[69] Seneca himself draws the paradoxical inference from this (45): 'If I believe Nausiphanes then this one thing is certain – that nothing is certain.'[70]

Whether Nausiphanes himself drew such a sceptical inference is debatable. If he was a self-proclaimed sceptic, then Epicurus' use of the *content* of the *Tripod* for the basis of his own epistemology is highly unlikely, and Epicurus' insistence that he took nothing from Nausiphanes' theory is quite understandable. It is also possible that Seneca's view of a sceptical Nausiphanes is taken from Epicurean sources which saw parallels between Nausiphanes' thought and Democritus B9.

---

[67] Alongside *nihil esse magis quam non esse* (Nausiphanes), he lists *nihil esse* (Zeno), which perhaps reflects Eudemus' interpretation of Zeno noted by Simplicius at *in Phys.* 139.16–19 (DK 29 A 21). See Furley (1967) 66. The third absurd conclusion is: *nihil scire* (Pyrrhonists, Megarians, Eretrians, Academics). The Eretrici were the school founded by Menedemus (DL 2.125ff.) whose methods were later said to have been adopted by Arcesilaus (DL 4.33).

[68] On οὐ μᾶλλον arguments and their role in ancient atomism in particular, see Makin (1993) and cf. above p. 17.

[69] Cf. Furley (1993) 82.

[70] Isnardi Parente (1984) 113 n. 14 suggests that Seneca confuses Nausiphanes with Metrodorus.

Epicurus' abuse ... 'Jellyfish'

Epicurus was infamous for his critical and abusive attitude towards his own teacher Nausiphanes. Even Sedley, who finds Epicurus less hostile to his 'professional rivals' than is often thought, comments that 'it is only against Nausiphanes that we find Epicurus in truly vitriolic mood'.[71] His abuse of Nausiphanes is well documented by Sextus at *M*. 1.1ff. in the context of a discussion of the uselessness of *mathēmata*.

Two schools have made strong cases against *mathēmata*, says Sextus, the Epicureans and the Pyrrhonists. The Epicureans claim that such proficiency is of no help in attaining *sophia*, perhaps (Sextus speculates) as a result of Epicurus' own lack of culture (*M*. 1.1). Then Sextus turns to Nausiphanes.

οὐκ ἀπέοικε δὲ καὶ διὰ τήν πρὸς Ναυσιφάνην τὸν Πύρρωνος ἀκουστὴν ἔχθραν· πολλοὺς γὰρ τῶν νέων συνεῖχε καὶ τῶν μαθημάτων σπουδαίως ἐπεμελεῖτο, μάλιστα δὲ ῥητορικῆς. (*M* 1.2)

It is possible that [Epicurus renounced learning] also because of his antipathy towards Nausiphanes, the pupil of Pyrrho. For Nausiphanes used to attract many young men and concerned himself seriously with the liberal studies – with rhetoric in particular.

It is interesting that Sextus has introduced Nausiphanes as a follower of Pyrrho, since the Pyrrhonists themselves are introduced at *M* 1.5 as the second of two groups (the Epicureans are the first) to attack the dogmatic assertion of the usefulness of *mathēmata*. Nausiphanes clearly advocated their use, and so we might wonder what kind of 'Pyrrhonist' he is meant to represent. We should make a distinction between Nausiphanes the 'pupil of Pyrrho' (Πύρρωνος ἀκουστής, *M*. 1.2) and those described as 'coming from Pyrrho' (οἱ ἀπὸ τοῦ Πύρρωνος, *M*. 1.1, 1.5ff.). The first five chapters of this work are setting up a number of conflicts in a characteristically Sextan manner: between those *pro-mathēmata* and those *anti-mathēmata* (Nausiphanes and Epicurus), between (of those *anti-mathēmata*) the Epicureans and the Pyrrhonists and possibly between the 'Pyrrhonist' Nausiphanes and the Pyrrhonists supported by Sextus.[72]

[71] Sedley (1976a) 135.   [72] Cf. Decleva Caizzi (1992a) 295.

Sextus goes on to describe how when Epicurus became Nausiphanes' pupil he wished to appear self-taught in every respect and therefore sought to undermine Nausiphanes' reputation and de-emphasise any Nausiphanean influence on Epicurean theory. So already there are two proposed motivations for Epicurus' hostility: a point of philosophical disagreement on the usefulness of various sorts of expertise, and a question of publicity and self-presentation.

There is a link between the theoretical and public-relations issues. Presumably it is far easier for a philosopher like Nausiphanes who advocated and practised an extremely visible form of self-advertisement such as public speaking to win a large following than it would be for a philosopher like Epicurus who retreated into the security of the Garden. In this battle to win over more young men, Epicurus launches a two-pronged attack. He criticises the theoretical basis of the practice which Nausiphanes uses to win followers, and then presents himself as an antidote to this second-hand reception of philosophical truth, by insisting instead that he was self-taught:

οἶμαι δὲ ἔγωγε τοὺς βαρυστόνους καὶ μαθητήν με δόξειν τοῦ πλεύμονος εἶναι, μετὰ μειρακίων τινῶν κραπαιλώντων ἀκούσαντα. (*M.* 1.4)

I suppose that the moaners will also think that I am a pupil of the Jellyfish, because I sat listening to him with some hung-over young men.

It is tempting to see here a further resonance of the *topos* of the young men (μειράκια) 'enthralled' by the rhetorical power of a philosopher; just as Nausiphanes was said to be 'enthralled' by Pyrrho (θηραθῆναι, DL 9.64) so Nausiphanes claimed a philosopher with the correct theoretical understanding would be able to command the attention and opinion of a crowd. Epicurus rejects any claim Nausiphanes might make that the philosopher's rhetorical power and entitlement to give ethical advice derive from his understanding of the physics of the world and physiology of the audience, but is therefore faced with a secondary problem: he was clearly known to have been a pupil of Nausiphanes.

His method of dissociating himself from the teacher whose theories he reviled is in turn indicative of their theoretical disagreement. Epicurus did not deny that he heard Nausiphanes (cf. Cic.

ND 1.73, discussed above p. 175), but there is a great difference between listening to someone lecture and being their pupil. This is the distinction emphasised in the passage from Sextus (*M.* 1.4). Although Epicurus certainly sat with the other young men and heard Nausiphanes speaking, he learned nothing from him.[73] Now that we have a picture of *why* and on what points Epicurus disagreed so violently with Nausiphanes, we can see why this claim could be made. Epicurus denies that anyone *can* be taught by Nausiphanes' method: Nausiphanes has no *technē*, no systematic body of knowledge which can be imparted. No one can learn anything in this way.

The content of the abuse stemming from this disagreement is also intriguing. Diogenes notes that Nausiphanes is branded a jellyfish (πλεύμων), illiterate, deceitful, and a whore (DL 10.7). Corroborating evidence that Epicurus himself used the first of these terms of abuse comes in Sextus, who adds a short explanatory tag: 'as something which cannot perceive' (ὡς ἀναίσθητον, *M.* 1.4). Sextus' explanation is corroborated by Aristotelian biological investigations. He says that jellyfish and related species which have no perception live like plants (*PA* 681a19). We should remember Plato *Phlb.* 21c6, where someone with no ability to reason is said to live a life of a jellyfish, not the life of a human.[74] Perhaps we should read the insult as a further critique of the kind of life which Nausiphanes advocated, or of the particular view of the best life which emerged from his writings. Philodemus' criticism of Nausiphanes in the *Rhetoric* focused on the earlier philosopher's insistence on the sufficiency of a knowledge of the physiology and elemental motions of pleasure and pain for infallible persuasive skill and ethical advice. Such a conception might be presented as the *reduction* of the human life to the life of something less than human,[75] and if Plato reaches for 'jellyfish' as a pertinent placeholder for 'less-than-human', why not Epicurus? This 'reduction' has clear echoes of Pyrrho's exhortation to ἐκδῦναι τὸν ἄνθρωπον,

---

73 This distinction was noted well by Laks (1976) 68.

74 Cf. Laks (1976) 58, Laurenti (1996) 54–5, Blank (1998a) 79. Lefebvre (1999) 79–86 has an extended discussion of jellyfish, and their possible significance in the *Philebus* passage.

75 As in von Arnim's reconstruction of XVI.4–12.

to which the Epicureans also objected. Perhaps Nausiphanes took this suggestion from Pyrrho and teamed it with Democritean *physiologia*.

The other insults are less obscure. To accuse Nausiphanes of being a whore (πόρνη) is to equate him with the lowest class of prostitute. These women were far removed from the *hetairai* maintained by wealthy Athenians, and were paid for their services with no continuing tie of affection or obligation. Similarly the success of Nausiphanes' orator-philosopher depends on his pandering to the needs of the masses, on his fulfilling their desires.[76] Philodemus quotes Metrodorus:

καρ|πὸν οὐ μισθὸν, ἀλλὰ κε|[ν]ῶν δοξῶν ἀπαλλα|[γή]ν. (XLIV.18–20 Blank)

The reward is not payment, but the removal of empty opinions.

This could mean both that the benefit of philosophy for the philosopher is not the accumulation of wealth, but the release from his *own* empty opinions, and also that the 'fruits' of philosophy are not wealth and associated trappings of power but the release of *the students* from *their* empty opinions. Either way, it is a swipe against Nausiphanes' insistence that the philosopher will take up a public career and, presumably, rise to a position of public prominence: that is not the route to *eudaimonia* for the philosopher himself, nor his audience. It merely prostitutes the philosopher, who panders to the desires of his public.

---

[76] At DL 10.8 Epicurus calls him a slave.

CONCLUSION. EPICURUS AND DEMOCRITEANISM: DETERMINISM, SCEPTICISM, AND ETHICS

At the beginning of my study (pp. 7–9, 70) I drew attention to the difference of opinion between Epicurus and Democritus over 'metaphysical' or 'ontological' questions. Primarily the disagreement centres around the reality of macroscopic sensible objects and qualities. Remember Democritus B9:

νόμῳ γλυκύ, νόμῳ πικρόν, νόμῳ θερμόν, νόμῳ ψυχρόν, νόμῳ χροιή, ἐτεῇ δὲ ἄτομα καὶ κενόν. (Democritus B9 (SE *M*.7.135))

By convention sweet, by convention bitter, by convention hot, by convention cold, by convention coloured, but in truth atoms and void.

As far as Epicurus was concerned, this demonstrates that Democritus eliminated everything but atoms, void, and their respective *per se* attributes.[1] All other qualities and properties – here represented by sweetness, heat, and the rest – do not exist in reality, but merely 'by convention'. It might be wondered why I should now return to this issue as the key to understanding the ethical tradition of Democriteanism. But it is never the case that the ethical theories of ancient philosophers can be divorced entirely from the metaphysical and theological aspects of their respective systems, and moreover, the Epicurean attack on Democritus for his attitude to macroscopic phenomena has an ethical import, most obviously found in Colotes' work *On the fact that it is impossible to live according to the views of the other philosophers* (περὶ τοῦ ὅτι κατὰ τὰ τῶν ἄλλων φιλοσόφων δόγματα οὐδὲ ζῆν ἔστιν).[2] The doctrines treated in that work are censured by the Epicureans because they prevent one from living a life. In the case of Democritus, the criticisms surround a particular assertion:

---

[1] For the suggestion that Epicurus over-emphasised Democritean 'reductionism/eliminativist materialism' in contrast to his own view see Brunschwig's preface to Morel (1996) 11–12 and 22–9.

[2] Plut. *Adv. Col.* 1107E.

CONCLUSION

ὅτι τῶν πραγμάτων ἕκαστον εἰπὼν οὐ μᾶλλον τοῖον ἢ τοῖον εἶναι συγκέχυκε
τὸν βίον. (Plut. *Adv. Col.* 1108f)[3]

Because in saying that each of the things is no more like this than like that, he
confused all of life.

The evidence for Democritus' denial of distinctions between
things (πράγματα) is based upon his famous pronouncement in
what we know as B9, that atoms and void are in truth, ἐτεῇ, but
colour, sweetness, and the like are by convention, νόμῳ. However,
in Colotes' formulation of B9 (at 1110E–F) a further point is added:
all combination (σύγκρισις) is by convention also. This is a more
radical thesis than is found in Sextus: all macroscopic bodies *per
se* are excluded from the class of true existents, ὄντα. Colotes
concludes from this that Democritus cannot even conceive of himself – a human[4] – as one of τὰ ὄντα, nor *a fortiori* is it possible
to live a human life following Democritus. Whether σύγκρισις appeared originally in Democritus' assertion is dubious. However,
Colotes' interpretation of the force of such statements as B9 is very
instructive.[5] The Epicureans interpreted Democritus as an eliminativist. They took B9 to imply that everything in the world is
'nothing but' atoms and void. All other putative existents are not
truly ὄντα, but are merely by convention, νόμῳ.

For now we should see how this interpretation drives Epicurus'
two major criticisms of Democritus, his anti-determinism and anti-
scepticism. These two issues are intimately related, since in order
to maintain both the freedom of human action, and the possibility of arriving at true opinions about the world through the
senses, Epicurus must insist on the reality and causal efficacy of
macroscopic bodies and qualities. The intervening years between
Democritus and Epicurus saw much philosophical work on the possibility of change, *genesis*, and destruction, items which Eleaticism

---

3 Cf. Diog. Oin. 7.II.2ff. Smith. Arrighetti (1979) 8 compares *SV* 57.
4 Plut. *Adv. Col.* 1110E ἄνθρωπος *suppl.* Pohlenz.
5 Cf. Vander Waerdt (1989) 250–1 considers σύγκρισις to be an interpolation by Colotes.
Wardy (1988a) 139 and n. 20 is keen to retain this as an 'accurate reflection of the
[sc. early] atomists' thesis in its full strength'. Furley (1993) 76 n. 7 thinks it is likely
to be anachronistic. Cf. Gemelli Marciano (1998) 108–9, 117–18; Taylor (1999) 151
n. 141. Morel (1998) 161 doubts this is Democritus' own expression, but compares DL
9.44: ἀρχὰς εἶναι τῶν ὅλων ἀτόμους καὶ κενόν, τὰ δ' ἄλλα πάντα νενομίσθαι. Also see
DL 9.106.

had banned.[6] But Epicurus insists on the possibility of qualitative change and the like while maintaining a version of atomism. He insists that the world is made of atoms arranged in the void, but that the world is not, *pace* Democritus, 'nothing but' atoms and void. Instead, atoms and void are *responsible* for macroscopic phenomena, but those macroscopic phenomena are nevertheless real, and can exert real causal effects on the world.[7]

Democritus, on this reading, explains the phenomena of perception as 'nothing but' the epiphenomena of physical interactions between atoms at a microscopic level. A sceptical view of the ability of the senses to gather information about the world is the result. However, Epicurus wishes to maintain that when I see a red coloured object, the redness of the object is a real property of the streams of atoms (*eidōla*) flowing from it which *qua* that property causes me *qua* perceiver to 'see red'.[8] While atoms are responsible for this macroscopic process, were I to give a microscopic explanation of the event I would make no reference to me as a perceiver nor to the 'redness' which I perceive, both of which Epicurus insists are ὄντα.

This much is familiar, and in the case of perception at least, uncontroversial. Perception is a case of what I will call 'horizontal' causation.[9] A macroscopic perceptible quality causes a macroscopic event (my φαντασία), this whole process being 'supervenient' on a parallel microscopic process of atomic interactions.[10]

---

[6] For Epicurean reception of Eleaticism: Capasso (1987) 111ff. Works perhaps available to Epicurus dealing with not-being and change include Plato's *Sophist*, and Aristotle's *Physics*. Cf. Wardy (1988a) 131–2 n. 11, Furley (1993) 93.

[7] See e.g. SE *M*. 10.42–4. Theophrastus *De sensibus* 79–82 offers a critique of Democritus' theory of colours. It is not coincidental that the Epicurean explanation of the ontological status of colours at Plut. *Adv. Col.* 1110c comes from Epicurus' work πρὸς Θεόφραστον (perhaps confirming that Epicurus' disagreements with Democritus were fuelled by Peripatetic criticism). The verb used to describe atoms' production of sensible qualities is: γεννᾶν. Cf. Philod. *De sign.* XXXVII.1–6 De Lacy; Diog. Oin. 6.I.6, 67.II.9–11 Smith. Lucretius' Latin equivalent is *gignere*: 1.767, 778; 2.228, 759, 808, 855, 870, 893, 901, 923, 930. The term used in *On Nature* XXV for Sedley's proposed 'emergent' properties of the mind is the cognate ἀπογεγεννημένα. Cf. Laursen (1988) 10, Annas (1993c) 55, Hankinson (1998) 226–32. Purinton (1996) 156 notes that the phrase suggests an emergent property but decides that it describes the animal itself *qua* emergent entity.

[8] Note *Ep. Hdt.* 49: ὁμοχρόων.

[9] For 'upwards', 'horizontal', and 'downwards' causation, cf. Sedley (1983b) 39–40, and (1988) 316–18.

[10] Generally on the sense in which it is possible to talk of causation between supervenient macroscopic states: Kim (1984). He does not relate this issue to questions of determinism

It has been suggested, however, that Epicurus wishes to insist on the possibility of 'downwards' causation: the ability of macroscopic items *per se* to affect microscopic atomic arrangements.[11] This thesis would most clearly be at work in the assertion of free will, especially if considered as a reaction to the kind of eliminativist position taken by Democritus. Perception is passive process; I am affected by the world. The 'parallelism' of the macro- and microscopic levels need not worry Epicurus here. However, if this parallelism is applied to cases of human action, determinism threatens. Epicurus wishes in some sense to insist on the aetiological primacy of the atomic level, even if he rejects Democritean eliminativist consequences. If this aetiological primacy is thoroughly maintained, it becomes impossible to argue that I *qua* (macroscopic) agent am primarily responsible for my behaviour. That behaviour supervenes on a microscopic process which is primarily the cause of my action. Even if *contra* Democritus, Epicurus denies that human actions are 'mere' epiphenomena, he has more work to do in order to prevent those actions being determined by atomic processes. They must be independent of the atomic level in the sense of having real causal power over the microscopic level.[12]

A fragmentary portion of Epicurus' *On Nature* 25 contains arguments for the self-refutation of a determinist thesis based on eliminative materialism, and has also been claimed to refer to an 'emergent' theory of the will such that the required 'downwards' causation may be produced.[13] It is not my concern here to evaluate

in that paper, but does offer some sceptical remarks on the possibility of psychophysical ('downwards') causation. On downwards causation see Kim (1992).

[11] This is a stronger notion than the downwards causation which Sharples (1991–93) 183–6 claims is also possible in deterministic systems, because in cases such as that under discussion here the one level (the atomic) is aetiologically prior. Kim (1992) 137 notes that Cartesian (or Platonic) dualism does not require downwards causation although it insists on mental–physical causation.

[12] If psychic events P_1 and P_2 are correlated with atomic events A_1 and A_2, to which the psychic events are aetiologically reducible, P_1 cannot be said to be the cause of A_2 (what 'downwards causation' requires), since *ex hypothesi* P-events are already aetiologically reducible to A-events, and if downwards causation is allowed P_2 becomes *overdetermined*, by both P_1 and A_2. (See Caston (1997) 316.) Rather A_1 is responsible for P_1 and is also the cause of A_2, which is then responsible for P_2. Compare: Kim (1984), (1992) 136, (1993) 203–10.

[13] Asmis (1990) 290–1 points out that 'emergence' is said in many ways – i, not yet existing at the level of the atoms (in which case *all* secondary qualities are emergent);

the various theses and responses that this has generated.[14] More important for me is the generally recognised fact that Epicurus is specifically trying to avoid consequences of Democritean atomism.[15] Furthermore, the parallels between the self-refutation argument used against determinism in this book of *On Nature* and that against scepticism found in Lucretius (*DRN* 4.469ff.), have led some to suggest that Epicurus in both of these arguments reacts against the entire Democritean tradition: Metrodorus, Anaxarchus, and Nausiphanes.[16]

The preceding discussions of Anaxarchus noted the scarcity of evidence that he was an atomist (above p. 73). Nevertheless, there were indications in the doxography which might point to interpretations of his thought which would make him a target for the Epicurean arguments detailed here. Anaxarchus' comparison of the world about us to scene-paintings (SE *M.* 7.88), while I wished to insist on its moral significance, was interpreted by Sextus and perhaps by Epicurus also as a species of general metaphysical reduction. If we require a reason for a doxographical deformation of Anaxarchus' thought from a predominantly moral to a general metaphysical position, then we should probably make the Pyrrhonian tradition responsible. We have seen that Timon in particular can be made responsible for the parallel extension of Pyrrho's indifference from a moral to a general metaphysical claim, and thus invited replies such

ii, inexplicable in atomic terms (what is also termed 'epistemological non-reduction');
iii, emergent dualism (at certain complexities of material organisation properties are generated which are not logically reducible to the atomic level and can have independent causal efficacy). Compare Nagel (1979) esp. 186. The instability of any non-reductive physicalism is well illustrated by Kim (1989). It constantly must struggle not to collapse into epiphenomenalism on the one hand, and substance dualism on the other. Cf. Loar (1992) 242, 249; Caston (1997) esp. 309.

[14] Sedley (1983b) first provided a text and discussion of the then *Lib. de nat. incertus* (Long and Sedley (1987) §§20 B, C, j). This was followed by Sedley (1988). Laursen (1987) identified the book as *De nat.* 25. The latest text is in Laursen (1997). Sedley (1983b) argues for a kind of emergent dualism on the basis of this text, but this has been disputed by Laursen (1988); Annas (1992) 132–3, (1993a) 58 n. 30; Sharples (1991–93) 183ff.; Hankinson (1998) 226–32; Bobzien (2000).

[15] Sedley (1983b) 32, Long and Sedley (1987) vol. I, 108, Annas (1992) 128.

[16] For a discussion of the possible relationship between this and Metrodorus B1, see Burnyeat (1976) 56–7; Sedley (1983b) 26–7, 33; and cf. Brunschwig (1996). Vander Waerdt (1989) 241–2 is not impressed by the similarity of the arguments and doubts that the Lucretian passage derives directly from Epicurus himself. Sedley (1998b) 85–7 has strong arguments to counter this. Compare for the dialectical self-refutation argument: Llewelyn (1966).

as those found in Aristocles which attack Pyrrho's attitude in much the same way that Epicurus attacks Democritus'.[17] Both make a human life unlivable by banishing moral and metaphysical distinctions. Once this tradition had become established, the interpretation of Anaxarchus, Pyrrho's mentor and a known Democritean, was likely to follow suit.

As for Nausiphanes, we know little about his metaphysical thought, although Seneca suggests that he held a view of perceptible qualities like that found in Democritus B9 (see above pp. 187–8). If Epicurus interpreted the Democritean position as eliminativist, then presumably he took a similarly critical attitude towards Nausiphanes. However, I have outlined some clear developments within the Democritean tradition which are under-emphasised by the Epicurean reception. The thought which originated in phrases such as B9 was extended first by Anaxarchus and Pyrrho into a vision of a blank moral canvas, and later by Timon and Nausiphanes into a broad metaphysical thesis. Epicurus rejected all of these conclusions, and saw Democritus himself as the source of the general malaise.

Epicurus' argument with Nausiphanes over the technicity of rhetoric was a reaction to the figure of an ideal natural philosopher-orator, whose *physiologia* is a sufficient basis for compelling and objectively grounded ethical advice. Epicurus objected that persuasion works only on the level of opinions: the orator wins his audience's approval by building on and pandering to their established opinions, not by working with a 'bottom up' theory of what is objectively good for everyone.

This last disagreement points to the key distinction between Epicurus and his Democritean predecessors. I noted that Democritus' own ethical thought was at least consistent with his physics, and that the occurrence of 'physical' or 'atomist' vocabulary within the ethical fragments could be read both metaphorically, and as pointing to a connection between the atomist view of the world and the ethical theses Democritus wished to defend.[18] Even if there is no clear evidence for the systematic deduction of ethics

[17] E.g. Aristoc. *apud* Eus. *PE* 14.18.5–13.
[18] As I have already suggested, this connection might perhaps be made through Democritus' view of (moral) psychology.

from physics in Democritus, there were clear suggestions of the promise of such a deduction in Nausiphanes. Epicurus' distaste for Nausiphanean *physiologia*-based ethical advice (as expressed in *SV* 45, for example) stems from the same motivations as his dislike of the sceptical and determinist consequences of Democritean atomism. Moreover, these all derive from what Epicurus takes to be the starting point of philosophy, namely ethics in general, and the drive for *ataraxia* in particular.

Epicureanism, like the other Hellenistic schools, takes the primary goal of philosophical thought to be the attainment of the goal of human life, a goal which Epicurus identifies as pleasure, the absence of pain.[19] That this is the goal of philosophy entails that philosophy is a discipline which deals with humans, their actions, and their interaction with the world. Democritean eliminativism conflicts immediately with this, and so must be modified. Similarly, Epicurus denied *a priori* Pyrrho's claim that the best human life is the one in which one 'removes what is human'. (However, we should notice that Epicurus also found much to agree with in the pre-Timonian Pyrrhonism he probably learned about from Nausiphanes, particularly its resultant state of equanimity.)

Epicureanism begins with an ethical goal, and builds a natural philosophy in order to attain that goal. *KD* 11 implies that the primary rôle of natural philosophy is to banish the anxieties which are the primary obstacle to *ataraxia*: the *tetrapharmakos* is applied via *physiologia*.[20] As far as we can tell, if Democritus' ethics and physics are related at all, they are connected in a less systematic fashion; the physical system is plausibly interpreted as a reaction to Eleaticism, and is an attempt to provide a cosmology which observes as many Eleatic precepts as possible, while the ethical thoughts offer advice for living a good human life within

---

[19] E.g. SE *M*. 11.169. The first four *Kyriai Doxai*, and the *tetrapharmakos*, arguably the central tenets of Epicureanism, make no reference to atomism.

[20] *KD* 11, 12; *Ep. Hdt.* 37, 78, 83; *Ep. Pyth* 84, 87. Polyst. *De Cont. Irrat.* XXIX.2–XXX.22 Indelli, and cf. Indelli (1978) 31–5. Cf. Barnes (1983b) 149–50. Lucretius insists on the need for *naturae species ratioque* (= φυσιολογία: Clay (1969) 43, Sedley (1998b) 37) to dispel anxiety and *religio*: *DRN* 1.62ff., 146–8ff. (and 2.55–61, 3.87–93, 6.35–41); also Cic. *Fin.* 1.28, 63–4. The therapeutic and instrumental nature of Epicurean natural philosophy is stressed by Nussbaum (1994) 110–11, 123–4. Long (1997) 129 finds this emphasis excessive and argues that Epicurean natural philosophy was also intrinsically good for the inquirer.

a contemporary *polis* which is generally consistent with the relevant consequences of the physics (that death is annihilation, that if there are gods they do not punish or benefit humans and so on). Of course, between Democritus and Epicurus there was also an enormous amount of progress in ethical theory, particularly in the Academy and Lyceum. Just as Epicurus must have been aware of the Peripatetic criticisms of Democritean physics and psychology, so I think it reasonable that he was also aware of the ethical thought of the Platonic and Aristotelian tradition. The growth of ethics as a more or less well defined area of thought in its own right must account in part for Epicurus' reorientation of his philosophy away from the concerns of these Democriteans. But the story of Epicurus' relationship with the Platonic and Aristotelian texts – particularly with their discussions of pleasure – is one which I will not pursue here.

By now it might have become perplexing just why Epicurus espoused atomism of any sort. Why did he not simply reject atomism wholesale as a physical system? The answer, I think, is connected with certain ethical consequences of atomism, above all Democritus' stand against teleology, against eschatology and immaterial souls, and against interventionist deities. These were consequences of Democritean theory to which Epicurus was attracted, and so was disposed to maintain atomism in modified form. Democritean atomism, as viewed by Anaxarchus, Pyrrho, and Epicurus at least, describes a world which rejects moral realism and confines values along with all other secondary qualities to a merely 'conventional' (νόμῳ) existence. Later members of the tradition were attracted to this denial of values 'in nature', and proceeded to construct from that basis various alternative routes to *eudaimonia*. Epicurus wished to retain atomism but reinstate a natural goal (συγγενικὸν τέλος, *Ep. Men.* 128–9), to be attained by fulfilling natural and necessary desires. This wish forced him to reject the moral and/or metaphysical indifference (ἀδιαφορία) of his predecessors, and is therefore the root of many of his disagreements with them.

BIBLIOGRAPHY

Abel, K. (1987) 'Panaitios bei Plutarch *de tranquillitate animi?*', *RhM* 130: 128–52

Adam, H. (1974) *Plutarchs Schrift Non posse suaviter vivi secundum Epicurum* (Amsterdam)

Adorno, F. (1980) 'Polistrato e il suo tempo. Termini Platonici e Aristotelici in nuovi "significati"', *Elenchos* 1: 151–60

Alberti, A. (1995) 'The Epicurean theory of law and justice', in M. Schofield and A. Laks (eds.) *Justice and Generosity* (Cambridge): 161–90
(1996) 'Polistrato e il realismo etico epicureo', in G. Giannantoni and M. Gigante (eds.) *Epicureismo greco e romano* (Naples): 487–509

Alesse, F. (1994) *Panezio e la tradizione stoica* (Naples)

Alfieri, V. E. (1936) *Gli Atomisti* (Bari)
(1957) 'Per la cronologia della scuola di Abdera', in *Estudios de la historia de la filosofia* for R. Mondolfo, (Tucuman) vol. 1: 149–67
(1979) *Atomos Idea²* (Galatina)

Algra, K. A., Barnes, J., Mansfeld, J., and Schofield, M. (eds.) (1999) *The Cambridge history of Hellenistic philosophy* (Cambridge)

Algra, K. A., Koenen, M. H., and Schrijvers, P. H. (eds.) (1997) *Lucretius and his intellectual background* (Amsterdam)

Andria, R. G. (1989) *I frammenti delle 'successioni dei filosofi'* (Naples)

Angeli, A. (1988) *Filodemo agli amici di scuola* (Naples)

Annas, J. (1986) 'Doing without objective values: ancient and modern strategies', in Schofield and Striker (eds.) (1986): 3–30
(1987) 'Epicurus on pleasure and happiness', *Philosophical Topics* 15: 5–21
(1992) *Hellenistic philosophy of mind* (Berkeley)
(1993a) *The morality of happiness* (Oxford)
(1993b) 'Response to F. Decleva Caizzi (1993a) and C. Gill (1993)', in Bulloch et al. (eds.) (1993): 354–68
(1993c) 'Epicurus on agency', in Brunschwig and Nussbaum (eds.) (1993): 53–71

Annas, J. and Barnes, J. (1985) *The modes of scepticism* (Cambridge)

Arnim, H. von (1898) *Leben und Werke des Dion von Prusa* (Berlin)

Aronadio, F. (1990) 'Due fonti laerziane: Sozione e Demetrio di Magnesia', *Elenchos* 11: 203–55

Arrighetti, G. (1955) 'Filodemo ΠΕΡΙ ΘΕΩΝ III frr. 74–82 (Pap. Herc. 157)', *PP* 10: 322–56

(1979) 'Uno passo dell'opera "Sulla Natura" di Epicuro, Democrito e Colote', *CErc* 9: 5–10

Asmis, E. (1983) 'Rhetoric and reason in Lucretius', *AJPh* 104: 36–66

    (1984) *Epicurus' scientific method* (Ithaca)

    (1986) '*Psychagogia* in Plato's *Phaedrus*', *ICS*, 11: 153–72

    (1990) 'Free action and the swerve' (Review of W. Englert (1987), *OSAPh* 7: 275–91

    (1991) 'Philodemus' poetic theory and *On the Good King According to Homer*', *ClAnt* 10: 1–45

Ausland, W. H. (1989) 'The moral origin of the Pyrrhonian philosophy', *Elenchos* 10: 359–434

Ax, W. (1991) 'Timons Gang in die Unterwelt. Ein Beitrag zur Geschichte der antiken Literaturparodie', *Hermes* 119: 177–93

Ayache, L. (1996) 'Le cas de Démocrite: du diagnose médical à l'évaluation philosophique', in R. Witten and P. Pellegrin (eds.) (1996) *Hippokratische Medezin und antike Philosophie* (Hildesheim): 63–75

Badaloni, N. (ed.) (1984) *La storia della filosofia come sapere critico: studi offerti a Mario Dal Pra* (Milan)

Bailey, C. (1928) *The Greek atomists and Epicurus* (Oxford)

Balaudé, J.-F. (1994) *Épicure: lettres, sentences, maximes* (Paris)

Baldwin, B. (1983) *The Philogelos, or, Laughter-Lover* (Amsterdam)

Baltussen, H. (1998) 'The purpose of Theophrastus' *de Sensibus* reconsidered', *Apeiron* 31: 167–99

Bar-Kochva, B. (1996) *Pseudo-Hecataeus On the Jews: legitimising the Jewish diaspora* (Berkeley)

Barigazzi, A. (1969) 'Épicure et le scepticisme', in *Actes du VIIIe congrès de l'association Georges Budé* (Paris): 286–93

Barker, A. (1989) *Greek musical theory vol. II: harmonic and acoustic theory* (Cambridge)

Barnes, J. (1979) *The Presocratic philosophers*, 2 vols. (London)

    (1983a) 'The beliefs of a Pyrrhonist', *Elenchos* 4: 5–44

    (1983b) 'Ancient skepticism and causation', in Burnyeat (ed.) (1983): 149–203

    (1986a) 'Diogene Laerzio e il Pirronismo', *Elenchos* 7: 383–428

    (1986b) 'Is rhetoric an art?' *Darg newsletter* (Univ. Calgary) 2.2: 2–22

    (1990a) 'La διαφωνία Pyrrhonienne', in Voelke (ed.) (1990): 97–106

    (1990b) *The toils of scepticism* (Cambridge)

    (1990c) 'Scepticism and naturalism', *Annales universitatis scientiarum Budapestensis de Rolando Eötvös nominatae, sectio philosophica et sociologica* 22–3: 5–19

    (1994) 'Scepticism and relativism', in A. Alberti (ed.) (1994) *Realtà e Ragione* (Florence): 51–83

Barns, J. (1950–51) 'A new Gnomologium: with some remarks on gnomic anthologies', *CQ* 44: 126–37 and N.S. 1: 1–19

Benakis, L. G. (ed.) (1984) *Proceedings of the first International congress on Democritus*, 2 vols. (Xanthi)

Bernard, P. (1984) 'Anaxarque et Nicocréon', *Journal de savants*: 3–49

Bertelli, L. (1980) 'Per le fonti dell'antropologia di Democrito (68 B5 DK)', in Romano (ed.) (1980): 527–32

Berti, E. (1981) 'La critica allo scetticismo nel IV libro della *Metafisica*', in Giannantoni (ed.) (1981b): 61–80

Bett, R. (1988) 'Is modern moral scepticism essentially local?', *Analysis* 48: 102–7

  (1994a) 'What did Pyrrho think about "the nature of the divine and the good"?', *Phronesis* 39: 303–37

  (1994b) 'Aristocles on Timon on Pyrrho: the text, its logic and its credibility', *OSAPh* 12: 137–82

  (1994c) 'Sextus' *Against the Ethicists*: scepticism, relativism, or both?', *Apeiron* 27:123–61

  (1997) *Sextus Empiricus: Against the Ethicists* (Oxford)

  (1998) 'The sceptics and the emotions', in J. Sihvola and T. Engberg-Pedersen (eds.) (1998) *The emotions in Hellenistic philosophy* (Dordrecht): 197–218

  (1999) 'On the pre-history of Pyrrhonism', *PBACAP* 15: 137–66

  (2000) *Pyrrho, his antecedents and his legacy* (Oxford)

Bicknell, P. J. (1968) 'The seat of the mind in Democritus', *Eranos* 66: 10–23

  (1982) 'Melissus' way of seeming?', *Phronesis* 27: 194–201

Blanchard, A. (1991) 'Épicure, "Sentence Vaticane" 14: Épicure ou Métrodore?', *REG* 104: 394–409

Blanchard-Lemée, M. and Blanchard, A. (1993) 'Épicure dans une anthologie sur mosaïque à Autun', *CRAI* for 1993: 964–84

Blank, D. (1995) 'Philodemus on the technicity of rhetoric', in Obbink (ed.) (1995): 178–88

  (1998a) *Sextus Empiricus: against the Grammarians* (Oxford)

  (1998b) 'Versionen oder Zwillinge? Zu den Handschriften von Philodems *Rhetorik*', in G. Most (ed.) (1998) *Editing Texts, Texte edieren* Aporemata: Kritische Studien zur Philologiegeschichte bd. 2 (Göttingen): 123–40

Bobzien, S. (2000) 'Did Epicurus discover the free will problem?', *OSAPh* 19: 287–337

Bodnár, I. (1997) 'Demokriteer', *Der Neue Pauly* 3: 455

Bollack, J. and Laks, A. (eds.) (1976) *Études sur l'épicurisme antique*, Cahiers de Philologie 1 (Lille)

Bossu, B. (1982) 'La crainte dans la morale de Démocrite', *RPh* 56: 287–300

Bostock, D. (1986) *Plato's Phaedo* (Oxford)

Bouquiaux-Simon, O. (1992) 'Additamenta pour une anthologie mutilée (P.Berol. inv. 21312 + P.Schubart 27)', in *Proceedings of XIX international congress of Papyrology* (Cairo) vol. 1: 461–80

Bouquiaux-Simon, O. and Rutten, C. (1992) Edition of P.Berol. inv. 21312 = P.Schubart 27 fr. a, 2–6 in *Corpus dei Papiri Filosofici* I.1** (Florence): 158–61

Boyancé, P. (1963) *Lucrèce et l'épicurisme* (Paris)

Brancacci, A. (1977) 'Le orazione diogeniane di Dione Crisostomo', in G. Giannantoni (ed.) (1977) *Scuole socratiche minori e filosofia ellenistica* (Rome): 141–72

(1980) 'Democrito e la tradizione cinica', in Romano (ed.) (1980): 411–25

(1981) 'La filosofia di Pirrone e le sue relazioni con il cinismo', in Giannantoni (ed.) (1981b): 211–42

(1987) ' "Askesis" e "logos" nella tradizione cinica', *Elenchos* 8: 439–47

Branham, R. Bracht and Goulet-Cazé, M.-O. (eds.) (1996) *The Cynics* (Berkeley)

Brennan, T. (1998) 'Pyrrho on the criterion', *AncPhil* 18: 417–34

(1999) *Ethics and epistemology in Sextus Empiricus* (New York)

Brittain, C. and Palmer, J. (2001) 'The New Academy's appeals to the Presocratics', *Phronesis* 46: 38–72

Brochard, V. (1923) *Les sceptiques grecs* (Paris)

(1954) 'La théorie du plaisir d'après Épicure', in his *Études de philosophie ancienne et de philosophie moderne* (Paris): 252–93

Brumfield, A. (1997) 'Cakes in the Liknon: votes from the sanctuary of Demeter and Kore on Acrocorinth', *Hesperia* 76: 147–72

Brunschwig, J. (1984) 'Démocrite et Xéniade', in Benakis (ed.) (1984) vol. II: 109–24

(1986) 'The cradle argument in Epicureanism and Stoicism', in Schofield and Striker (eds.) (1986): 113–44

(1992a) 'The Anaxarchus case: an essay on survival', *PBA* 82: 59–88

(1992b) 'Pyrrhon et Philista', in M.-O. Goulet-Cazé, G. Madec, and D. O'Brien (eds.) (1992) ΣΟΦΙΗΣ ΜΑΙΗΤΟΡΕΣ *"Chercheurs de sagesse"*, *Hommage à Jean Pépin* (Paris): 133–46

(1994a) 'Once again on Eusebius on Aristocles on Timon on Pyrrho', in his *Papers in Hellenistic philosophy* (Cambridge): 190–211

(1994b) 'The title of Timon's *Indalmoi*: from Odysseus to Pyrrho', in his *Papers in Hellenistic philosophy* (Cambridge): 212–23

(1996) 'Le fragment DK 70 B1 de Métrodore de Chio', in K. A. Algra, P. W. van der Horst, D. T. Runia (eds.) (1996) *Polyhistor: studies in the history and historiography of ancient philosophy presented to Jaap Mansfeld on his sixtieth birthday* (Leiden): 21–38

(1997) 'L'aphasie pyrrhonienne', in C. Lévy and L. Pernot (eds.) (1997) *Dire l'évidence (philosophie et rhétorique antiques)*, Cahiers de philosophie de l'Université de Paris XII – Val de Marne no. 2 (Paris): 297–320

(1999a) 'Livre IX: introduction, traduction et notes', in Goulet-Cazé (ed.) (1999a): 1025–1145

(1999b) 'The beginnings of Hellenistic epistemology', in Algra, Barnes, Mansfeld, and Schofield (eds.) (1999): 229–59

Brunschwig, J. and Nussbaum, M. (eds.) (1993) *Passions and perceptions* (Cambridge)

Buck, A. (1963) '*Democritus ridens et Heraclitus flens*', in *Wort und Text* for Fr. Schalk (Frankfurt): 167–86

Bulloch, A. W. et al. (eds.) (1993) *Images and ideologies: self-definition in the Hellenistic world* (Berkeley)

Burkert, W. (1972) *Lore and science in early Pythagoreanism* (Cambridge, Mass.)
(1997) 'Logik und Sprachspiel bei Leukippos/Demokritos: οὐ μᾶλλον als These und Denkform', in Gunther and Rengakos (eds.) (1997): 23–33

Burkert, W., Gemelli Marciano, L., Matelli, E., and Orelli, L. (eds.) (1998) *Fragmentsammlungen philosophischer Texte / Le raccolte dei frammenti di filosofici antichi*, Aporemata bd. 3 (Göttingen)

Burnet, J. (1911) *Plato: Phaedo* (Oxford)

Burnstein, S. M. (1992) 'Hecataeus of Abdera's History of Egypt', in J. H. Johnson (ed.) (1992) *Life in a multi-cultural society: Egypt from Cambyses to Constantine and beyond* (Chicago): 45–9

Burnyeat, M. F. (1976) 'Protagoras and self-refutation in later Greek philosophy', *PhR* 85: 44–69
(1978) 'The upside-down, back-to-front sceptic of Lucretius 4.472', *Philologus* 112: 197–206
(1979) 'Conflicting appearances', *PBA* 65: 69–111
(1980a) 'Tranquillity without a stop: Timon fragment 68', *CQ* 30: 86–93
(1980b) 'Can the sceptic live his scepticism?', in M. Schofield et al. (eds.) (1980) *Doubt and dogmatism* (Oxford): 20–53
(1982) 'Idealism and Greek philosophy: what Descartes saw and Berkeley missed', *PhR* 91: 3–40
(ed.) (1983) *The skeptical tradition* (Berkeley)
(1984) 'The sceptic in his place and time', in R. Rorty et al. (eds.) (1984) *Philosophy in History* (Cambridge): 225–54

Burton, A. (1972) *Diodorus Siculus book one: a commentary* (Leiden)

Canfora, L. (1994) 'Clemente di Alessandria e Diogene Laerzio', in *Storia, poesia e pensiero nel mondo antico, studi in onore di M. Gigante* (Naples): 79–81

Capasso, M. (1976) 'L'opera polistratea sulla filosofia', *CErc* 6: 81–4
(1987) *Comunità senza rivolta: quattro saggi sull' epicureismo* (Naples)
(1991) *Manuale di papirologia ercolanese* (Lecce)

Cappelletti, A. J. (1979) *Ensayos sobre los atomistas griegos* (Caracas)

Casertano, G. (1983a) *Il piacere, l'amore e la morte nelle dottrine dei presocratici* vol. 1 (Naples)
(ed.) (1983b) *Democrito dall' atomo alla città* (Naples)
(1984) 'Pleasure, desire and happiness in Democritus', in Benakis (ed.) (1984) vol. 1: 347–53

Cassin, B. and Narcy, M. (1989) *La décision du sens: le livre Gamma de la Métaphysique d'Aristote* (Histoire des doctrines de l'antiquité classique 13) (Paris)

Caston, V. (1997) 'Epiphenomenalisms, ancient and modern', *PhR* 106: 309–63

Chadwick, H. (1966) *Early Christian thought and the classical tradition* (Oxford)

Chantraine, P. (1956) *Études sur le vocabulaire grec* (Paris)

Chiesara, M. L. (2001) *Aristocles of Messene: testimonies and fragments* (Oxford)

Chilton, W. (1971) *Diogenes of Oenoanda: the fragments* (Oxford)

Clay, D. (1969) 'Greek *Physis* and Epicurean *Physiologia* (Lucretius 1.1–148)', *TAPhA* 100: 31–47

    (1972) 'Epicurus' ΚΥΡΙΑ ΔΟΞΑ XVII', *GRBS* 13: 59–66

    (1973) 'Sailing to Lampsacus: Diogenes of Oinoanda, New Fragment 7', *GRBS* 14: 49–59

    (1986) 'The cults of Epicurus', *CErc* 16: 11–28

    (1992) 'Lucian of Samosata: four philosophical lives', *ANRW* 2.36.5: 3406–50

    (1996) 'The anatomy of a Lucretian metaphor', in Gigante and Giannantoni (eds.) (1996): 779–93

    (1998) *Paradosis and survival: three chapters in the history of Epicurean philosophy* (Ann Arbor)

Cole, T. (1967) *Democritus and the sources of Greek anthropology*, APA Philological monographs 25

Conche, M. (1993) 'Métrodore de Chio', in D. Huisman (ed.) (1993) vol. II: 1821

Cooper, J. (1999) 'Pleasure and desire in Epicurus', in his (1999) *Reason and emotion: essays on ancient moral psychology and ethical theory* (Princeton): 485–514

Cortassa, G. (1976) 'Due giudizi di Timone di Fliunte', *RF* 104: 312–26

    (1978) 'Note ai *Silli* di Timone di Fliunte', *RF* 106: 140–55

Couissin, P. (1929) 'L'origine et l'evolution de l' ἐποχή', *REG* 42: 373–97

Couloubaritsis, L. (1980) 'Considérations sur la notion de NOUS chez Démocrite', *AGPh* 62 :129–45

    (1984) 'Pensée et action chez Démocrite', in Benakis (ed.) (1984) vol. I: 327–37

Crönert, W. (1906a) *Kolotes und Menedemos* (Leipzig)

    (1906b) '*Lectiones Epicureae*', *RhM* 61: 414–26

Curd, P. (1998) *The legacy of Parmenides: Eleatic monism and later Presocratic thought* (Princeton)

Dal Pra, M. (1989) *Lo scetticismo greco*[3] (Rome–Bari)

Dalfino, M. C. (1993) 'Ieronimo di Rodi: la dottrina della *vacuitas doloris*', *Elenchos* 14: 277–303

Davison, J. A. (1953) 'Protagoras, Democritus, and Anaxagoras', *CQ* 3: 33–45

De Lacy, P. H. (1941) 'Cicero's invective against Piso', *TAPhA* 72: 49–58

    (1958a) 'οὐ μᾶλλον and the antecedents of ancient scepticism', *Phronesis* 3: 59–71

    (1958b) 'Pigs and Epicureans', *CB* 34: 55–6

    (1964) 'Colotes' first criticism of Democritus', in J. Mau and E. G. Schmidt (eds.) (1964) *Isonomia* (Berlin): 67–77

De Lacy, P. H. and D. A. (1978) *Philodemus on methods of inference* (Naples)

BIBLIOGRAPHY

De Martino, F. (1986) 'Cherilo, Timone e la cultura "da maiale"', *QUCC* 52 (NS 23): 137–46

Decleva Caizzi, F. (1980a) 'τῦφος: contributo alla storia di un concetto', *Sandalion* 3: 53–66

(1980b) 'Democrito in Sesto Empirico', in Romano (ed.) (1980): 393–410

(1981a) *Pirrone: Testimonianze* (Naples)

(1981b) 'Prolegomeni ad una raccolta delle fonti relative a Pirrone di Elide', in Giannantoni (ed.) (1981b): 93–128

(1984a) 'Timone di Fliunte: I frammenti 74, 75, 76 Diels', in Badaloni (ed.) (1984): 92–105

(1984b) 'Pirrone e Democrito: gli atomi un "mito"', *Elenchos* 5: 5–24

(1986) 'Pirroniani ed Accademici nel III secolo a.C.', in Flashar and Gigon (eds.) (1986): 147–83

(1990) 'Timone e i filosofi: Protagora', in Voelke (ed.) (1990): 41–53

(1992a) 'Sesto e gli scettici', *Elenchos* 13: 279–317

(1992b) 'Il libro IX delle "Vite dei Filosofi" di Diogene Laerzio', *ANRW* 2.36.6: 4218–40

(1993a) 'Early Hellenistic images of philosophical life', in Bulloch et al. (eds.) (1993): 303–29

(1993b) 'L'elogia del cane. Sesto Empirico, *Schizzi pirronniani* I 62–78', *Elenchos* 14: 305–30

(1995) 'Aenesidemus versus Pyrrho: il fuoco scalda 'per natura' (Sextus *M.* VIII 215 e XI 69)', in L. Ayres (ed.) *The passionate intellect: essays on the transformation of classical traditions presented to Prof. I. G. Kidd* (New Brunswick): 145–59

(1998) 'Pirrone, pirroniani, pirronismo', in Burkert et al. (eds.) (1998): 336–53

Deichgräber, K. (1930) *Die griechische Empirikerschule* (Berlin)

Delia, D. (1993) 'Response to A. E. Samuel (1993)', in Green (ed.) (1993): 192–204

Deschamps, L. (1998) 'Un bon mot de Cicéron en *fin.*, 5,38?', *REA* 100: 191–8

Di Marco, M. (1982) 'Riflessi della polemica antiepicurea nei *Silli* di Timone 1: Epicuro ΓΡΑΜΜΟΔΙΔΑΣΚΑΛΙΔΗΣ', *Elenchos* 3: 325–46

(1983) 'Riflessi della polemica antiepicurea nei *Silli* di Timone 2: Epicuro, Il porco e l'insaziablie ventre', *Elenchos* 4: 59–91

(1989) *Timone di Fliunte: Silli* (Rome)

Diano, C. (1974) *Scritti Epicurei* (Florence)

Diels, H. (1880) 'Über Leukipp und Demokrit' *Verhandlungen der 35. Versamunlung deutscher Philologen und Schulmänner* (Leipzig): 97–109 (repr. in his (1969) *Kleine Schriften* (ed.) W. Burkert, (Darmstadt): 185–98)

(1916) *Philodemos über der Götter: erstes buch* (Berlin)

(1917) *Philodemos über der Götter: drittes Buch* (Berlin)

Dierauer, U. (1977) *Tier und Mensch im Denken der Antike* (Amsterdam)

Dietz, K. M. (1970) *Protagoras von Abdera: Untersuchungen zu seinem Denken* (Berlin)

207

Diller, H. (1934) *Wanderzart und Aitiologie: Studien zur hippokratischen Schrift* ΠΕΡΙ ΑΕΡΩΝ ΥΔΑΤΩΝ ΤΟΠΩΝ, *Philologus* suppl. bd. 26, Heft 3

Dillery, J. (1998) 'Hecataeus of Abdera: Hyperboreans, Egypt, and the *interpretatio Graeca*', *Historia* 47: 255–75

Dillon, J. M. (1996) 'Speusippus on pleasure', in A. Keimpe, A. Algra, P. W. van der Host, D. T. Runia (eds.) *Polyhistor: studies in the history and historiography of ancient philosophy presented to Jaap Mansfeld on his sixtieth birthday* (Leiden): 99–114

Dixsaut, M. (ed.) (1999) *La fêlure du plaisir. Études sur le* Philèbe *de Platon. 1. commentaires* (Paris)

Dorandi, T. (1982a) *Filodemo: il buon re secondo Omero* (Naples)

(1982b) 'Filodemo. Gli Stoici (PHerc. 155 e 339)', *CErc* 12: 91–133

(1990) 'Per una ricompozisione dello scritto di Filodemo *Sulla Retorica*', *ZPE* 82: 59–87

(1991a) *Filodemo: Storia dei filosofi, Platone e l'Academia (PHerc. 1021 e 164)* (Naples)

(1991b) *Ricerche sulla cronologia dei filosofi ellenistici* (Naples)

(1994a) 'I frammenti di Anassarco di Abdera', *AATC* 49: 11–58

(1994b) 'Prolegomeni per una edizione dei frammenti di Antigono di Caristo II', *MH* 51: 5–29

(1995a) 'Prolegomeni per una edizione dei frammenti di Antigono di Caristo I', *RhM* 138: 347–68

(1995b) 'Prolegomeni per una edizione dei frammenti di Antigono di Caristo III', *ZPE* 106: 61–90

(1999) *Antigone de Caryste: fragments* (Paris)

Dörer, K. (1997) 'Bryson, der Lehrer des Philosophen Pyrrhos', *Der Neue Pauly* 2: 807–8

Dudley, J. A. (1984) 'The ethics of Democritus and Aristotle', in Benakis (ed.) (1984) vol. I: 371–85

Dumont, J.-P. (1972) *Le scepticisme et le phénomène* (Paris)

(1987) 'Les modèles de la conversion à la philosophie chez Diogène Laërce', *Augustinus* 32: 79–97

(1993) 'Abdéritains, ou l'école d'Abdère', in Huisman (ed.) (1993) vol. I: 4–7

Edwards, R. B. (1979) *Pleasures and pains: a theory of qualitative hedonism* (Ithaca)

Englert, W. G. (1987) *Epicurus on the swerve and voluntary action* (Atlanta)

Erler, M. and Schofield, M. (1999) 'Epicurean ethics', in Algra, Barnes, Mansfeld, and Schofield (eds.) (1999): 642–74

Everson, S. (ed.) (1998) *Ethics* (Cambridge)

Farrar, C. (1988) *The origins of democratic thinking* (Cambridge)

Fay, E. de (1906) *Clément d'Alexandrie: étude sur les rapports du Christianisme et de la philosophie grecque au IIe siècle*[2] (Paris)

Ferrari, G. A. (1968) 'Due fonti sullo scetticismo antico', *SIFC* 40: 200–24

(1981) 'L'immagine dell' equilibrio' in Giannantoni (ed.) (1981b): 337–70

Ferrari, G. F. (1987) *Listening to the cicadas* (Cambridge)

Ferrario, M. (1981) 'La concezione della retorica da Epicuro a Filodemo', in *Proceedings of the XVIth annual international congress of papyrology* (Chico): 145–52

Festugière, A.-J. (1946) *Épicure et ses dieux* (Paris)

Fischer, J. M. (ed.) (1993) *The metaphysics of death* (Stanford)

Flashar, H. (ed.) (1994) *Die Philosophie der Antike 4: Die hellenistische Philosophie*, 2 vols. (Basle)

Flashar, H. and Gigon, O. (eds.) (1986) *Aspects de philosophie hellénistique*, Entretiens Hardt 32 (Geneva)

Flintoff, E. (1980) 'Pyrrho and India', *Phronesis* 25: 88–108

Floridi, L. (1997) 'Scepticism and animal rationality: the fortune of Chrysippus' dog in the history of western thought', *AGP* 79: 27–57

Flower, M. A. (1994) *Theopompus of Chios: history and rhetoric in the fourth century BCE* (Oxford)

Foucault, M. (1972) *The archaeology of knowledge* (trans. A. M. Sheridan-Smith) (London)

Fowler, D. P. (1983) 'A commentary on Lucretius *de rerum natura* Book 2, lines 1–322', Oxford D.Phil. thesis

(1984) 'Sceptics and Epicureans' (Review of Gigante (1981)), *OSAPh* 2: 237–67

(1989) 'Lucretius and Politics', in Griffin and Barnes (eds.) (1989): 120–50

(1993) 'Review of Mitsis (1988)', *JHS* 113: 169–74

Fowler, H. N. (1890) 'Plutarch on εὐθυμία', *HSPh* 1: 139–52

Fränkel, H. (1955) *Wege and Formen frügriechischen Denkens²* (Munich)

Fraser, P. M. (1972) *Ptolemaic Alexandria*, 3 vols. (Oxford)

Frede, M. (1982) 'The sceptic's beliefs', in his *Essays in ancient philosophy* (Oxford): 179–200

(1999) 'The sceptics', in D. J. Furley (ed.) (1999) *Routledge history of philosophy vol. II: from Aristotle to Augustine* (London): 253–86

Freeman, K. (1948) *Ancilla to the Pre-Socratic philosophers* (Oxford)

Fritz, K. von (1934) 'Theodosius, (3)', *RE* V. 2: 1929–30

(1935) 'Nausifanes', *RE* XVI.2: 2021–7

(1937) 'Numenius (8)', *RE* XVII.2: 1296–7

(1938) *Philosophie und sprachlicher Ausdruck bei Demokrit, Plato und Aristoteles* (New York)

(1963) 'Pyrrhon', *RE* XXIV: 89–106

Furley, D. J. (1967) *Two studies in the Greek atomists* (Princeton)

(1985) 'Strato's theory of the void', in J. Wiesner (ed.) (1985) *Aristoteles Werk und Wirkung vol. I 'Aristoteles und seine Schule'* (Berlin): 594–609

(1993) 'Democritus and Epicurus on sensible qualities', in Brunschwig and Nussbaum (eds.) (1993): 72–94

Gaiser, K. (1988) *Philodems Academica* Supplementum Platonicum 1 (Stuttgart)

Gale, M. R. (1994) *Myth and poetry in Lucretius* (Cambridge)

Gallop, D. (1975) *Plato: Phaedo* (Oxford)

Gargiulo, T. (1982) 'Epicuro e "il piacere del ventre" (fr. 409 Us. = [227] Arr.)', *Elenchos* 3: 153–8

Gemelli Marciano, L. (1998) 'Wörtliche Zitate aus Demokrit in der skeptischen Überlieferung', in Burkert et al. (eds.) (1998): 106–27

Giannantoni, G. (1981a) 'Pirrone, la scuola scettica e il sistema delle "successioni"', in Giannantoni (ed.) (1981b): 11–34

  (ed.) (1981b) *Lo scetticismo antico*, 2 vols. (Naples)

  (1984) 'Il piacere cinetico nell' epicureismo', *Elenchos* 5: 25–44

  (1990) *Socratis et socraticorum reliquiae* vol. IV (Naples)

Giannantoni, G. and Gigante M. (eds.) (1996) *Epicureismo greco e romano*, 2 vols. (Naples)

Gigante, M. (1981) *Scetticismo e epicureismo* (Naples)

  (1983) *Ricerche filodemee*² (Naples)

  (1986) 'Biografia e dossografia in Diogene Laerzio', *Elenchos* 7: 7–102

  (1990) 'Quelques précisions sur le scepticisme e l'épicurisme', in Voelke (ed.) (1990): 69–83

  (1992) *Cinismo e epicureismo* (Naples)

  (1995) *Philodemus in Italy* (Ann Arbor)

  (1996) '*Sigfridus Sudhaus Philodemeorum studiosus*', *CErc* 26: 15–26

  (1997) 'La Scuola di Aristotele', in Gunther and Rengakos (eds.) (1997): 255–70

Gigante, M. and Dorandi, T. (1980) 'Anassarco e Epicuro "*Sul Regno*"', in Romano (ed.) (1980): 479–97

Gigante, M. and Indelli, G. (1980) 'Democrito nei papiri ercolanesi di Filodemo', in Romano (ed.) (1980): 451–66

Gigon, O. (1946) 'Antike Erzählungen über die Berufung zur Philosophie', *MH* 3: 1–21

  (1961) 'Review of Spoerri (1959)', *Gnomon* 33: 771–6

Gill, C. (1993) 'Panaetius on the virtues of being yourself', in Bulloch et al. (eds.) (1993): 330–53

  (1994) 'Peace of mind and being yourself: Panaetius to Plutarch', *ANRW* 2.36.7: 4599–640

Glad, C. E. (1995) *Paul and Philodemus: adaptability in Epicurean and early Christian psychagogy* (Leiden)

  (1996) 'Frank speech, flattery, and friendship in Philodemus', in J. T. Fitzgerald (ed.) (1996) *Friendship, flattery, and frankness of speech* (Leiden): 21–59

Glucker, J. (1978) *Antiochus and the late Academy* (Göttingen)

Goldschmidt, V. (1977) *La doctrine d'Épicure et le droit* (Paris)

Goodenough, E. K. (1928) 'The political philosophy of Hellenistic kingship', *YClS* 1: 55–102

Görler, W. (1985) 'Review of Decleva Caizzi (1981a)', *AGPh* 67: 320–35

  (1994) 'Älterer Pyrrhonismus, jungere Akademie, Antiochus aus Askalon', in Flashar (ed.) (1994) vol. II: 717–74

Gosling, J. C. B. and Taylor, C. C. W. (1982), *The Greeks on pleasure* (Oxford)

Gottschalk, H. (1971) 'Soul as *harmonia*', *Phronesis* 16: 179–98

(1986) 'Democritus *FV* 68 B1: an amputation', *Phronesis* 31: 90–1

(1987) 'Aristotelian philosophy in the Roman world from the time of Cicero to the end of the second century AD', *ANRW* 2.36.2: 1079–1174

Goukowsky, P. (1978–81) *Essai sur les origines du mythe d'Alexandre* (Nancy)

Goulet, R. (ed.) (1994) *Dictionnaire de philosophes antiques* (Paris)

Goulet-Cazé, M.-O. (ed.) (1999a) *Diogène Laërce: vies et doctrines des philosophes illustres* (various translators) (Varese)

(1999b) 'Introduction générale', in Goulet-Cazé (ed.) (1999a): 9–27

(1999c) 'Livre VI: Introduction, traduction et notes', in Goulet-Cazé (ed.) (1999a): 655–772

Graeser, A. (1970) 'Demokrit und die skeptische Formel', *Hermes* 98: 300–17

Graham, A. J. (1992) 'Abdera and Teos', *JHS* 112: 44–73

Green, P. (ed.) (1993) *Hellenistic history and culture* (Berkeley)

Griffin, M. and Barnes, J. (eds.) (1989) *Philosophia togata* (repr. 1997 as *Philosophia togata I*) (Oxford)

Grilli, A. (1978) 'Il naufragio di Epicuro', *RSF* 33: 116–18

(1983) 'ΔΙΑΘΕΣΙΣ in Epicuro', in ΣΥΗΤΗΣΙΣ: *studi sull'epicureismo greco e romano offerti a M. Gigante* (Naples) vol. I: 93–109

(1992) 'Sul proemio del II libro di Lucrezio', in his *Stoicismo, epicureismo, letteratura* (Brescia): 65–72

Grimal, P. (1986) 'Les éléments philosophiques dans l'idée de monarchie à Rome à la fin de la République', in Flashar and Gigon (eds.) (1986): 233–73

(1992) 'Le vocabulaire de l'intériorité dans l'œuvre de Sénèque', in *La langue Latine, langue de la philosophie*, Collection de l'École française à Rome 161 (Rome): 141–59

Groarke, L. (1990) *Greek scepticism: anti-realist trends in ancient thought* (Montreal and Kingston)

Gruen, E. S. (1993) 'Introduction to Part One', in Bulloch et al. (eds.) (1993): 3–6

(1996) 'Hellenistic kingship: puzzles, problems, and possibilities', in P. Bilde, T. Engberg-Pedersen, L. Hannestad, and J. Zahle (eds.) (1996) *Aspects of Hellenistic kingship* (Cambridge): 116–25

Gunther, H.-C. and Rengakos, A. (eds.) (1997) *Beiträge zur antiken Philosophie für W. Kullmann* (Stuttgart)

Guthrie, W. K. C. (1965) *History of Greek philosophy* volume II (Cambridge)

Hammerstaedt, J. (1992) 'Der Schlussteil von Philodems Drittem Buch über Rhetorik', *CErc* 22: 9–117

Hankinson, R. J. (1995) *The Sceptics* (London)

(1998) *Cause and explanation in ancient Greek thought* (Oxford)

Hardie, P. (1986) *Virgil's Aeneid: cosmos and imperium* (Oxford)

Haslam, M. W. (1993) 'Two philosophic barbs', *AJPh* 113: 43–46

Heinze, R. (1890) 'Ariston von Chios bei Plutarch und Horaz', *RhM* 45: 497–523

Herschbell, J. P. (1982) 'Plutarch and Democritus', *QUCC* 39: 81–111

Hirzel, R. (1879) 'Demokrits Schrift περὶ εὐθυμίης', *Hermes* 14: 354–407
   (1882) 'Der Demokriteer Diotimos', *Hermes* 17: 326–8
   (1883) *Untersuchungen zu Ciceros philosophischen Schriften b. 3* (Stuttgart)

Holtsmark, E. B. (1967) 'On Lucretius 2.1–19', *TAPhA* 98: 193–204

Hornblower, J. (1981) *Hieronymus of Cardia* (Oxford)

Hossenfelder, M. (1986) 'Epicurus – hedonist *malgré lui*', in Schofield and Striker (eds.): 248–64

Hubbell, H. M. (1916) 'Isocrates and the Epicureans', *CPh* 11: 405–18
   (1926) 'The *Rhetorica* of Philodemus', *Transactions of the Connecticut Academy of Arts and Sciences* 23: 243–382

Huby, P. M. (1978) 'Epicurus' attitude to Democritus', *Phronesis* 23: 80–6

Huffman, C. (1993) *Philolaus of Croton: Pythagorean and Presocratic* (Cambridge)

Huisman, D. (ed.) (1993) *Dictionnaire des philosophes*[2], 2 vols. (Paris)

Hussey, E. L. (1985) 'Thucydidean history and Democritean theory', in P. A. Cartledge and F. D. Harvey (eds.) (1985) *Crux: essays in Greek history presented to G. E. M. de Ste. Croix*, History of political thought 6.1: 118–38

Ibscher, G. (1983) *Demócrito y sus sentencias sobre ética y educación* (Lima–Peru)
   (1996) *Demokrit: Fragmente zur Ethik* (Stuttgart)

Indelli, G. (1977) 'Polistrato contro gli scettici', *CErc* 7: 85–95
   (1978) *Polistrato sul disprezzo irrationali delle opinioni populari* (Naples)
   (1995) *Plutarco: le bestie sono esseri razionali* (Naples)
   (1996) 'Plutarco *bruta ratione uti*: una "risposta" a Polistrato *de irrationali contemptu*?', in Giannantoni and Gigante (eds.) (1996): 939–49

Indelli, G. and Tsouna-McKirahan, V. (1995) *[Philodemus]* [On choices and avoidances] (Naples)

Inwood, B. (1990) '*Rhetorica disputatio*: the strategy of *de finibus* 2', in M. Nussbaum (ed.) *The poetics of therapy*, Apeiron 23.4: 143–64
   (1995) 'Seneca in his philosophical milieu', *HSPh* 97: 63–76

Ioppolo, A.-M. (1980a) *Aristone di Chio e lo stoicismo antico* (Naples)
   (1980b) 'Anassarco e il cinismo', in Romano (ed.) (1980): 494–506
   (1986) *Opinione e scienza: il dibattito tra Stoici ed Accademici nel III e II secolo a.C* (Naples)

Irwin, T. (1986) 'Socrates the Epicurean?', *ICS* 11: 85–112

Isnardi Parente, M. (1966) *Techne: momenti del pensiero greco da Platone ad Epicuro* (Florence)
   (1971) 'L'epicureo Polistrato e le categorie', *PP* 139: 280–9
   (1984) 'I democritei e l'antiscetticismo di Epicuro', in Badaloni (ed.) (1984): 106–21

Jacoby, F. (1912) 'Hekataios (4)', *RE* 7: 2750–69
   (1943) *Fragmente der griechische Historiker*, vol. 3A (Leiden)

Janácek, K. (1992) *Indice delle vite dei filosofi di Diogene Laerzio* (Florence)

Janko, R. (2000) *Philodemus* On Poems: *book one* (Oxford)

Kahn, C. H. (1983) 'Arius as doxographer', in W. W. Fortenbaugh (ed.) (1983) *On Stoic and Peripatetic ethics: the work of Arius Didymus* (New Brunswick): 3–13

(1984a) 'Democritus and the origins of moral psychology', *AJP* 106: 1–31

(1984b) 'Democritus on moral psychology', in Benakis (ed.) (1984) vol. 1: 307–16

(1985) 'Democritus and the origins of moral psychology', *AJP* 106 :1–31

(1998) 'Pre-Platonic ethics', in Everson (ed.) (1998): 27–48

Karadimas, D. (1996) *Sextus Empiricus against Aelius Aristides: the conflict between philosophy and rhetoric in the second century A.D.* (Lund)

Kenney, E. (1971) *Lucretii de rerum natura liber III* (Cambridge)

Kerferd, G. B. (1971) 'Epicurus' doctrine of the soul', *Phronesis* 16: 80–96

Keuls, E. C. (1975) '*Skiagraphia* once again', *AJA* 79: 1–16

(1978) *Plato and Greek painting* (Leiden)

Kidd, I. G. (1992) *Plutarch: essays* (Introduction and notes) (Harmondsworth)

Kienle, W. von (1961) *Die Berichte über die Sukzessionen der Philosophen in der hellenistichen und spätantiken Literatur* (Berlin)

Kim, J. (1984) 'Epiphenomenalism and supervenient causation', *Midwest studies in philosophy* 9: 57–70, repr. in his (1993) *Supervenience and mind* (Cambridge): 92–108

(1989) 'The myth of non-reductive materialism', *Proceedings and addresses of the American Philosophical Society* 63: 31–47, repr. in his (1993) *Supervenience and mind* (Cambridge): 265–84

(1992) ' "Downwards causation" in emergentism and nonreductive physicalism', in A. Beckermann, H. Flohr, and J. Kim (eds.) (1992) *Emergence or reduction? Essays on the prospects of nonreductive physicalism* (Berlin): 119–38

(1993) 'The non-reductionist's troubles with mental causation', in J. Heil and A. Mele (eds.) *Mental causation* (Oxford): 189–210, repr. in his (1993) *Supervenience and mind* (Cambridge): 336–57

Kirk, G., Raven, J., and Schofield, M. (1983) *The Presocratic philosophers*, 2nd edn (Cambridge)

Kleve, K. (1963) *Gnōsis theōn*, *SO* fasc. suppl. 19

(1978) 'The philosophical polemics in Lucretius. A study in the history of Epicurean criticism', in O. Gigon (ed.) (1978) *Lucrèce* Entretiens Hardt 24 (Geneva): 39–71

Kleve, K. and Longo Auricchio, F. (1992) 'Honey from the Garden of Epicurus', in M. Capasso (ed.) (1992) *Papiri letterari greci e latini* (Lecce): 211–26

Koenen, L. (1993) 'The Ptolemaic king as a religious figure', in Bulloch et al. (eds.) (1993): 25–115

Konstan, D. (1973) *Some aspects of Epicurean psychology* (Leiden)

Konstan, D., Clay, D., Glad, C. E., Thom, J. C., and Ware, J. (1998) *Philodemus on frank criticism* (Atlanta)

Krämer, H. J. (1971) *Platonismus und Hellenistische Philosophie* (Berlin)

Kullmann, W. (1969) 'Zur Nachwirkung des homo-mensura-Satzes des Protagoras bei Demokrit und Epikur', *AGPh* 51: 128–44

Laks, A. (1976) 'Édition critique de la 'vie d'Épicure' dans Diogène Laërce 10.1–34', in Bollack and Laks (eds.) (1976): 121–59

(1981) 'Une légèreté de Démocrite (Epicurus *de natura liber incertus* 34.30.7–15 Arrighetti[2])', *CErc* 11: 19–24

(1983) *Diogène d'Apollonie: la dernière cosmologie présocratique*, Cahiers de philologie 9 (Lille)

(1990) "The more" and "the full": on the reconstruction of Parmenides' theory of sensation in Theophrastus' *de sensibus*', *OSAPh* 8: 1–18

(1993) 'Annicéris et les plaisirs psychiques: quelques préalables doxographiques', in Brunschwig and Nussbaum (eds.) (1993): 18–49

Langerbeck, H. (1935) ΔΟΞΙΣ ΕΠΙΡΥΣΜΙΗ (Berlin)

Lasserre, Fr. (1975) 'Un papyrus sceptique méconnu (P. Louvre 7733 Rº)', in J. Bingen, G. Cambier, and G. Nactergael (eds.) (1975) *Le monde grec: hommages à Claire Préaux* (Brussels): 537–48

Laurenti, R. (1980) 'L'*euthymia* di Democrito in Seneca', in Romano (ed.) (1980): 533–52

(1985) 'La questione Bolo–Democrito', in *L'Atomo fra scienza e letteratura* Università di Genova Facoltà di Lettere (Genoa): 55–74

(1996) 'Il *Filebo* di Plutarco', in P. Cosenza (ed.) (1986) *Il Filebo di Platone e la sua fortuna. Atti del convengo di Napoli 4–6 novembre 1993* (Naples): 53–71

Laursen, S. (1987) 'Epicurus, On Nature book XXV', *CErc* 17: 77–8

(1988) 'Epicurus On Nature XXV (Long–Sedley 20 B, C and j)', *CErc* 18: 7–18

(1997) 'The later parts of Epicurus On Nature 25th book', *CErc* 27: 5–82

Lefebvre, D. (1999) 'Qu'est-ce qu'une vie vivable? La découverte de la vie mixte dans le *Philèbe* (20b–22b)', in Dixsaut (ed.) (1999): 61–88

Leone, G. (1984) 'Epicuro *della Natura* XIV' *CErc* 14: 17–107

Lévy, C. (1980) 'Un problème doxographique chez Cicéron: les indifférentistes', *REL* 58: 238–51

(1997) 'Lucrèce avait-il lu Énésidème?', in Algra, Koenen, and Schrijvers (eds.) (1997): 115–24

Lewis, E. (1999) 'Commentary on Bett [1999]', *PBACAP* 15: 167–75

Lilja, S. (1976) *Dogs in ancient Greek poetry* (Helsinki)

Llewelyn, J. E. (1966) 'The inconceivability of pessimistic determinism', *Analysis* 27: 39–44

Lloyd, G. E. R. (1987) *The revolutions of wisdom* (Berkeley)

Loar, B. (1992) 'Elimination versus non-reductive physicalism', in D. Charles and K. Lennon (eds.) (1992) *Reduction, explanation, and realism* (Oxford): 239–63

Löbl, R. (1976) *Demokrits Atome* (Bonn)

Long, A. A. (1968) 'Aristotle's legacy to Stoic ethics', *BICS* 15: 72–85

(1978) 'Timon of Phlius: Pyrrhonist and satirist', *PCPhS* 24: 68–91

(1981) 'Aristotle and the history of Greek scepticism', in D. J. O'Meara (ed.) (1981) *Studies in Aristotle* (Washington): 79–106

(1984) 'Review of Decleva Caizzi (1981a)', *CR* 34: 219–21

(1986) 'Pleasure and social utility – the virtues of being Epicurean', in Flashar and Gigon (eds.) (1986): 283–316

(1993) 'Hellenistic ethics and philosophical power', in Green (ed.) (1993): 138–56

(1996) 'Diogenes, Crates, and Hellenistic ethics', in Bracht Branham and Goulet-Cazé (eds.) (1996): 28–46

(1997) 'Lucretius on nature and the Epicurean self', in Algra, Koenen, and Schrijvers (eds.) (1997): 125–39

Long, A. A. and Sedley, D. N. (1987) *The Hellenistic philosophers*, 2 vols. (Cambridge)

Longo Auricchio, F. (1977) 'Edition of Philodemus *Rhetorica I and II*', in F. Sbordone (ed.) *Ricerche sui papiri ercolanesi*, vol. III (Naples)

(1978) 'La scuola di Epicuro', *CErc* 8: 21–37

(1984) 'Epicureismo e scetticismo sulla retorica', in *Atti del XVII congresso internazionale di papirologia* (Naples) vol. 2: 453–72

(1985) 'Testimonianze della "Retorica" di Filodemo sulla concezione dell' oratoria nei primi maestri epicurei', *CErc* 15: 31–61

(1994) 'New readings in the fragments of *PHerc*. 832/1015', in A. Bülow-Jacobsen (ed.) (1994) *Proceedings of the 20th international congress of Papyrology* (Copenhagen): 389–95

(1996) 'Nuovi elementi per la riconstruzione della *Retorica* di Filodemo', *CErc* 26: 169–72

(1997) 'New elements for the reconstruction of Philodemus' *Rhetorica*', in B. Kramer, W. Luppe, H. Maehler, and G. Poethke (eds.) (1997) *Akten des 21. internationalen Papyrologenkongresses* (Berlin) vol. 2: 631–5

Longo Auricchio, F. and Tepedino Guerra, A. (1980) 'Per un riesame della polemica epicurea contro Nausifane', in Romano (ed.) (1980): 467–78

(1981) 'Aspetti e problemi della dissidenza epicurea', *CErc* 11: 25–40

Longo, F. (1969) 'Nausifane nei papiri ercolanesi', in F. Sbordone (ed.) *Ricerche sui papiri ercolanesi* (Naples) vol. I: 9–21

Lovejoy, A. O. and Boas, G. (1965) *Primitivism and related ideas in Antiquity* (New York)

Luria, S. R. (1936) 'Zur Leukipp–Frage', *SO* 15: 19–22

(1964) *Zur Frage der materialistischen Begründung der Ethik bei Demokrit*, Deutsche Akademie der Wissenschaften zu Berlin, Schriften der Sektion für Altertumswissenschaft 44

(1970) *Democritea* (Leningrad)

Lutz, C. H. (1953–54) 'Democritus and Heraclitus', *CJ* 49: 309–14

Mackie, J. L. (1977) *Ethics: inventing right and wrong* (Harmondsworth)

MacKintyre, A. (1984) *After virtue: a study in moral theory*[2] (London)

Mainoldi, C. (1984) *L'image du loup et du chien dans la Grèce ancienne* (Paris)

Makin, S. (1993) *Indifference arguments* (Oxford)

Mangoni, C. (1993) *Filodemo: il quinto libro della poetica (PHerc. 1423 and 1538)* (Naples)

Manolidis, G. (1987) *Die Rolle der Physiologie in der Philosophie Epikurs* (Frankfurt)

Mansfeld, J. (1986) 'Aristotle, Plato and the Peripatetic doxography and chronography', in G. Cambiano (ed.) *Storiografia e dossografia nella filosofia antica* (Turin): 1–59

   (1992) *Heresiography in context: Hippolytus'* Elenchos *as a source for Greek philosophy* (Leiden)

   (1994) *Prolegomena: questions to be settled before the study of an author or text* (Leiden)

   (1996) 'Aristote et la structure du *de sensibus* de Théophraste', *Phronesis* 41: 158–88

Mansfeld, J. and Runia, D. T. (1997) *Aetiana: the method and intellectual context of a doxographer* (Leiden)

McCabe, M. M. (2000) *Plato and his predecessors: the dramatisation of reason* (Cambridge)

McGibbon, D. (1960) 'Pleasure as the 'criterion' in Democritus', *Phronesis* 5: 75–77

   (1965) 'The religious thought of Democritus', *Hermes* 93: 385–97

McPherran, M. L. (1987) 'Skeptical homeopathy and self-refutation', *Phronesis* 32: 290–328

   (1989) '*Ataraxia* and *eudaimonia* in ancient Pyrrhonism: is the sceptic really happy?', *PBACAP* 5: 135–71

   (1990) 'Pyrrhonism's arguments against value', *PhStud* 60: 127–42

Méhat, A. (1966) *Études sur les "Stromates" de Clément d'Alexandrie*, Patristica Sorbonensia 7 (Paris)

Mejer, J. (1978) *Diogenes Laertius and his Hellenistic background*, Hermes Einzelschriften 40 (Wiesbaden)

   (1992) 'Diogenes Laërtius and the transmission of Greek philosophy', *ANRW* 2.36.5: 3556–3602

Mesiano, F. (1951) *La morale materialistica di Democrito di Abdera* (Florence)

Michaelides, S. (1978) *The music of ancient Greece: an encyclopedia* (London)

Militello, C. (1997) *Memoriee epicuree (PHerc. 1418 e 310)* (Naples)

Mill, J. S. (1861) *Utilitarianism* (London)

Mitsis, P. (1988) *Epicurus' ethical theory: the pleasures of invulnerability* (Ithaca)

Molte, A. (1984) 'Le nécessaire, le naturel et l'agir humain selon Démocrite', in Benakis (ed.) (1984) vol. II: 329–45

Momigliano, A. (1935) 'Su alcuni dati della vita di Epicuro', *RFIC* 13: 302–16

Montiglio, S. (2000) 'Wandering philosophers in classical Greece', *JHS* 120: 86–105

Moraux, P. (1967) 'Aristoteles, der Lehrer Alexanders von Aphrodisias', *AGPh* 49: 169–82

(1984) *Der Aristotelismus bei den Griechen von Andronikos bis Alexander von Aphrodisias* vol. II (Berlin)

(1985) 'Ein neues Zeugnis über Aristoteles, den Lehrer Alexanders von Aphrodisias', *AGPh* 67: 266–9

Morel, P.-M. (1996) *Démocrite et la recherche des causes* (Paris)

(1998) 'Démocrite: connaissances et apories', *RPhilos* 188: 145–64

Moutsopolos, E. (1984) 'La morale de Démocrite, est-elle une morale de *'kairos'*?: summary', in Benakis. (ed.) (1984) vol. I: 325–6

Mühll, P. von der (1919) 'Epikurs κύριαι δόξαι und Demokrit', in *Festgäbe für Kägi* (Frauenfeld): 172–8

Müller, C. (1848) *Fragmenta Historicorum Graecorum*, vol.II (Paris)

Müller, R. (1980a) 'Le rapport entre la philosophie de la nature et la doctrine morale chez Démocrite et Épicure', in Romano (ed.) (1980): 325–52

(1980b) 'Naturphilosophie und Ethik im antiken Atomismus', *Philologus* 124: 1–17

(1994) 'Demokrit – der "lachende Philosoph"', in S. Jäkel and A. Timonem (eds.) (1994) *Laughter down the centuries* (Turku) vol. I: 39–52

Murray, O. (1965) 'Philodemus on the Good King according to Homer', *JRS* 55: 161–82

(1970) 'Hecataeus of Abdera and Pharaonic kingship', *JEA* 56: 141–71

(1971) 'Περὶ βασιλείας: studies in the justification of monarchic power in the Hellenistic world', Oxford D.Phil. thesis

(1975) 'Review of Burton (1972)', *JHS* 95: 214–15

(1984) 'Rileggendo *il buon re secondo Omero*', *CErc* 14: 157–60

Mutschmann, H. (1911) 'Inhaltsangabe und Kapitelüberschrift im antiken Buch', *Hermes* 46: 93–107

(ed.) (1912) *Sexti Empirici opera* vol.I (Leipzig)

Nagel, T. (1979) 'Panpsychism', in his *Mortal questions* (Cambridge): 181–95

Natorp, P. (1893) *Die Ethika des Demokritos* (Marburg)

(1905) 'Diogenes (44) von Sinope', *RE* 5: 765–73

Nestle, W. (1932) 'Metrodorus (14)', *RE* 15.2 1475–6

Nill, M. (1985) *Morality and self-interest in Protagoras, Antiphon, and Democritus* (Leiden)

Nussbaum, M. C. (1979) 'Eleatic conventionalism and Philolaus on the conditions of thought', *HSPh* 83: 63–108

(1986) *The fragility of goodness* (Cambridge)

(1994) *The therapy of desire* (Princeton)

(1995) 'Aristotle on human nature and the foundations of ethics', in J. E. J. Altham and R. Harrison (eds.) (1995) *World, mind and ethics: essays on the ethical philosophy of Bernard Williams* (Cambridge): 86–131

O'Keefe, T. (1997) 'The ontological status of sensible qualities for Democritus and Epicurus', *AncPhil* 17: 119–34

Obbink, D. (1989) 'The atheism of Epicurus', *GRBS* 30: 187–223

(ed.) (1995) *Philodemus and poetry* (Oxford)

(1996) *Philodemus On Piety* (Oxford)

(1997) 'The mooring of philosophy' (Review of G. Indelli and V. Tsouna–McKirahan (1995)), *OSAPh* 15: 259–82

Padel, R. (1992) *In and out of the mind: Greek images of the tragic self* (Princeton)

(1995) *Whom the gods destroy* (Princeton)

Palmer, J. A. (2001) 'A new *testimonium* of Diogenes of Apollonia, with remarks on Melissus' cosmology', *CQ* 51: 7–17

Pandermalis, D. (1983) 'Sul programa della decorazione scultorea', in *La Villa dei Papiri, CErc* 13 suppl 2: 19–50

Pemberton, E. G. (1976) 'A note on *skiagraphia*', *AJA* 80: 82–4

Philippson, R. (1909) 'Polystratos' Schrift über die grundlose Verachtung der Volkmeinung', *Neue Jahr. f.d. Klass. Alt.* 12: 487–509

(1924) 'Demokrits Sittensprüche', *Hermes* 59: 369–419

(1928) 'Verfasser und Abfassungszeit der sogennanten Hippokratesbriefe', *RhM* 77: 293–328

(1929) 'Panaetiana', *RhM* 78: 337–60

(1931) 'Diogenes (47b)', *RE* suppl. 5: 170–2

Pigeaud, J. (1981) *La maladie de l'âme* (Paris)

Pollitt, J. J. (1974) *The ancient view of Greek art* (New Haven and London)

Porter, J. I. (1996) 'The philosophy of Aristo of Chius', in Bracht Branham and Goulet-Cazé (eds.) (1996): 156–89

Powell, J. G. F. (1995) 'Cicero's translations from Greek', in his (ed.) *Cicero the philosopher* (Oxford): 273–300

Pratesi, R. (1988) 'Note ai *"Silli"* di Timone di Fliunte', *Prometheus* 12: 39–56 and 123–38

Procopé, J. F. (1971) 'Democritus the moralist and his contemporaries', Cambridge Ph.D. thesis

(1989a) 'Democritus on politics and the care of the soul', *CQ* 39: 307–31 and (1990) 'Appendix', *CQ* 40: 21–45

(1989b) 'Review of G. Casertano ed. (1983b) and G. Ibscher (1983)', *JHS* 109: 238–9

Purinton, J. S. (1993) 'Epicurus on the *telos*', *Phronesis* 38: 281–321

(1996) 'Epicurus on the degrees of responsibility of "Things Begotten" for their actions: a new reading of *on Nature* XXV', in Giannantoni and Gigante (eds.) (1996): 155–68

Race, W. H. (1981) 'On *kairos*', *TAPhA* 111: 197–213

Reale, G. (1981) 'Ipotesi per una rilettura della filosofia di Pirrone di Elide', in Giannantoni (ed.) (1981b): 243–336

Reinhardt, K. (1912) 'Hekataios von Abdera und Demokrit', *Hermes* 47: 492–513

Richter, G. M. A. (1965) *The portraits of the Greeks* (London)

Ridings, D. (1995) *The Attic Moses: the dependency theme in some early Christian writers* (Göteborg)

Robin, L. (1944) *Pyrrhon et le scepticisme grec* (Paris)

Rodis-Lewis, G. (1975) *Épicure et son école* (Paris)

Rohde, E. (1901) 'Über Leukipp und Demokrit', in his *Kleine Scriften* (Tübingen and Leipzig), vol. I: 205–55

Romano, F. (ed.) (1980) *Democrito e l'atomismo antico* (Catania)

Romilly, J. de (1992) *The great sophists in Periclean Athens* (trans. J. Lloyd) (Cambridge)

Romm, J. S. (1989) 'Herodotus and mythic geography: the case of the Hyperboreans', *TAPhA* 119: 97–113

(1992) *The edges of the earth in ancient thought: geography, exploration and fiction* (Princeton)

Russell, B. (1957) *Human society in ethics and politics* (London)

Russell, D. (1990) '"Only the other day"', in E. M. Craik (ed.) (1990) *Owls to Athens: essays on classical subjects presented to Sir Kenneth Dover* (Oxford): 293–4

Rütten, T. (1992) *Demokrit – lachender Philosoph und sanguinischer Melankoliker: eine pseudhippokratische Geschichte* Mnemosyne suppl. 118 (Leiden)

Ryan, G. E. (1989) 'Commentary on McPherran (1989)', *PBACAP* 5: 172–80

Sacks, K. S. (1990) *Diodorus Siculus and the first century* (Princeton)

Salem, J. (1996) *Démocrite: grains de poussière dans un rayon de soleil* (Paris)

Samuel, A. E. (1993) 'The Ptolemies and the ideology of kingship', in Green (ed.) (1993): 168–92

Sandbach, F. H. (1985) *Aristotle and the Stoics, PCPhS* suppl.10

Sassi, M. M. (1978) *Le teorie della percezione in Democrito* (Florence)

Scatozza-Höricht, L. A. (1986) *Il volto dei filosofi antichi* (Naples)

Schächter, R. (1927) '*Philodemus quid de psychagogia docuerit*', *Eos* 30: 170–3

Schaps, D. (1996) 'Piglets again', *JHS* 116: 169–71

Schmid, W. (1977) '*Lucretius ethicus*', in O. Gigon (ed.) (1977) *Lucrèce*, Entretiens Hardt 24 (Geneva): 123–57

(1979) 'Problemi ermeneutici della papirologia ercolanese da Gomperz a Jensen', in C. Jensen, W. Schmid, and M. Gigante (eds.) (1979) *Saggi di papirologia ercolanese* (Naples): 27–44

Schofield, M. (1991) *The Stoic idea of the city* (Cambridge)

(1999) 'Social and political thought', in Algra, Barnes, Mansfeld, and Schofield (eds.) (1999): 739–70

Schofield, M. and Striker, G. (eds.) (1986) *The norms of nature* (Cambridge)

Schrijvers, P. H. (1992) 'Philosophie et paraphrase: Lucrèce et les sceptiques', in *La langue latine, langue de la philosophie*, Collection de l'École française de Rome 161 (Rome): 125–47

Schuhl, P. M. (1968) *Aristote: cinq œuvres perdues* (Paris)

Schwartz, E. (1885) 'Hekataios von Teos', *RhM* 40: 223–62

Scott, D. (1989) 'Epicurean illusions', *CQ* 39: 360–74

Seaford, R. (1984) *Euripides:* Cyclops (Oxford)

Sedley, D. N. (1976a) 'Epicurus and his professional rivals', in Bollack and Laks (eds.) (1976): 121–59

(1976b) 'Epicurus and the mathematicians of Cyzicus', *CErc* 6: 23–54

(1982) 'Two conceptions of vacuum', *Phronesis* 27: 175–93

(1983a) 'The motivation of Greek skepticism', in Burnyeat (ed.) (1983): 9–30

(1983b) 'Epicurus' refutation of determinism', in ΣΥΖΗΤΗΣΙΣ: *studi sull'epicureismo greco e romano offerti a M Gigante* (Naples) vol. I: 11–51

(1983c) 'Review of G. Indelli (1978)', *CR* 33: 355–6

(1988) 'Epicurean anti-reductionism', in J. Barnes and M. Mignucci (eds.) (1988) *Matter and metaphysics* (Naples): 295–327

(1989) 'Philosophical allegiance in the Greco–Roman world', in Griffin and Barnes (eds.) (1989): 97–119

(1992) 'Sextus Empiricus and the atomist criteria of truth', *Elenchos* 13: 19–56

(1995) 'The *dramatis personae* of Plato's *Phaedo*', in T. J. Smiley (ed.) *Philosophical dialogues* (Oxford): 3–26

(1996) 'The inferential foundations of Epicurean ethics', in Giannantoni and Gigante (eds.) (1996): 313–39, reprinted in Everson (ed.) (1996): 129–50

(1997) '"Becoming like god" in the *Timaeus* and Aristotle', in T. Calvo and L. Brisson (eds.) (1997) *Interpreting the Timaeus–Critias: proceedings of the IV Symposium Platonicum* (Sankt Augustin): 327–40

(1998a) 'Theophrastus and Epicurean physics', in J. M. van Ophuijsen and M. van Raalte (eds.) (1998) *Theophrastus: reappraising the sources* (New Brunswick): 331–54

(1998b) *Lucretius and the transformation of Greek wisdom* (Cambridge)

Segal, C. P. (1990) *Lucretius on death and anxiety* (Princeton)

Sharples, R. W. (1991–93) 'Epicurus, Carneades, and the Epicurean swerve', *BICS* 38: 174–90

Shorey, P. (1917) 'A lost Platonic joke [*Politicus* 266D]', *CPh.* 12: 308–10

(1919) 'Note on Metrodorus fr. 1', *CPh* 14: 393–4

Sider, D. (1997) *The epigrams of Philodemos* (Oxford)

Siefert, G. (1908) *Plutarchs Schrift* περὶ εὐθυμίας (Naumburg)

Silvestre, M. L. (1985) *Democrito e Epicuro: il senso di una polemica* (Naples)

Silvestre-Pinto, M. L. (1983) 'La sensazione spiegata coi principi della fisica', in Casertano (ed.) (1983b): 31–60

Smith, M. F. (1993) *Diogenes of Oinoanda: the Epicurean inscription* (Naples)

(1996) *Diogenes of Oinoanda: the philosophical inscription*, Österreichische Akademie der Wissenschaften Ergänzungsbände zu den *Tituli Asiae Minoris* NR. 20 (Vienna)

Smith, W. D. (1990) *Hippocrates: Pseudepigrapha* (Leiden)

Sorabji, R. (1993) *Animal minds, human morals* (London)

Spinelli, E. (1991) 'ΠΛΟΥΤΟΣ Η ΠΕΝΙΗ: il pensiero economico di Democrito', *Philologus* 135: 290–319

(1997) 'On using the past in Sextus Empiricus: the case of Democritus', *Hyperboreus* 3: 151–73

Spoerri, W. (1959) *Späthellenistiche Berichte über Welt, Kultur, und Götter* (Bonel)

Steckel, M. (1970) 'Demokrit', *RE* suppl. 12: 191–223

Stella, L. A. (1942) 'Valore e posizione storica dell'etica di Democrito', *Sophia* 10: 207–58

Stern, H. and Murray, O. (1973) 'Hecataeus of Abdera and Theophrastus on Jews and Egyptians', *JEA* 59: 159–68

Stewart, Z. (1958) 'Democritus and the Cynics', *HSPh* 63: 179–91

Stokes, M. C. (1995) 'Cicero on Epicurean pleasures', in J. G. F. Powell (ed.) *Cicero the philosopher* (Oxford): 145–70

Stopper, M. R. (1983) 'Schizzi pirroniani', *Phronesis* 28: 265–97

Striker, G. (1983) 'The ten tropes of Aenesidemus', in Burnyeat (ed.) (1983): 95–115, reprinted in Striker (1996): 116–34

(1990) '*Ataraxia*: happiness as tranquillity', *Monist* 73: 97–111, reprinted in Striker (1996): 183–95

(1993) 'Epicurean hedonism', in Bruschwig and Nussbaum (eds.) (1993): 3–17, reprinted in Striker (1996): 196–208

(1996) *Essays on Hellenistic epistemology and ethics* (Cambridge)

Stückelberger, A. (1984) *Vestigia democritea: die Rezeption der Lehre von der Atomen in der Antiken Naturwissenschaft und Medezin* (Basel)

Sudhaus, S. (1892/6) *Philodemi volumina rhetorica*, 2 vols. (Leipzig)

(1893) 'Nausiphanes', *RhM* 48: 321–41

Susemihl, F. (1901) 'Aphorismen zu Demokritos', *Philologus* 60: 180–91

Tarrant, H. (1993) *Thrasyllan Platonism* (Ithaca)

Taylor, C. C. W. (1967) 'Pleasure, knowledge and sensation in Democritus', *Phronesis* 12: 6–27

(1999) *The atomists: Leucippus and Democritus* (Toronto)

Teodorsson, S. T. (1990) 'Theocritus the sophist, Antigonus the one-eyed and the limits of clemency', *Hermes* 118: 380–2

Tepedino Guerra, A. (1991) 'Filosofia e società a Roma', *CErc* 21: 125–32

Thesleff, H. (1961) *An introduction to the Pythagorean writings of the Hellenistic period* (Abo)

Thierfelder, A. (1968) *Philogelos: der Lachfreund* (Munich)

Thrams, P. (1986) *Die Morallehre Demokrits und die Ethik des Protagoras* (Heidelberg)

Todd, R. B. (1976) *Alexander of Aphrodisias on Stoic physics* (Leiden)

Tortora, G. (1983) '*Nous* e *Kairos* nell'etica democritea', in Casertano (ed.) (1983b): 101–34

(1984) 'ΦΥΣΙΣ and ΔΙΔΑΧΗ in Democritus' ethical conception', in Benakis (ed.) (1984) vol. I: 387–97

Trabucco, F. (1958–59) 'La polemica di Aristocle di Messene contro Protagora e Epicuro', *AAT* 93: 473–515

(1960) 'La polemica di Aristocle di Messene contro lo scetticismo e Aristippo e i Cirenaici', *RSF* 15: 115–40

Trimpi, W. (1978) 'Early metaphorical uses of σκιαγραφία and σκηνογραφία', *Traditio* 34: 403–14

Tsouna, V. (1998a) 'Doubts about other minds and the science of physiognomics', *CQ* 48: 175–86

(1998b) 'Remarks about other minds in Greek philosophy', *Phronesis* 43: 245–63

(1998c) *The epistemology of the Cyrenaic school* (Cambridge)

Turner, E. G. (1971) 'The need for new work on the papyri from Herculaneum', *CErc* 1: 7–10

Turrini, G. (1982) 'Il fr.34 di Senofane e la tradizione dossografica', *Prometheus* 8: 117–35

Untersteiner, M. (1954) *The sophists* (Oxford)

(1971) 'L'incontro fra Pirrone e Timone', in his *Scritti Minori* (Brescia): 640–4

Usener, H. (1887) *Epicurea* (Leipzig)

Van Straaten, M. (1962) *Panaetii Rhodii Fragmenta*[3] (Leiden)

Vander Waerdt, P. A. (1989) 'Colotes and the Epicurean refutation of scepticism', *GRBS* 30: 225–267

(ed.) (1994) *The Socratic movement* (Ithaca)

Velleman, J.P. (1993) 'Well-being and time', in Fischer (ed.) (1993): 329–57

Viano, C. (1993) 'L'applicazione dei principi dell' ὅμοιον e dell' ἐναντίον nell'argomentazione dossografica del *de sensibus* di Teofrasto', in A. M. Battegazzore (ed.) (1993) *Dimostrazione, Argomentazione: dialettica e argomentazione retorica nel pensiero antico* (Genoa): 424–40

Vlastos, G. (1945–46) 'Ethics and physics in Democritus', *PhR* 54 :578–92 and 55: 53–64

(1946) 'On the pre-history in Diodorus', *AJPh* 47: 51–9

Voelke, A.-J. (ed.) (1990) *Le scepticisme antique: perspectives historiques et systématiques*, Cahiers de la revue de théologie et de philosophie 15 (Lausanne)

Voros, F. K. (1973) 'The ethical fragments of Democritus: the problem of authenticity', *Hellenika* 26: 193–206

Wachsmuth, C. (1885) *Sillographorum graecorum reliquiae* (Leipzig)

Wallbank, F. W. (1984) 'Monarchies and monarchic ideas', *Cambridge Ancient History*[2] 7.1: 62–100

Wardy, R. B. B. (1988a) 'Eleatic pluralism', *AGPh* 70: 125–46

(1988b) 'Lucretius on what atoms are not', *CPh* 83: 112–28

(1990) *The chain of change* (Cambridge)

(1996) *The birth of rhetoric* (London)

Warren, J. I. (2000a) 'Epicurean immortality', *OSAPh* 18: 231–61

(2000b) 'Aristocles' first refutations of Pyrrhonism (Eus. *PE* 14.18.1–10)', *PCPhS* 46: 140–64

(2001) 'Epicurus and the pleasures of the future', *OSAPh* 21: 135–79

Wehrli, F. (1946) 'Der erhabene und der schlichte Stil in der poetisch–rhetorischen Theorie der Antike', in O. Gigon et al. (eds.) (1946) *Phyllobolia für P. von der Mühll* (Basle): 9–34

(1978) *Die Schule des Aristoteles: Supplementband II, Sotion* (Basle)

West, D. (1969) *The imagery and poetry of Lucretius* (Edinburgh)

Westman, R. (1955) *Plutarch gegen Kolotes*, Acta Philosophica Fennica 7

Wigodsky, M. (1995) 'The alleged impossibility of philosophical poetry', in Obbink (ed.) (1995): 58–68

Wilamowitz-Moellendorf, U. von (1965) *Antigonos von Karystos*² (Berlin)

Wilke, K. (1905) *Polystrati Epicurei* περὶ ἀλόγου καταφρονήσεως *libellus* (Leipzig)

Williams, B. (1985) *Ethics and the limits of philosophy* (London)

(1995) 'Ethics and the fabric of the world', in his *Making sense of humanity* (Cambridge): 172–81

Williams, B. A. O. (1959) 'Pleasure and belief', *PAS* suppl. vol. 33: 57–72

Wilson, J. R. (1980) 'KAIROS as "due measure"', *Glotta* 58: 177–204

Wojcik, M. R. (1986) *La Villa dei Papiri ad Ercolano* (Rome)

Wolff, F. (1997) 'Être disciple de Socrate', in M. Narcy and G. Giannantoni (eds.) (1997) *Lezioni socratiche* (Naples): 29–79

Woodruff, P. (1988) 'Aporetic Pyrrhonism', *OSAPh* 6: 139–68

(1993) 'Response to Long (1993)', in Green (ed.) (1993): 157–62

Zacher, K.-D. (1982) *Plutarchs Kritik an der Lustlehre Epikurs* (Königstein)

Zanker, P. (1995) *The mask of Socrates* (Berkeley)

Zeller, E. and Mondolfo, R. (1969) *La filosofia dei greci nel suo sviluppo storico* 1.5 (Florence)

Zeppi, S. (1971) 'Significato e posizione storica dell' etica di Democrito', *AAT* 105: 499–540

(1984) 'Le radici presocratiche della gnoseologia scettica di Pirrone', in Badaloni (ed.) (1984): 75–91

INDEX LOCORUM

227

237

GENERAL INDEX